Set Margins' #71

TROJAN HORSE EXIT STRATEGIES

A Compendium, Inside the Belly of Contemporary Art Institutions

by **-ATI**
Natalia Agati, Matteo Locci,
Başak Tuna, Merve Yücel

Contents

An Existential and Elusive Guide on How to Activate and Get Out of the Trojan Horse

Natalia Agati, Matteo Locci, Merve Yücel, Başak Tuna

"...they were all silent..."
Homer

The Trojan Blueprint

After years of struggle, the cunning Achaeans devised a brilliant ruse: they left behind a massive wooden horse as a deceptive token of defeat. Once drawn inside Troy's fortified walls, soldiers stealthily emerged from its hollow belly under the cover of night, overwhelming the guards and setting the city aflame. We've all heard the tale, and whether events unfolded exactly as told in the *Iliad* remains uncertain and, perhaps, irrelevant. We possess no patent on the truth, and we often prefer myth over facts. Archaeological evidence suggests that a conflict on the scale of the Trojan War occurred at Troy around 1200 BCE. Regardless of historical accuracy, the Trojan Horse endures as a powerful symbol of subversion, a timeless strategy that has become a metaphor for infiltration and transformation. In the halls of modern museums, it finds new life, offering a blueprint for those who seek to disrupt. This book is intended to remind us that the concept of breaking and escape, whether physical or ideological, begins from

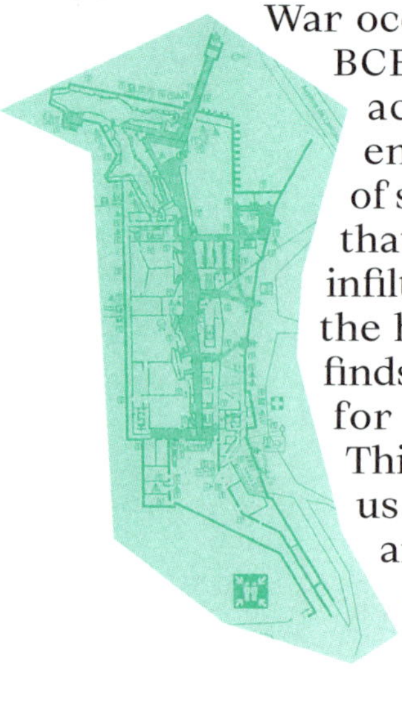

Photo (detail), Centre International de l'Art Pariétal, Lascaux.

within. We propose to explore the Trojan Horse not only as a historical ruse but as a symbolic site where the contradictory desires of engagement and escape are tested, where complicity and critique intersect.

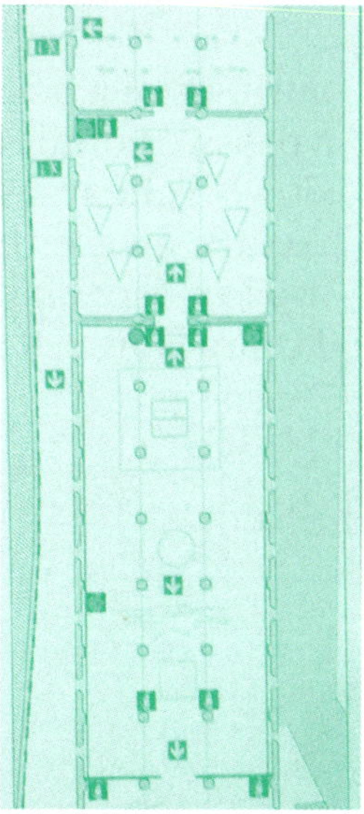

Photo (detail), Arsenale, La Biennale di Venezia, Venice.

Dwelling in the Belly

Some believe that understanding our creative involvement with the world requires a position of detachment, as if we must step outside to gain true insight. This book suggests an alternative: understanding arises from adopting the right posture, a relational one that embraces a *dwelling perspective* entangled with the world's flows and complexities.[1]

This split-level existence, caught between the inside and the outside, between observer and participant, shapes much of human activity. From within this liminal space, resembling the belly of the Trojan Horse, we begin to understand how to navigate both involvement and withdrawal. This metaphorical space within the human-made beast offers a unique vantage point from which a shift in perspective can begin. Cramped, dark, and suspended in anticipation, it is not only a container of bodies, but a crucible for thought where we begin to grasp how to navigate contradictions, embracing a mode of knowing that emerges from within the very structure one may wish to escape. This enclosed threshold between stillness and eruption offers both a vantage and a pressure point between complicity and dissent. From here, one can listen differently, plan resistance, or trace the

. To speak of dwelling is to resist he fantasy of pure exteriority, the nyth that one can critique without peing complicit. Anthropologist Tim Ingold offers a compelling provocation here: instead of standing above or outside the world o understand it, we must "dwell" within it, moving with its textures, naterials, and rhythms. Ingold's shift from a building perspective o a dwelling one emphasizes that our engagement with the world is always already situated, an invitation o stay with the discomfort of peing inside. This idea resonates trongly with those who operate nside institutions, not as neutral observers or accidental guests, but s embedded agents, navigating the nurky terrain between subversion nd survival. The belly of the Trojan Horse, then, is not only a trap or a rick. It becomes a metaphorical home—tense, uncomfortable, and emporary—from which one plots n impossible exit or a radical eorientation. Ingold, *Perception of the Environment.*

outlines of a possible exit. Dwelling in the belly is not a passive condition, but a state of alert readiness that slowly rehearses transformation.

We are aware that the metaphor can be stretched too far, especially given the historical fiction of the Trojan Horse. It likely never existed; neither in wood nor in words.[2] Once we accept that the hoax may not have been a horse and that Ulysses was "no one," the only certainty was the construction with a hidden space, a container, a body, for this book, a belly. The Horse is a myth inflated over time with yeast, and hardly with Homer's consent. Storytelling continues to ferment, inflating the figure of Ulysses, the architect of the ruse, while the thing itself, the hollow belly and its dark crawl space of silent waiting men remains a shadow behind the legend. Our perspective is not to celebrate the bloated hero, but to pay attention to the dwellers and the ways they inhabit and reshape spaces.

2 According to maritime archaeologist Francesco Tiboni, the so-called Trojan Horse may never have been a horse at all. The object described by Homer was likely a ship. In ancient Greek, the word hippos (ἵππος), typically translated as "horse", was also a technical term for a type of Phoenician cargo vessel. Tiboni argues that this confusion led to one of the most enduring translation errors in Western literature: a boat mistaken for a beast, a seafaring infiltration recast as equine deception. Tiboni, *The Hippos of Troy*.

Moreover, our gastro-détournement (our consumption and repurposing of concepts and strategies) disregards the original spirit or the identity embedded in both the textual corpus and wooden body of the horse. To continue the process of de-Ulyssesizing the myth, we propose something elemental: to silence the brain in order to think with the guts. In this book, the body is no longer an instrument of mind, language and behavior; the belly becomes our primary epistemological organ. Somewhere between going out and staying in, the Trojan belly emerges as a site for intestine-led thought, fermentation, nausea, and rebellion. What might it mean to practice critique as digestion? Literal *gut feelings*, as stomach-situated thoughts, are forms of pre-cognitive dissent. Not light weight

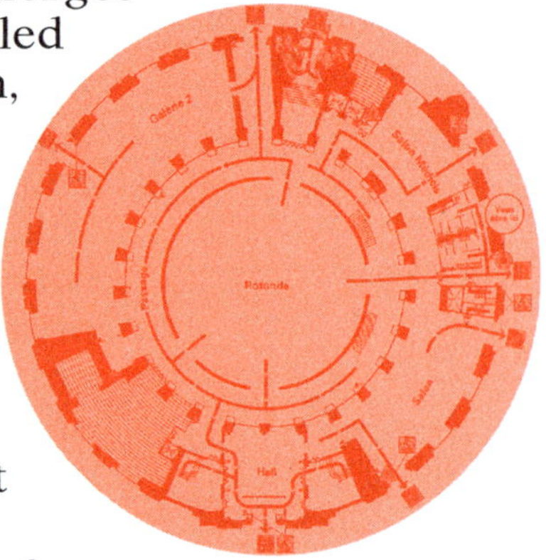

Photo (detail), Bourse de Commerce, Pinault Collection, Paris.

instinct, but deliberate thinking from the gut. To free the phrase from the commonplace and avoid misunderstanding, we propose a new word. *Gut feelings* that unsettle and disturb, in their excessive manifestation, might be called *dissentery*, a neologism that collides *dysentery* and *dissent*, fusing bodily disruption with ideological resistance. This leads us into the contradictions of the horse metaphor by including embodied struggle, where oppositions become somatic, corrosive, eruptive. Beyond biological recognition, the belly is an epistemological site of instinctual refusal, intuitive decision, or embodied protest.

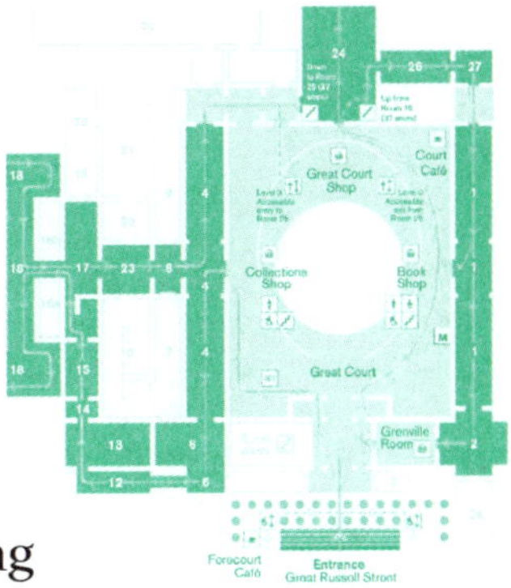

Photo (detail), The British Museum, London.

This reading asks readers to take the metaphor not merely as a symbol but as an organ that metabolizes information, ferments contradictions and churns through systems of meaning until they are broken down or expelled. Bile, nausea, blockage, gas might be misunderstood as pathologies, but here they are epistemic states, performative devices for this book. The intestinal perspective forces critique to confront its own embodiment. What does it mean when resistance is not a shout, but a cramp? When art is not performed but chemically hidden? When destruction strategies build intestinal tunnels? Not an argument, but an acidic revolt? Like an *alla turca* toilet, we've collectively chosen to bring ambiguities to the fore and face them head-on.[3] Throughout these pages, we unpack the many subtleties of the Trojan metaphor, challenging both ourselves and our contributors to confront the paradoxes of critiquing systems from within.

3 In contrast to Western toilets discussed by Slavoj Žižek, the *alla turca* toilet does not typically allow the visual inspection of one's waste. In Žižek's terms, the German toilet exposes, the French one conceals, and the Anglo-American lets it float in between; writing such a book in a Turkish context pushes the reflection toward immediate evacuation, a squatting multisensorial effort, into a kind of black hole. Put differently, the *alla turca* stance privileges release over display. Precision is rarely guaranteed; not every landing is centered. Žižek, *The Plague of Fantasies*.

Silent Strategists

Beyond the heroic legends of warfare and well-worn narratives lies a layer of intrigue often overlooked: what transpired just before the warriors burst out of the Horse? Before the eruption of action, there is always a moment of silence, heavy with anticipation and the weight of what's to come. Virgil speaks of a tense, silent crowd in hiding, where tension is palpable: a space in which strategy and courage are quietly tested.

Just as the warriors within the wooden belly waited for the right moment to strike, many contemporary artists, curators, and critics operate in that same deliberate silence, challenging power, where plans are laid and tactics refined, forcing institutions to reckon with the dynamics they would prefer to leave unnoticed. These quiet but powerful acts of infiltration mirror a *queer use* of space, where an unexpected, disorienting act forces the institution to confront the rigid structures it seeks to uphold.[4] In such moments, silence becomes an active tool of subversion, a force that challenges from within.

The mythical assault on Troy, however, also mirrors the persistence of a widespread colonial *cultural hegemony*. Even as these institutions claim openness, they continue to maintain power structures that uphold dominant narratives and values. The Trojan Horse whispers of a deeper possibility, where opposites can collaborate to build a *counter-hegemonic force*.[5] This silent disruption reveals both the fragility of

4 The idea of queer use is about taking something that was designed for one purpose and using it otherwise. It bends function, stretches intention, and makes room for something unexpected to emerge. It doesn't have to be loud or confrontational; sometimes it's a quiet redirection, a way of inhabiting a structure without fully aligning with it. In the context of contemporary art institutions, this becomes a potent silent strategy. Artists and cultural workers often operate from within the very systems they seek to challenge -galleries, museums, funding bodies- repurposing their own tools in unexpected ways. Sara Ahmed reminds us that this kind of quiet disobedience can expose the rigidity of institutional norms and gently press against their edges, creating cracks where other ways of thinking, being, and relating can begin to take hold. Ahmed, *What's the Use?*

5 Dominant powers shape what is seen as normal, acceptable, or valuable in society, not just through politics or laws, but through culture itself. This means that even art institutions that may seem open and progressive, can still reinforce the same hierarchies and values that benefit the powerful. They might showcase diversity on the surface while continuing to support the same voices, aesthetics, or ways of thinking underneath. Chantal Mouffe invites us to consider *cultural hegemony* not as a problem of bad intentions, but as part of a broader political struggle in which real change happens by opening space for conflict, difference and alternative narratives. When silent strategists challenge institutions, they're not just asking to be included, instead, they're questioning the whole framework of what counts as legitimate, visible or valuable. Mouffe, *Agonistics*.

the systems designed to uphold them and these institutions' capacity for transformation.

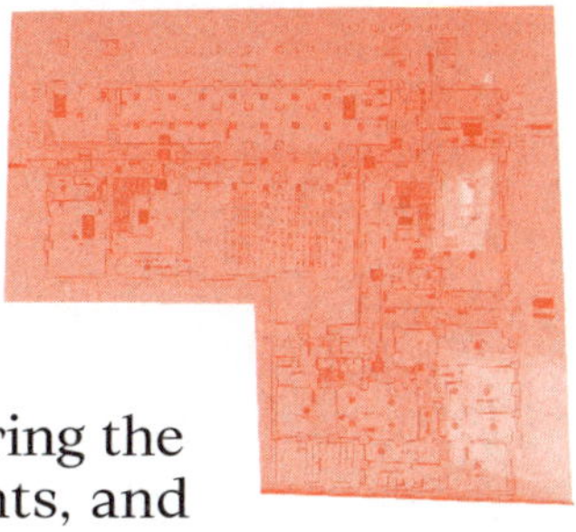

Photo (detail), MUSA, Vienna.

This book delves into that contradictory silence, exploring the unspoken, minor movements, and the moments pregnant with anticipation. It examines the artistic and subversive exit strategies of those who embody this metaphor, confronting both the physical and symbolic challenges they face. Our ambition to juxtapose these ancient strategies with contemporary artistic practice has pushed us to the edge of our curatorial limits, stretching our expertise and resilience. It is within this tension, much like the calm before the storm, that we find space to navigate.

The Story of the Phantom Exit

At this point, the question naturally arises: why do we seek escape from the very situations we create? This paradox of desiring both immersion and liberation reflects the idiosyncrasies of how we engage with art and life. In our attempt to overturn, we risk being absorbed; in our desire to transform, we might find ourselves trapped. To make sense of this approach and outline a possible research path, it became necessary to go through a series of logical and practical steps, one of which led us to museums, spaces where this paradox is quietly rehearsed every day. They function as intricate escape rooms that invite both critique and participation, yet ultimately confront us with the dilemma: How does one actually get out? The exit becomes a symbol. It reminds us that our engagement with these institutions is inherently temporary and transitional. We are encouraged to occupy their halls with a clear understanding that the goal is not to settle, but to transcend the boundaries they impose.

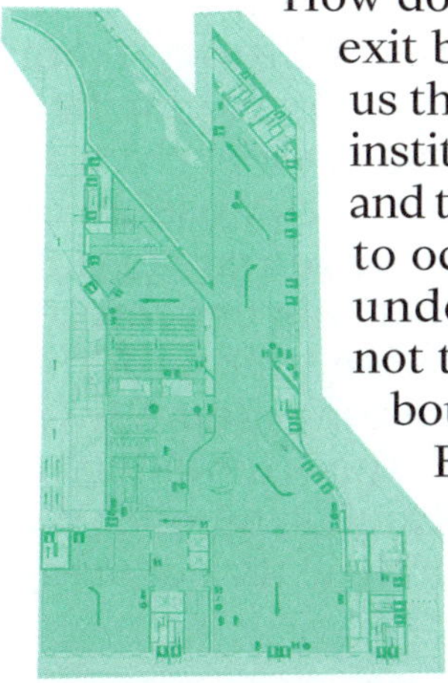

Exit routes are obvious safety protocols and therefore usually attract little to no

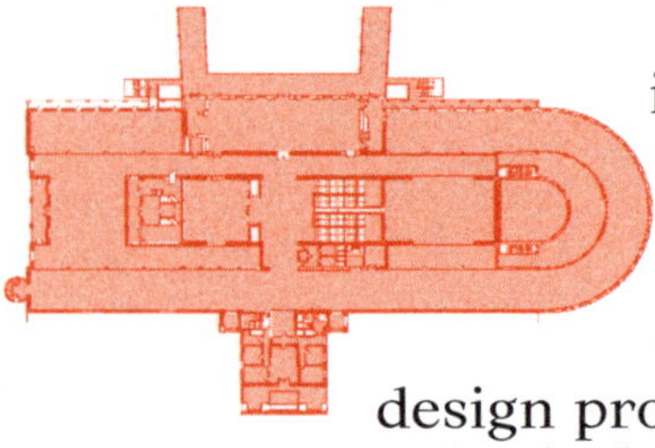

Photo (detail), Triennale Milano, Milan.

interest from visitors and museum critics. However mundane they seem, they carry significant relevance in the design process because they mark a physical and legislative boundary between the curated, controlled environment and the outside world. The exit functions as a threshold archetype, whose technical and symbolic complexities extend beyond the door. Born of code compliance and dimensioned by regulation, it is also where authority can be tested. It operates as a transition point by offering visitors a choice: to continue engaging with the institution's narrative and its principles or to step away from it entirely. As critical architects, we like to reinterpret those legislative boundaries as potential portals to autonomy, where stepping outside also signifies a refusal to be confined by the museum's power structures.

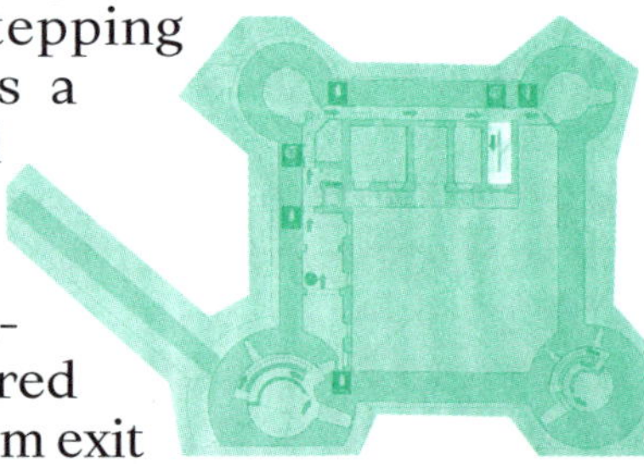

Photo (detail), Rocca Pia, Tivoli.

It was precisely this visitor's paradox that inspired us to photograph museum exit plans over the past two years, a process that formed the visual spine of this book. The collection began as a pedagogical experiment at the Paleolithic center in Lascaux, where we treated evacuation maps not only as safety protocols, but also as speculative diagrams.[6] As the project evolved so did its critical lens, transforming it into an inquiry into institutional exits. Following a reverse-engineered, intuitive drift through art history, from animals at Lascaux to glorified wooden animals, we arrived at the Archaeological Museum of Troy, where the initial version of this project was conceived. To our surprise, the building did not have emergency exit signage, and this coincidental absence became symbolic. We learned, with time, that in many

6 On the occasion of a workshop hosted by ÉESI (École européenne supérieure de l'image), we developed the Out of Image Tour, an invitation to rethink our relationship with images, starting from how they have been conceived over the past centuries and how they shape the cognitive and political lives we inherit. This archaeological approach, informed by Graeber and Wengrow's research, seeks to deconstruct the dominant and monolithic origin narrative and to open new hypotheses for the present. Graeber and Wengrow, *The Dawn of Everything.*

art institutions evacuation plans are not available to visitors. This lack of signage is particularly paradoxical, given that cultural institutions are typically spaces of control that exert their power through coded behaviors and internalized self-surveillance. This absence might seem irrelevant at first glance, but we charged it with meaning beyond rationality, and analyzed it with the same obsessive fervor as UFO hunters scanning the skies for elusive signals.

The desire behind this existential and elusive guide is to elevate these seemingly irrelevant signs as a way to reckon with the absence of escape routes in the burning present. Seen in this light, the omission no longer feels accidental; recognizing it reignited our resolve. We brought art workers into the fold, gathering heterogeneous, situated practices that disrupt mechanisms of control in an effort to trace the contours of what we may call *artistic escapology.*[7]

7 In the first two decades of the twentieth century, the French illusionist Harry Houdini began staging artistic escapes later known as escapology. From Paris to New York, he performed with great success as he freed himself from handcuffs, chains, and straitjackets. Hanging upside down from a rope, submerged in water, or under the watchful eyes of the audience, Houdini developed a refined art in which spectators watched as he enacted his escapes. What we take from his art is the premise that in every situation of capture and control, a different force or a specific method is needed to break free. In some cases, we tie additional knots to support the escape; in others, we have to find the proper key.

Slippery Tactics: On Illusion and Deception

The Trojan legend is but one example in a long history of strategies designed to deceive and outmaneuver entrenched power. From political coups to avant-garde art, the act of smuggling ideas into the heart of the establishment is a recurring theme in human history. War, politics, and art all share a profound connection to the art of illusion, exemplifying the intricate relationship between deception, perception, and power. In this light, the Trojan Horse stands as one of the earliest known examples of political subversion through deception.

The reference is not free of uncomfortable undertones, though. Rooted in a deeply colonial, patriarchal, and Eurocentric tradition, the Achaean ruse bears the weight of these critical

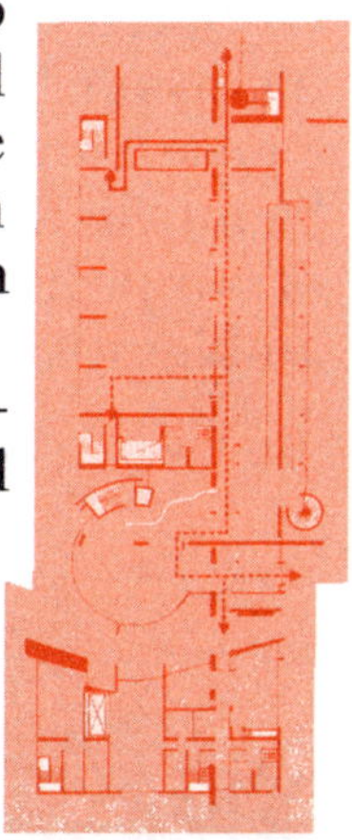

Photo (detail), MACBA, Barcelona.

frameworks. However, it is precisely this ambiguity that gives the metaphor its power. It was a penetrative war strategy and, yes, the Greeks were a colonial army. It was as patriarchal as they come, but it was also the first recorded illusionistic act of political consequence, one to which we offer a decontextualized homage.

The artists and thinkers featured in this book grapple with this ambiguity, using it in ways that both acknowledge and transcend its problematic origins. Stripped of its original historical intent, the horse transcends its roots, becoming an adaptable, non-ideological conjuring tool, usable in different contexts and meanings, and a compelling symbol for subversion, critique, and transformation.

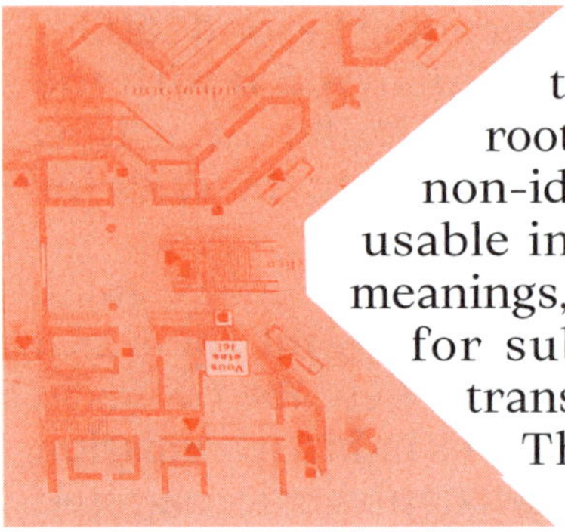

Photo (detail), Louvre Museum, Paris.

This malleability of the Trojan disguise may be the key to its longevity, but it's also where our sharpest self-criticism lies. Within our curatorial team and among contributors, we grappled with the fact that, while we use the figure to stand for experimental, desiring, bottom-up, parasitical interventions—what our circle might call "good subversion"—it can just as easily be co-opted by destructive forces. We find ourselves once again on slippery ground. In the face of rising post-fascist discourse and its infiltration into projects of institutional transformation, we cannot ignore how this tool of disruption has also become a reference point for darker ideologies. The word EXIT itself has become a banner in right-wing, exclusionary European political frameworks, co-opted to insinuate a negation of openness and inclusion. For all these reasons and many more, it is a precarious path we tread. While we recognize the beauty in the illusionistic post-ideological strength of our proposal, we remain cautious. Magnifying this ambiguity is not something we take lightly.

An Emotional Journey and Fugitive Planning

The metaphor of escape also challenges us to reconsider what we are escaping from: is it the institution itself, or the constraints of the societal structures it upholds? In navigating these spaces, are we only rehearsing a kind of symbolic departure while remaining complicit in the systems of power that shape them? This idiosyncratic behavior says much about the way we curate our lives. How many of us find ourselves caught in this contradiction? Who among us, free of inconsistency, is truly in a position to cast the first stone?

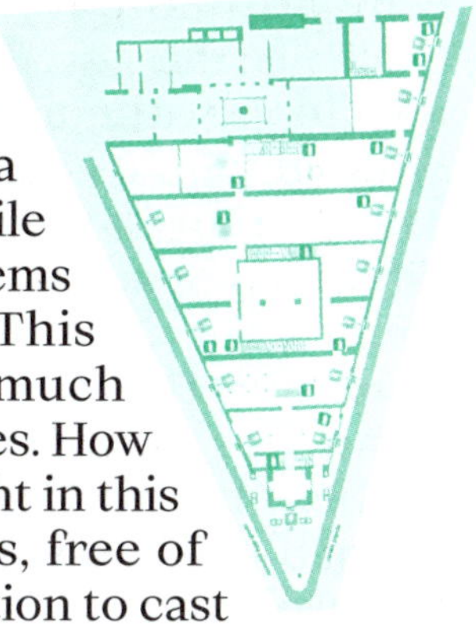

Photo (detail), Punta della Dogana, Pinault Collection, Venice.

Rather than offering simple answers, this book dives into the nuances of these questions, making doubts out of our contradictions. How do artists, curators, art workers, and thinkers balance their role within organizations while plotting their escape? How does the act of infiltration affect their psyche, their strategies, and their ethics?

Perhaps the most radical exits do not exist at all. They are the quiet refusals that happen from within, what some have called *fugitive planning:* a form of movement that doesn't announce itself, that resists capture, and instead stays close to the ground, improvising through friendship, study, and shared exhaustion. It is not a grand exodus, but an intimate, low-frequency insurgency, an ongoing recalibration of presence, of complicity, of distance, and of care beyond heroic gestures.[8]

This publication gathers reflections of those who have navigated this delicate and often risky path, providing insights into the psychological and strategic considerations that shape the planning of an effective escape strategy. Entering an institution with the intention to subvert requires more than just

8 Escape doesn't have to be loud or heroic. It can be slow, collective, even unnoticed. It can look like staying in the cracks, building trust, studying together, refusing without spectacle. It can mean showing up without fully showing yourself. Moreover, there are artists sans oeuvre, sabotaging the machinery gently from the inside, or designing gestures meant to dissolve rather than endure. Stefano Harney and Fred Moten's theories have been our quiet companions throughout this work. Like a compass in navigation, their words remind us that the courage to imagine an exit isn't a rupture, but can be a quiet movement of care, stealth, and shared opacity, right there, in the belly of the beast. Harney and Moten, *The Undercommons.*

strategic acumen; it demands psychological resilience. With every contributor and every act of subversion comes an ethical quandary: can we challenge the system using its own tools without becoming entangled in its machinery? The Trojan gambit, both a gift and a weapon, embodies this duality, forcing us to consider the cost of our strategies on our very own bellies. Institutions often absorb critiques, patching themselves up and pressing on, just as they have done time and time again. Just as the soldiers in the Horse were both part of and apart from the offering, so too are art workers who enter institutions with the intent to subvert. The fear of exposure, the anxiety of waiting for the right moment, and the hope that the effort will lead to real change all shape the inner life of those who dwell in the belly of the beast. Many covert agents of change wait for the right moment to emerge, and for them, planning an exit is as crucial as the infiltration itself.

9 Do we enter to endure the fire, or to help it burn? This question is what Giorgio Agamben encounters in *The Man Without Content*, where he suggests that it is only when the house is burning that its architecture truly reveals itself. In the same way, it is often at the moment of collapse that art discloses its original intent, not as form or object, but as gesture, as potential. When institutions ignite, whether by crisis or critique, what was once concealed by structure becomes visible in ruin. This is the fragile terrain in which this book moves: not merely asking how to critique from within, but what kind of clarity emerges when we no longer pretend the walls are stable. In that space, the choice is no longer just strategic, it becomes existential and ontological: whether to stay inside as witness or walk out and let the structure complete its own undoing. Agamben, *L'uomo senza contenuto*.

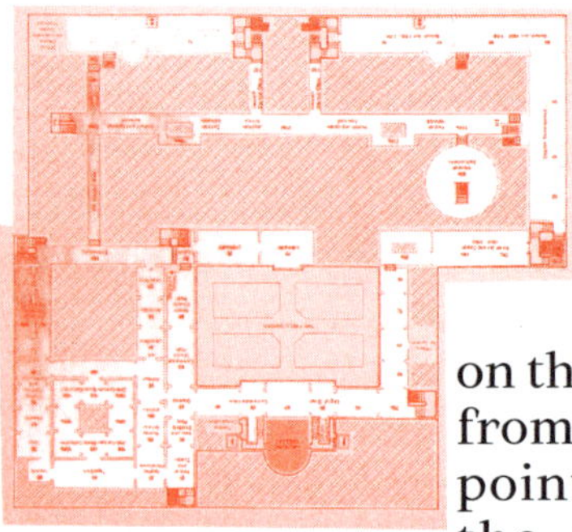

Photo (detail), Victoria and Albert Museum, London.

The personal narratives in this book underscore the psychological and strategic dimensions of such an endeavor. Each contributor was invited to share personal insights on their journey inside the belly, from which they had a vantage point to observe and analyze the distortion of the world while always keeping an eye on the exit. Some set clear goals, others focus on their well-being. Some express regret, others value their tactical success. Some plan breakouts from the outset without hesitation, while others spend years uneasily scanning the emergency exit signs of the institutions that employ them.

The Architecture of Collapse

As we have already clarified, the Trojan Horse is not proposed only as a metaphor for political critique and sabotage; it vividly represents the architecture of systemic collapse or the *house on fire*.[9] Institutions, like buildings, are constructed with specific purposes and constraints, yet they also carry the potential for their own undoing, both literally and conceptually. Far from being problematic, the flames of this ongoing fire present an array of possibilities, a spectrum of exit strategies to escape the status quo, illuminating the contradictions that run deep in the established Western art system.

Do we infiltrate institutions merely to navigate through the flames, or is the aim to ultimately dismantle their foundations? What appears as a tactical question is an existential dilemma, tied closely to the architecture of power itself. Emergency exit signs become symbols of choice, offering sudden clarity to the dilemma at the heart of this book: art's paradoxical role in its own dissolution is inevitably part of the spectacle.[10]

10 The spectacle doesn't simply mask reality, it replaces it, absorbing even its critiques and neutralizing oppositions by staging them. Guy Debord's lesson is well known: spectacle is not just something to resist, but something that dissolves everything it touches. In this sense, staying visible within institutional frameworks risks becoming part of their self-reinforcing image. The exit, then, is not merely an act of withdrawal, but a refusal to be dissolved into visibility. It is a gesture of opacity, a way of interrupting the endless circulation of signs and stepping beyond the loop of recognition. Debord, *La Société du spectacle*.

Throughout the contributions in this book, one sentiment stands out: our desire for change can't rely on blunt destruction. Instead, we propose a careful, complexity-driven practice of dismantling to prevent the rise of something worse. This stance acknowledges the prospect of breakdown while staying with, and accountable to, the communities affected. Whether the collapse happens through spontaneous combustion, an outside push, or a slow, internal crumble does not matter. What truly matters is finding alliances that allow us to dwell within these contradictions and foster a collective

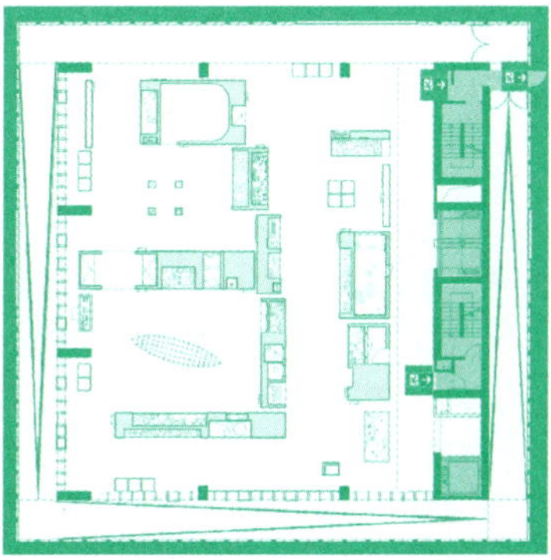

Photo (detail), Troy Museum, Çanakkale.

reflection on how to move beyond the museum apparatus. In this light, the escape routes act as involuntary self-injected antidotes to the self-preserving policies and procedures that institutions work so hard to maintain. More than pragmatic safety measures, they belong to the architecture itself, reminding us that every structure is designed with its own possible undoing. Change doesn't necessarily come from fighting within; sometimes it comes from walking out, letting the institution crumble under its own contradictions. The exit, therefore, becomes an architectural horizon, a philosophical strategy, and, with a touch of emphatic political performativity, a trigger that sounds the alarm.

The Snowball Curatorial Method

We can't be sure how you first encountered this book; perhaps someone who reached the exit passed it to you as a symbolic gift. Now that you are holding it, it's worth further reflecting on the methods used in the research and development of this book.
Many friends from a diverse group of artists, museum directors, art workers, curators, and thinkers shared unpublished and incisive takes on the exit strategies; others joined playful, unconventional, gastro-experimental interviews in order to enhance and push to its limits the metaphor. Between each individual contribution by the authors, there are also seventeen visual tributes. They extend the domain of our curatorial framework by paying homage to different forms of dwelling in the belly of modern institutions. In the middle of the book, you'll find the documentation from an orchestrated collective evacuation at the Troy Museum in October 2024, when, thanks to the museum director Rıdvan Gölcük and Çanakkale Biennial co-director Deniz Erbaş, the lights of the museum were turned off for a few minutes and visitors were invited to exit.

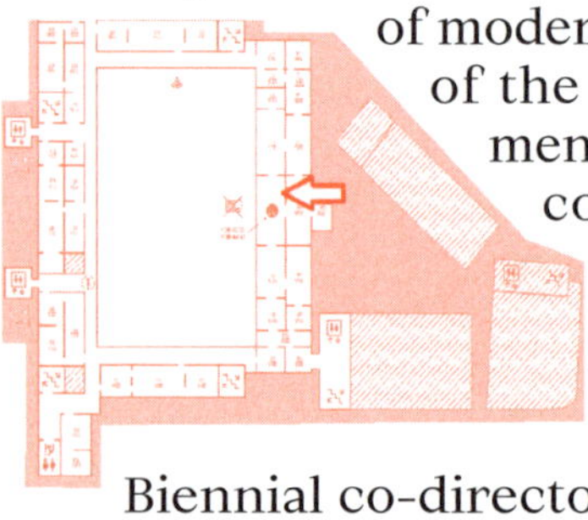

Photo (detail), Museo Nacional Centro de Arte Reina Sofía, Madrid.

What's especially important to highlight is that most of the curatorial decisions were guided by ties of friendship and solidarity, fostering mutual trust as we developed a discourse around something intrinsically ambiguous and dangerously post-ideological, such as the previously described Trojan Horse. In a world where the neoliberal establishment has infiltrated our most precious, intimate, and emotional spheres, manipulating emotions, and shaping responses, moving forward in a kinship-based way becomes the most essential escape strategy in institutional critique. Yet, like all delicate things, it must be handled with care. In trying to avoid fetishizing the concept of an *open process,* we embraced a relational method that reimagined the artistic space as something unfinished, capable of generating new conceptual ground for emerging forms of aesthetics.[11]

By involving the individual authors and shaping each interview with a sensitivity to this evolving process, we activated something akin to a *snowball effect*: each conversation flowed into the next, influencing and amplifying the ideas in play.[12] A snowball melts on its own, but when it gathers momentum, it can spark an avalanche. This gathering energy in motion is the spirit that has guided our curatorial choices. In this process, we avoided canonical interviews and perpetuation of heroic storytelling, and pushed for methodological shifts, non-functional props, declared manipulations, and playful interventions, or anything that would allow the contributors to pay homage to the Trojan Horse and its rebellious, pirate spirit.

11 This curatorial approach was shaped by a desire to stay close and give power to friendships. But as Bojana Kunst reminds us, proximity and openness are not immune to capture. The language of process, care, and horizontality, once radical gestures, has often been appropriated by the same cultural industries they were meant to resist. In a system where the performance of participation is easily monetized, and artistic labor is increasingly immaterial, even the most relational methods risk being absorbed. That's why we handled this process with caution. Not to close it off., but to avoid turning it into another form of spectacle. This book doesn't celebrate openness as a value in itself—it tests its limits, traces its tensions, and holds space for the mess that escapes framing. Kunst, *Artist at Work*.

12 Another important influence comes from the work of Vilém Flusser and his philosophical autobiography *Bodenlos* (1992), in which the philosopher, instead of speaking about himself, dedicates each chapter to a different friend. For him, the term "conversation" (*conversação*) often overlaps with the term "culture." This assimilation helps us to deconstruct the monolithic and unified block of Western culture, and instead conceive of it as an ocean crossed by multiple currents. From Flusser, we inherit the image of conversation and interviews contained in the book as a snowball (*Schneeball*): on its own, it melts, but when it gathers momentum, it can trigger an avalanche. Flusser, *Bodenlos*.

The book started with an open plan and transformed through a process of constant adaptation, guided by a shared commitment to stay open and malleable. What you hold in your hands is the quirky result of a structured method which, paradoxically, doesn't seek to represent an historical moment or the state of the art. Instead, it deploys ties of friendship and camaraderie to open up a sincere discourse on fatigue, difficulties, and problems encountered. These sparkling discussions, that don't follow a strictly rational line of reasoning, stem from a deeper, visceral place in our bodies, somewhere between the stomach and the heart.

References

Ahmed, Sara. *What's the Use? On the Uses of Use.* Duke University Press, 2019.

Agamben, Giorgio. *L'uomo senza contenuto.* Rizzoli, 1970.

Debord, Guy. *La Société du spectacle.* Buchet-Chastel, 1967.

Flusser, Vilém. *Bodenlos: Eine philosophische Autobiographie.* Bollmann, 1992.

Graeber, David, and David Wengrow. *The Dawn of Everything: A New History of Humanity.* Penguin Books, 2021.

Harney, Stefano, and Fred Moten. *The Undercommons: Fugitive Planning & Black Study.* Minor Compositions, 2013.

Ingold, Tim. *The Perception of the Environment: Essays on Livelihood,* Dwelling and Skill. Routledge, 2000.

Kunst, Bojana. *Artist at Work: Proximity of Art and Capitalism.* Zero Books, 2015.

Mouffe, Chantal. *Agonistics: Thinking the World Politically.* Verso, 2013.

Tiboni, Francesco. *The Hippos of Troy: Why Homer Never Talked about a Horse.* Archaeopress, 2021.

Žižek, Slavoj. *The Plague of Fantasies.* Verso, 1997.

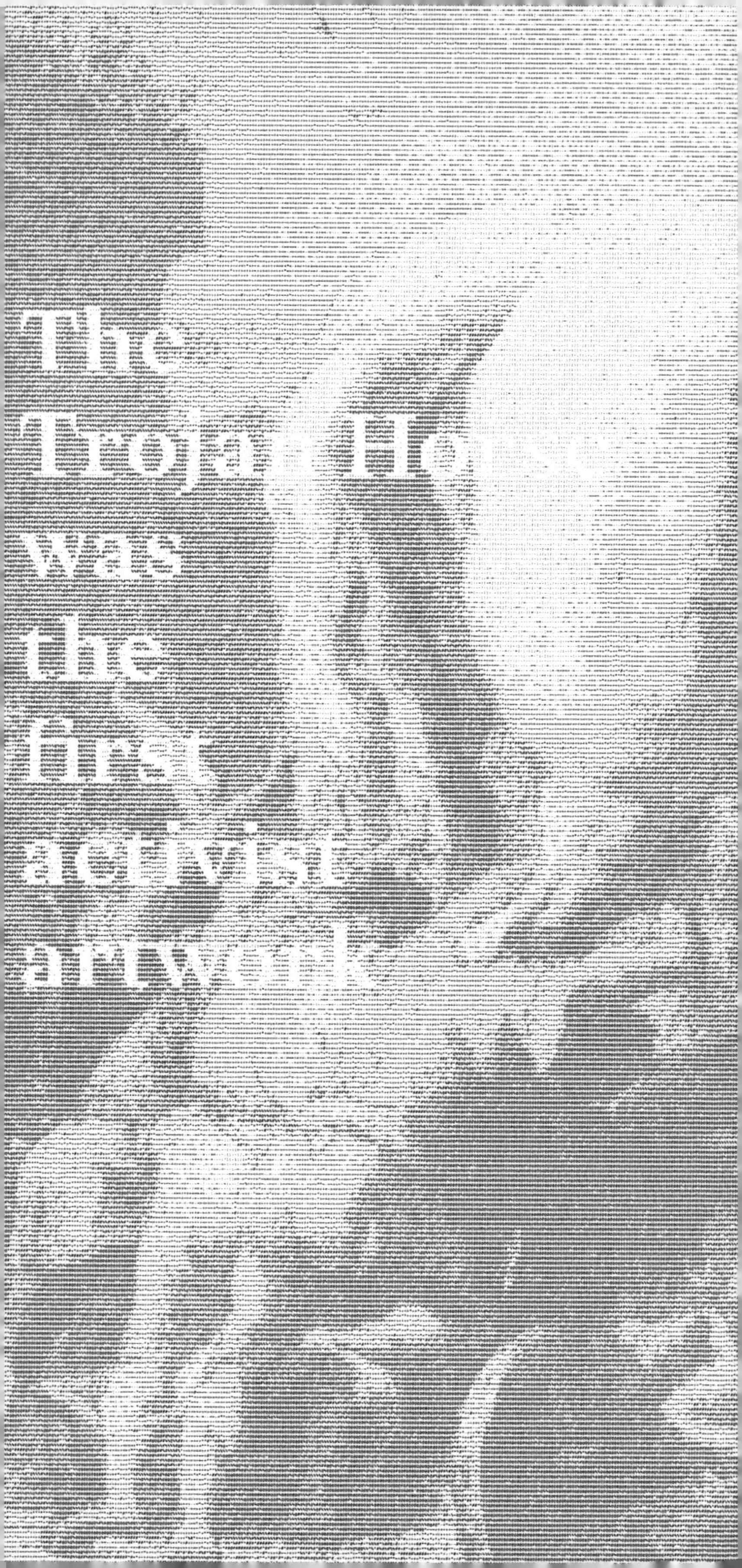
The Trojan Horse was the first activist artwork

In her 1984 essay "Trojan Horses: Activist Art and Power," Lucy Lippard reframes the Trojan Horse as a model for activist art, a way to subvert dominant structures from within. Art, in this view, is not just expressive but tactical: a tool for social change, blending aesthetics with activism to mobilize communities and challenge power. Lippard emphasizes the need for collective effort and the strategic role of artists in controlling and disseminating their work to empower marginalized voices. ***Processione del cavallo di Troia (detail), Giandomenico Tiepolo, National Gallery, London.***

Electrodes and Epiphanies: Navigating Institutional Change Under Stimulation

Interview with Cesare Pietroiusti

On June 24, 2024, we interviewed Cesare Pietroiusti in a session designed as a unique, multisensory experience. Our aim was not only to ask questions and exchange information, but to engage the senses and explore the interaction between mind and body. With his consent, a small four-electrode stimulator was applied to his abdomen. Throughout the afternoon, our conversation was accompanied by gentle abdominal massages intended to enhance gastrointestinal reflexes and prompt thinking from the body's core. We proposed this method in a playful spirit and made clear that he was free to decline or stop the experiment at any time. Each BEEP↑ BEEP↓ transcribed corresponds to a change in the intensity or type of electrostimulation we activated during the interview, adjusted in response to the theme or nature of Pietroiusti's answers.

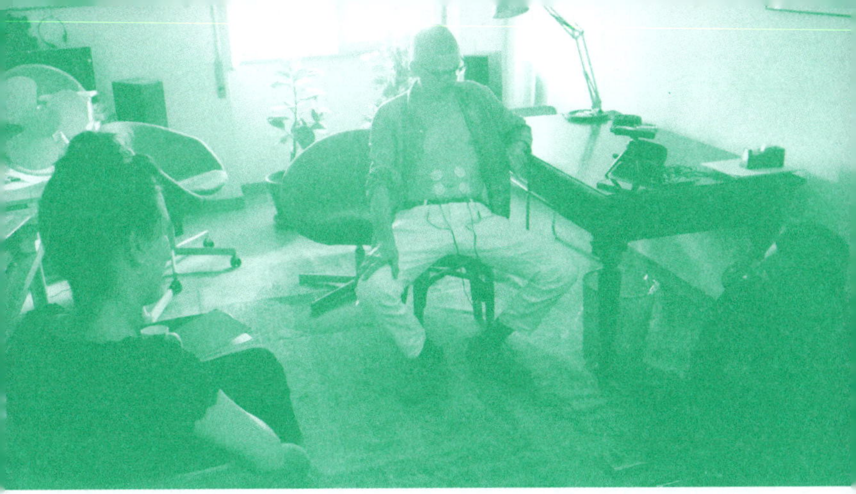

Why do you think we are here interviewing you today? What made you accept, and what do you think is worth "digesting" from what's been proposed?

First of all, the topic is compelling because it touches on the relationship between the individual and the institution. The metaphor of the Trojan Horse in relation to the institution raises some specific points for reflection. From the moment you invited me, I started thinking about three moments-better said forces, in which it operates and reveals itself:

First, the entrance: This is the moment when someone or some intention introduces a force, let's say, that isn't anticipated. No one knows how this force will manifest once inside a perimeter, a secure zone, or an institution.

Second, the intention of the one entering: Obviously, there's the intention of the one entering, which, in Homer's historical case, is an intention of conquest or destruction. To be clear, the Greeks weren't just trying to change the government, they weren't entering peacefully. They aimed to take back something they considered theirs, and they saw the horse as something destructive, not transformative. Moving beyond the metaphor, the force entering the perimeter has its own intention, beyond who, why, and how it happens.

Third, the internal force: This prompts reflection on what happens when the horse reveals itself, how does this internal force manifest?

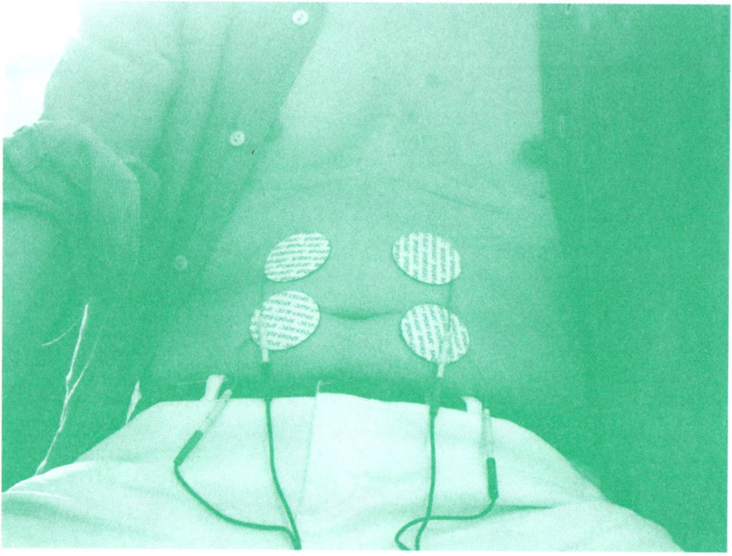

Obviously, the comparison between this story and my experience as president at Palaexpo fits.[1] I asked myself: what was the entrance, the first force? A city councilor from Rome introduces the character Cesare Pietroiusti, an atypical figure. This councilor wanted to stir the waters, promoting a vision of contemporary Rome, likely expecting an electoral image boost.

BEEP↑ BEEP↑ BEEP↑↑

Here's the first deviation from the initial scheme: it's not necessarily the case that the intentions of the one who opens the doors—the councilor—are the same as mine. So I asked myself, what were my intentions beyond personal ambition, or, better yet, vanity? A vanity that also manifests in relation to an institution that was fairly rigid, without big artistic production ambitions, which I instead proposed should focus on research and experimentation. I arrive and, either bold or naïve, suggest that funds and resources could be used to promote an attitude and concepts of experimentation and research... Unlike the Greeks, who won thanks to this stratagem, I didn't. And what little happened was partial and only for a brief period. Moreover, much

1 On behalf of the Rome municipality, Palaexpo manages the entire integrated system of public spaces and sub-institutions, namely: the Palazzo Esposizioni Roma, the MACRO, the Mattatoio, and the Museo delle Periferie.

of what I started was either erased or watered down. So, comparing it in military terms: the objective wasn't achieved, and the intentions of the inhabitants inside the horse's belly (it wasn't just me, but others, including you, who are interviewing me) didn't achieve the goal they set—to introduce some seeds into the institution, both temporarily and permanently.

BEEP↑ BEEP↑ BEEP↑↑

Unfortunately, Palaexpo has returned to being rigid and predictable, as it was before. During my presidency, I knew I was like a boat rowing upstream; some transformative seeds were planted, and that was why, despite difficulties and frustrations, there was something to defend and support, not to let those rowing against me win. This, in summary, is how I see your question and the epic metaphor.

By the way, what are you recording? (pointing to electrodes)

This is a firming program that doesn't record anything. Before being a temporary president, your performative work often explored the experimentation of psychophysical resistance and the understanding of limits or the reciprocal influences between mind and bodily stimuli. What are your expectations for this interview?

The opportunity to explore a gastroenterological language is irresistible, and it would be a shame to miss it. But there are some comparisons in the metaphor that work and others that don't. For example, in the digestive metaphor, what exactly is the "belly" in question? If we're talking about the intention of conquest and desire, the object of transformation would be Troy. There are digestive processes that take place, not so much in the horse but within the walls of institutions. The place where the horse enters as a foreign presence and finds, in fact, a hostile environment. There's a certain naïveté I noticed back then, which I know is part of my nature. You think you'll come in and make a big difference, but we all have limits and blind spots. That naïveté makes you believe that employees and workers will welcome the change with enthusiasm. It's not just a matter of government employees or bureaucratic inertia, hierarchical layers—there's also a mix of sadism, unnecessary malice, and obstacles crafted with precision. However, there are also the honest workers who see your arrival as an unnecessary upheaval.

What strategies did you use to subvert institutional norms from within?

As you can imagine, the position is ambiguous; you have to assert your place within the institution and its value, while simultaneously the very workers there are opposing you. They're hidden, not inside the horse's belly, but within the institution itself. You, on the other hand, are exposed. From the inside, they see you as a troublemaker, or, to use a more emphatic term, a revolutionary. From the outside, you're seen as a conservative because you feel or think you're forced to maintain a profile of not-too-extreme disruption, just to do the minimum that the institution allows.

BEEP↑ BEEP↑

Logically, you become both a defender and an antagonist of the very systems in which you operate. To understand the incompatibility, I'll tell you an anecdote: when I first spoke with the cultural commissioner, he said that Palazzo delle Esposizioni had no audience. I replied, "Why don't we think counterintuitively and say: politically, let's take responsibility and say that if this exhibition had very few visitors, it means it was a good exhibition!" He might have grasped the concept, but of course, he couldn't agree with me. In four years of activity, I think I managed to apply a counterintuitive logic successfully only once: in 2020, we organized an exhibition on Assange that was produced, set up, and never opened—or rather, it was opened only to remain closed. Obviously, it was a game. A little gem within a reactionary structure. The moral of the story is: it's easy to criticize from the outside about numbers, audience, fears, etc. But when you're inside, you start to adopt that logic too.

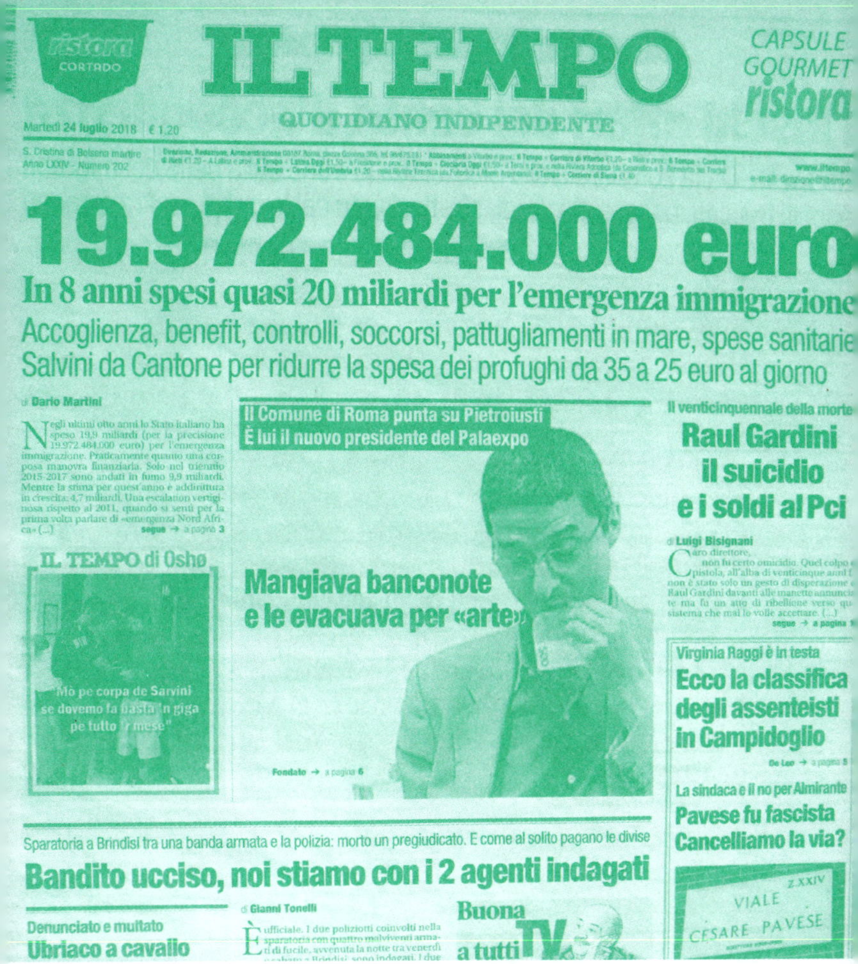

IL TEMPO
QUOTIDIANO INDIPENDENTE

Martedì 24 luglio 2018 | € 1,20

S. Cristina di Bolsena martire
Anno LXXIV - Numero 202

CAPSULE GOURMET ristora

19.972.484.000 euro

In 8 anni spesi quasi 20 miliardi per l'emergenza immigrazione

Accoglienza, benefit, controlli, soccorsi, pattugliamenti in mare, spese sanitarie
Salvini da Cantone per ridurre la spesa dei profughi da 35 a 25 euro al giorno

di Dario Martini

Negli ultimi otto anni lo Stato italiano ha speso 19,9 miliardi (per la precisione 19.972.484.000 euro) per l'emergenza immigrazione. Praticamente quanto una corposa manovra finanziaria. Solo nel triennio 2015-2017 sono andati in fumo 9,9 miliardi. Mentre la stima per quest'anno è addirittura in crescita: 4,7 miliardi. Una escalation vertiginosa rispetto al 2011, quando si sentì per la prima volta parlare di «emergenza Nord Africa» (...)

segue → a pagina 3

IL TEMPO di Oshø

"Mò pe corpa de Sarvini se dovemo fa pasta 'n giga pe tutto 'r mese"

Il Comune di Roma punta su Pietroiusti
È lui il nuovo presidente del Palaexpo

Mangiava banconote e le evacuava per «arte»

Fondato → a pagina 6

Il venticinquennale della morte

Raul Gardini il suicidio e i soldi al Pci

di Luigi Bisignani

Caro direttore,
non fu certo omicidio. Quel colpo di pistola, all'alba di venticinque anni fa, non è stato solo un gesto di disperazione di Raul Gardini davanti alle manette annunciate ma fu un atto di ribellione verso quel sistema che mai lo volle accettare. (...)

segue → a pagina

Virginia Raggi è in testa

Ecco la classifica degli assenteisti in Campidoglio

De Leo → a pagina 8

La sindaca e il no per Almirante

Pavese fu fascista Cancelliamo la via?

VIALE CESARE PAVESE

Sparatoria a Brindisi tra una banda armata e la polizia: morto un pregiudicato. E come al solito pagano le divise

Bandito ucciso, noi stiamo con i 2 agenti indagati

di Gianni Tonelli

È ufficiale. I due poliziotti coinvolti nella sparatoria con quattro malviventi armati di fucile, avvenuta la notte tra venerdì ...

Denunciato e multato

Ubriaco a cavallo

Buona a tutti TV

Did you feel afraid? Were your intentions clashing significantly with that field of tension?

Over time, I realized the important thing is to flip the fear and live the experience as if it were a work of art. You face opposition and say: "Oh really? So what, I'll push even harder." You, the institution, the administrator, anyone.

BEEP↑BEEP↑BEEP↑

A horrible and morally flawed position is that of the media because they push you to value only the most trivial things. Gossip and similar matters become the reasons through which the institution is known.

BEEP↑BEEP↑BEEP↑

Ah, I see! So, it's the idea of a thought that also absorbs this kind of stimulus. For example, the bile that comes when you see scandalized articles about our picnic on some Roman ruins... After so much effort to raise the bar, the only time you appear in an eight-column newspaper headline is because you ate a sandwich on four dirty stones, abandoned, that no one even knew existed. It's an unacceptable dynamic that forces you into a logic of fear. Differently, as an artist, if a media outlet gave me eight columns over such nonsense, I'd make it an artwork, I'd be happy. I don't fear it because I can depict the absurdity of the subject at stake. Do you remember that page from *Il Tempo*?[2] I'll show you... (He pulls out a newspaper from the archive.) A small masterpiece where, to criticize public spending, they show a photo of one of my performances in which I eat a €500 bill. No connection whatsoever! Yet I recognize it as a work of art that I sign and buy to anyone holding a copy.

Marvelous. Can we take a picture, do you mind? Another institutional loophole is related to responsibilities with the various heads of safety, emergency exits, and oversight.

If I had the awareness back then, I would have told the commissioner: I'll accept the directorship only if I have a majority on the board of directors to avoid spending my days convincing, pushing, debating, etc. and by changing the general director. Now that I think about it, the commissioner had actually suggested that to me, but I didn't pay attention because I thought: if I have to replace the director, I'll have to keep paying the old one, so that's another salary... 200,000 euros a year! Damn, I'd rather use that money for a research program. I didn't realize that compromises cost money. The issue is that the legal responsibility falls on the general director, and when I was appointed, I thought that was a guarantee for me...

BEEP↑BEEP↑BEEP↑

2 *Il Tempo* is conservative daily Italian newspaper published in Rome.

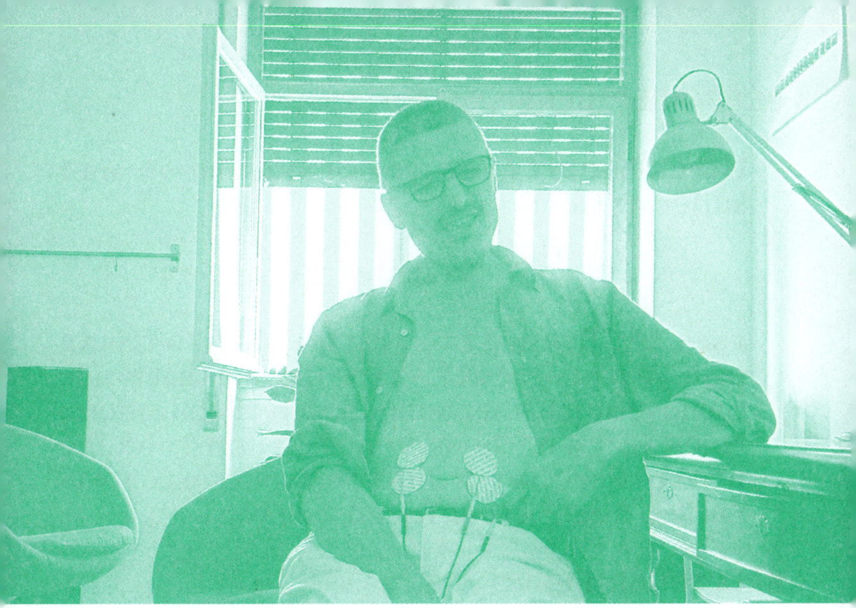

But over time, I realized that, in fact, the director had veto power. To give you an idea, anything outside the norms of safety, fire prevention, accessibility, or that might touch the "sensitivities of visitors," he could decide. As he always repeated: "I'm the legal responsible party; if something happens, the lawsuit comes to me, so let it go."

BEEP↑BEEP↑BEEP↑

Just think of the absurdity of Italy: despite most artists performing at exhibitions, as a museum, to authorize it, you have to call a technician, file a report, and pay office staff for paperwork.

BEEP↑BEEP↑BEEP↑

Ow, that hurts.

BEEP↓ ↓ **Sorry, should I lower it?** BEEP↓ ↓

Yes, please. In case of an exhibition (which is quite normal for a museum), it's mandatory to have two firefighters, paid from the museum's budget, in uniform for the entire duration of the exhibition. People who aren't needed, just sitting there twiddling their thumbs. Awk! Turn it down a bit...

BEEP↓BEEP↓BEEP↓

Here's better. What type of stimulation am I suffering from?

It is a treatment to make the pain go away.

I see, like fighting fire with fire, pain to relieve pain. Where were we? Ah yes, the fact that inside the institution, this complex web of obligations, rules, fears, tensions, contradictions, and the need to work on two different fronts makes you far less free. All your friends tell you...

BEEP↑BEEP↑BEEP↑

"Make it an artwork!" I've obviously thought about this Trojan Horse dynamic in abstract terms, but it's not that simple—there are fears, hesitations, ethics... As an artist, a bit of a rogue, you play for yourself; you take responsibility for being called mad, a buffoon, a genius. But as president of an institution with a €15 million budget, 60 employees, and ties to politics, it's normal to lose that bold, performative attitude and to sacrifice the performative mindset. Don't you agree? By the way...I feel a little bit ticklish...

BEEP↓ The question is, do YOU feel anything in your stomach?

The truth is, I've always suffered from gastritis, especially since I lived in New York. A triggering moment was the Tropicana fruit juices. Since then, I've learned to recognize my stomach's reactions to what I eat, so I think I've learned to eat healthier in response to that weakness. Prosecco is now taboo, after five minutes, I'm writhing in pain. White or red wine, no problem. Honestly, I don't think the gastritis worsened during my Trojan Horse experience, but insomnia definitely did. I always told myself...

BEEP↑BEEP↑BEEP↑ BEEP↑

Ahhh, I feel something different now, lower it a bit, please!

Of course.

BEEP↓BEEP↓BEEP↓BEEP↓

– breathing pause –

Insomnia was one of the reasons I thought of quitting a thousand times. As an artist, I always took whatever freedoms I wanted. I chose not to become a doctor partly for that reason.[3] Working in school gave me a freedom that I didn't think any job could offer, and I always took that liberty. But in these years in Palaexpo, I felt I didn't have it, and I didn't cope well with that. But I didn't quit because I had the feeling that the people I was in conflict with would have been happy if I did. Why let them win?

Any regrets?

Certainly, this feeling of fear of failure is a bit like a toxin that stays inside and takes the form of resentment. After the Palaexpo experience ended, I had a sort of bile overflow. For example, I don't set foot there anymore because I don't want to play the hypocrite with people I'd rather tell to go to hell. I hope the bitterness will pass; it's better not to dwell on it. The resentment is so deep that in some of my biographies, I've removed the title of Palaexpo president from 2018 to 2022. Erased, information removed. It feels like something toxic that I want to get rid of, but it's hard, and I realize it's a bit of a pointless act, so I'm ashamed of it. President with shame, not with merit, with shame.

Shame on you!

Why not? I often talk about shame with young artists because I know from experience that when you do strange, unconventional work, you hesitate and feel embarrassed. I'm aware that as an artist, that's exactly where you need to go. In shame, there's a lot to be found—a lot of density

3 Cesare Pietroiusti studied medicine and graduated from clinical psychiatry.

in meaning. The important thing is to turn shame into a practice of freedom. I already feel better; it's good to talk. Thank you.

Happy to contribute to your self-analysis. It's nice to express and name things. What do you find unspeakable about the experience?

The topic of the unspeakable reaches heights of thought and my artistic work that aren't the subject now; they have to do with the experience of death, with a totality that speaks. Returning to the metaphor, the soldiers inside the Trojan Horse almost don't breathe, to avoid being heard. In that sense, silence can also have a strategic function, not declaring intention.

BEEP↑BEEP↑BEEP↑

Also there is the negative silence, the loss of the freedom to speak. For me, any attitude that tends to close the mouth, based on criteria tied to morality, religion, etc., from any side, is very dangerous, at least as much, if not more, than the opposite excess. I don't trust anyone who claims to be on the side of righteousness. Maybe my cultural background teaches me, from a young age, to distrust priests. And that attitude is more important than the explicit content of the discourse.

BEEP↑BEEP↑BEEP↑

The famous political correctness, I've been feeling it these past few years like a blanket that tends to silence people.

BEEP↑BEEP↑BEEP↑

The conditions... Ow! Lower it a bit!...

BEEP↓

A little more, please.

BEEP↓BEEP↓↓↓

As I was saying, the conditions are such that even personal relationships are always mediated, hindered by many parallel things, so I don't know... well, I got a bit distracted.

I'm raising the pain threshold a little so you can listen better. Does it feel right? BEEP↓BEEP↓

Acceptable.

Good. BEEP↓BEEP↓ You can relax. Can you think of a word in your work that resonates with the exit from the horse?

Ah, it's hard to choose. The word that stimulates me most is *ecstacy*[4] because, perhaps in recent years, experiences like Lac o Le Mon[5] opened up a field of interest that wasn't so present in my artistic research before. It's kind of a new thing. In hindsight, I realized that certain joyful, beautiful moments always had this *ecstatic* component. Lac o Le Mon, for me, is a place where we create the conditions for this to happen—not, of course, at Palaexpo. There's potential linked to that kind of thing, which is fundamentally a foundation, an institution, but also tied to the physical conditions of the architecture, the surrounding land, the limitation of resources. As a co-director, the attempt I am making is to let the foundation grow with this freedom...

BEEP↑ BEEP↑

And let such community moments emerge. Because **ecstasy means to go out of the self.**

BEEP↑

A movement from place. To get out of... OUCH! It hurts...You try it every now and then, huh?

4 Not meant to convey mystical absorption, but rather the ancient Greek etymology of ἔκστασις (ekstasis), "to be or stand outside oneself, a removal to elsewhere" derived from ek- ("out") and stasis ("standing").

5 The Lac or Le Mon Foundation was established in late 2015 by artists Emilio Fantin, Luigi Negro, Giancarlo Norese, Cesare Pietroiusti, and Luigi Presicce in San Cesareo di Lecce, Italy.

I am sorry, I'll lower it. BEEP↓BEEP↓ Can we call it an *institutional alter ego*?

The word institution obviously has a Latin root, but it still gives the idea of a place of staying, of confirming positions. So, of course, there's a fundamental contradiction. ***Institutional ecstasy* as a way out.** *But what is this ecstatic component*? On an abstract level: the feeling of collectively thinking about a thought in which everyone there participates and no one particularly claims authorship of that thought. So, a thought that everyone feels is their own, or at least shared, that circulates and is felt joyfully because everyone is happy that the other person is thinking it too.

A *collective epiphany*?

Yes, something like that. They can be simple thoughts, but then there's that joyful moment, which is the sharing of something already seen together, and you especially see that others see it too.

A *resonance*?

Exactly. And this participation makes the thought the thing you're thinking: content with the circularity of the collective experience. Then, beyond this, the next step—and I realized this with the drunken lectures, the Dionysian experiences, etc.—is that ecstasy is thinking with the body.[6]

BEEP↑ BEEP↑

Suddenly, everything becomes one, let's say: mind and body. A unified whole in which bodily sensation contributes to thought and vice versa. A thing that works and resembles the erotic moment of falling in love. When the Eros works on various levels, not sure how to express this feeling.... We could say that it is almost more exciting if this Eros appears in a collective context. Because it's clear that it can

6 Cesare has co-led multi-day drunken seminars over the past several years.

happen one-on-one, but when it is collective... We indeed err in connoting the word orgy, the Greeks called it orgia and it is precisely that sensation, a kind of collective Eros of mind and body, mind and sense become a bit of a whole. What I discovered is that joy is not just intellectual, it is precisely a joyful sensation. The other level, to return to the unspeakable we talked about before, is the feeling of being part of the whole, where individuality is yes real, but it is as real as the inevitable belonging of each of our particles to a whole, for which the term we call life is just a parenthesis, partial as well. And even that, our cells will be different tomorrow thanks to the spaghetti or steak we eat tonight, and ten years from now, they'll be even more different. All these parts belong to a whole, and the thought that activates a thought about those mysteries is the same thought that makes you realize you're experiencing death. So, you no longer fear it because you've experienced that you're part of a whole. Easier said than done. For example, the experience with mushrooms is deeply connected to feeling part of a whole.

We will let you go now.

BEEP↓ BEEP↓ BEEP↓ BEEP↓ BEEP↓ BEEP↓ BEEP↓ BEEP↓ BEEP↓

BEEP↓ BEEP↓ BEEP↓ BEEP↓ BEEP↓ BEEP↓ BEEP↓ BEEP↓ BEEP↓

BEEP↓ BEEP↓ BEEP↓ BEEP↓ BEEP↓ BEEP↓ BEEP↓ BEEP↓ BEEP↓ BEEP↓ BEEP↓ BEEP↓ BEEP↓ BEEP↓ BEEP↓ BEEP↓ BEEP↓ BEEP↓

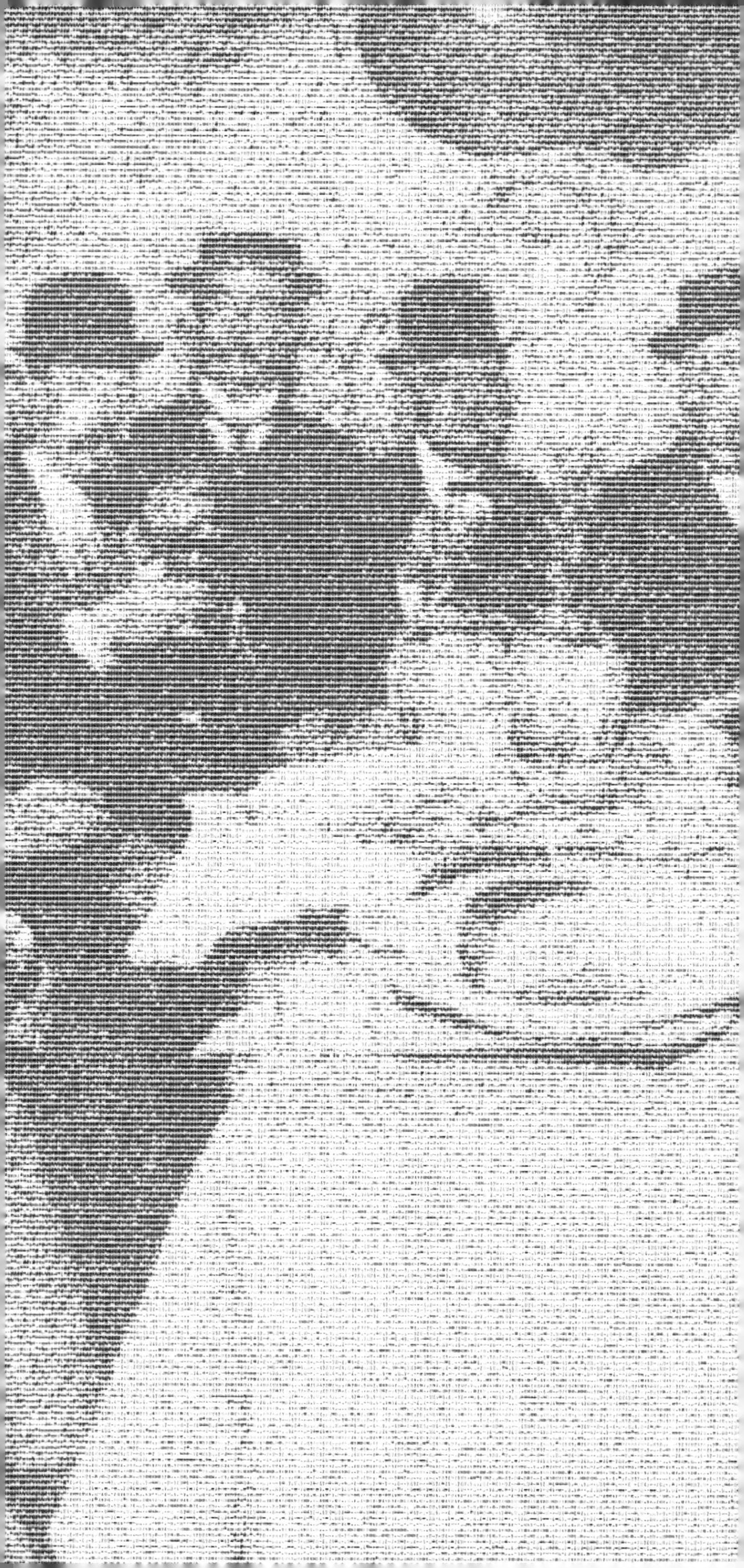

In 1911, a colossal bronze monument to King Vittorio Emanuele of Italy was unveiled near the Roman Forum. On inauguration day, two toasts were raised inside the belly of its sixteen-times-life-size horse. However, it appears there were actually two toasts. One was for the dignitaries including the mayor, Lord Torlonia, and the national minister, Bertolini. The other belonged to the foundry workers who built it. Twenty-one of them gathered at a table inside the monument, toasting the horse from within, unsanctioned but unforgettable.

Tales of Disillusions

Meriç Öner

Meriç Öner brings a nuanced perspective to discussions of institutional survival, subversion, and the emotional complexities of navigating the intricate spaces within cultural organizations. Drawing on her tenure as the Director of Research and Programs at Salt, one of Turkey's leading art and research institutions, she writes as a seasoned Trojan Horse belly-dweller. Through vivid metaphors of car crashes, skid marks, rearview mirrors and patches, Öner probes the disillusionment around the notion of "institutional death," an impossibility that both frustrates and fascinates her. Annoyed by the inner workings of these systems, she weaves personal experiences with broader reflections on institutional critique, crafting a narrative that engages on multiple registers and invites deeper contemplation.

Trojan Horse, a War Tactic, Really?

It is only befitting that we speak of culture and its many institutions using terminology borrowed from mythology—wars and gods. Yes, these concepts can easily be considered the epitome of human existence, covering both the physical and metaphysical. But isn't it a failure when the peace-making, love-promoting, long-term-thinking art world still relies on these analogies to make a point? For me, it's OK; it helps to deconstruct the polarities that originally construct the terminology. For every god, there is at least one believer in their power; for every war, there is at least one side ready to take and the other, well, not so ready to give. Culture is simply what is woven among these. It may be practical, useful, a whisper to the soul, a tingling sensation to the body, a real boost to the faculties of the brain—idolizing or commoning, tone-deaf or woke, cheerful and solemn, a second away from being cut financially or otherwise, contemporary yet allegedly timeless. All these, and the cracks in between. Then how dare I speak ill of the culture war when culture is but all that?

The Ever Unattainable Greater Good

In the early 2000s, I was working by day as an architect and drinking by night with 20-somethings like me. Still, I managed to wake up pretty early and had this routine of going to the office before the rest. There was only one computer connected to the internet. There, I would go online to acikradyo.com.tr to copy-paste and print the latest online texts—an article by Robert Fisk, George Monbiot, Paul Krugman, or Noam Chomsky, an interview with Arundhati Roy by Amy Goodman, etc. On those early mornings, I read pieces on 9/11, later followed by the war in Iraq, often with bits on global warming—as it was called back in the day. Each one contributed to my ongoing sense of shock. I was a young woman with no radical bone in my body. I remain a similar woman in my mid-40s. Yet I was deeply changed by learning the existence of two distinct things. One is a sense of immense and timeless despair, which easily leads first to confusion, then to anger.

I remember the peak of this feeling while reading about the killing of Rachel Corrie, a woman of my age defending Palestinians against Israeli settlers. The second is the rhetoric of good and evil. I had neither ties to religion nor a taste for classic literature. Those could be the only reasons why I missed the grand narrative of the world. As I said, I remained a silent observer, largely because I wasn't sold on the idea of absolute good and evil. Rather, they were our shared and infinite resources for the wars with one another. I'm not trying to portray our daily frustrations and struggles as acts out of supervillain movies. I'm simply acknowledging the greater good as an impossibility. Then its rhetoric can clearly be read as a war tactic of recomposing the ground. And, well, a war is nasty but always somehow justified.

Generations: Oh, but Sweet Domination

I'm definitely up for representing the world through memes. Probably because I always enjoyed cartoons—daily comic strips, moving ones on TV, surprised to learn some were translated into Turkish, relieved to know some were always the originals. My father especially loved one from that grim-looking black-and-white Cumhuriyet newspaper when I was a kid. He once said, "This is an article disguised in a few strokes." That perspective stayed with me. Today, it feels as if you're only as relevant as how much of the humor you truly understand, even deciphering the sting in a meme. It's a breath of fresh air, especially as I find lectures that value word count and thesaurus-level vocabulary most tiresome. One word sums up the friendly, invisible competition in the genre: Legacy. Yes, legacy might be the worst curse of the cultural thinker. They would like to be quoted, studied, selected, and praised in the future. These things do and most likely will continue to happen. It's almost the very bizarre nature of the work, to be evaluated later, in decades, or better centuries. How sad, if we all wait to be finally called the genius. The "one-incredible-person-whodunit-all" narrative, on the other hand, caters to the highly incentivized inspiration market. If it's actually about the work, well, it already happened, meaning it already did its magic on some minds, or not. It's a gamble to claim a grasp on a new generation's values. Just attempting it proves I belong to an older one. Still, in the case that reports point to a sensible direction, the youth within the realm of the cultural thinker don't seem to qualify as mentor hunters. Mentorship is a corporate operation, much like the inspiration market and the contemporary cultural institution.

Institutions or Mile-long Debris of a Car Crash

I came across debris from a car crash while driving this summer. It was a perfectly even road with a circular inclination of the slightest degree. The one particular difficulty was that on the left side, the road ended with a wall. The driver must have somehow calculated the angle wrong and probably could not get back on the lane once the wall started tearing up the car as its bits and pieces came into contact with it. I had already received this invitation to write about the "death of the institution." I studied the scene in my rearview mirror for the longest time that it took the debris to disappear from my sight. I realized then that it was never possible to speak of death when it came to an institution. If one reason is that they strive and strategize for, as well as are defined by, a common goal of reaching immortality, another is that it is unrealistically dramatic in light of the actual mechanics of their existence. In reality, the driver might have died on the scene or been rushed away by an ambulance. In the hopeful rare chance, they might have also walked out from the car at the exact point where I saw the end of the accident. Only in the final option will they have a visual of the incident. Maybe they would receive the crime scene report months later, a piece of paper written with technical specifications of the location, speed, the actual physical length of the skid marks, etc. In any case, they won't see what I saw—the thing that becomes less terrifying yet more obvious as you drive past. All in all, a car doesn't really die. It is either patched up or fully renewed following the insurer's willy-nilly questioning. It might be returned to the driver or the legal heir. At that point, it is both too late and too early to be suspicious of the road infrastructure or the upkeep of the vehicle. These elements, hushed away before an inquiry, help sustain the casual glimpses of immortality. They would prove their worth, of course, if they didn't fail in reality.

How Not to Wear Your Heart on Your Sleeve

I wished the unradical in me would provide me with fewer delusions and refrain me from grand expectations to remain real to life. Not possible. Is it just me, or was my whole generation trapped by the idea and image of cool? Did anyone really impress anyone, or were we just complicit in promoting legends that keep the vicious circle of good and evil spinning? Could we choose not to drive if the road looks slightly dark and the car feels a little dodgy?

Will the Next Proxy Please Stand Up

I never really quit drinking. I just had to phase out of that lifestyle with age. I also found a way to push past the despair, even if only minimally and temporarily. After I tucked away my degree in architecture and joined the ranks of the cultural workers I identified the institution as a proxy for the publics, those I imagined surrounding us. I saw it as a common ground for speaking to one another without the prerequisite of reaching consensus. In short, the institution wasn't us; it was a proxy for a larger group that we, as the managing people, couldn't fully represent. Neither would I dare to do so. Things kept changing, it seems. Over the next ten years, I noticed that individuals had to become proxies for the systems sustaining the institutions, which in return stood tall to continue the fight for the greater good. Some things remained the same, though. A very rare and fine example: Açık Radyo is still an independent broadcaster despite official attempts to silence it. It seems there are ways to exist differently...

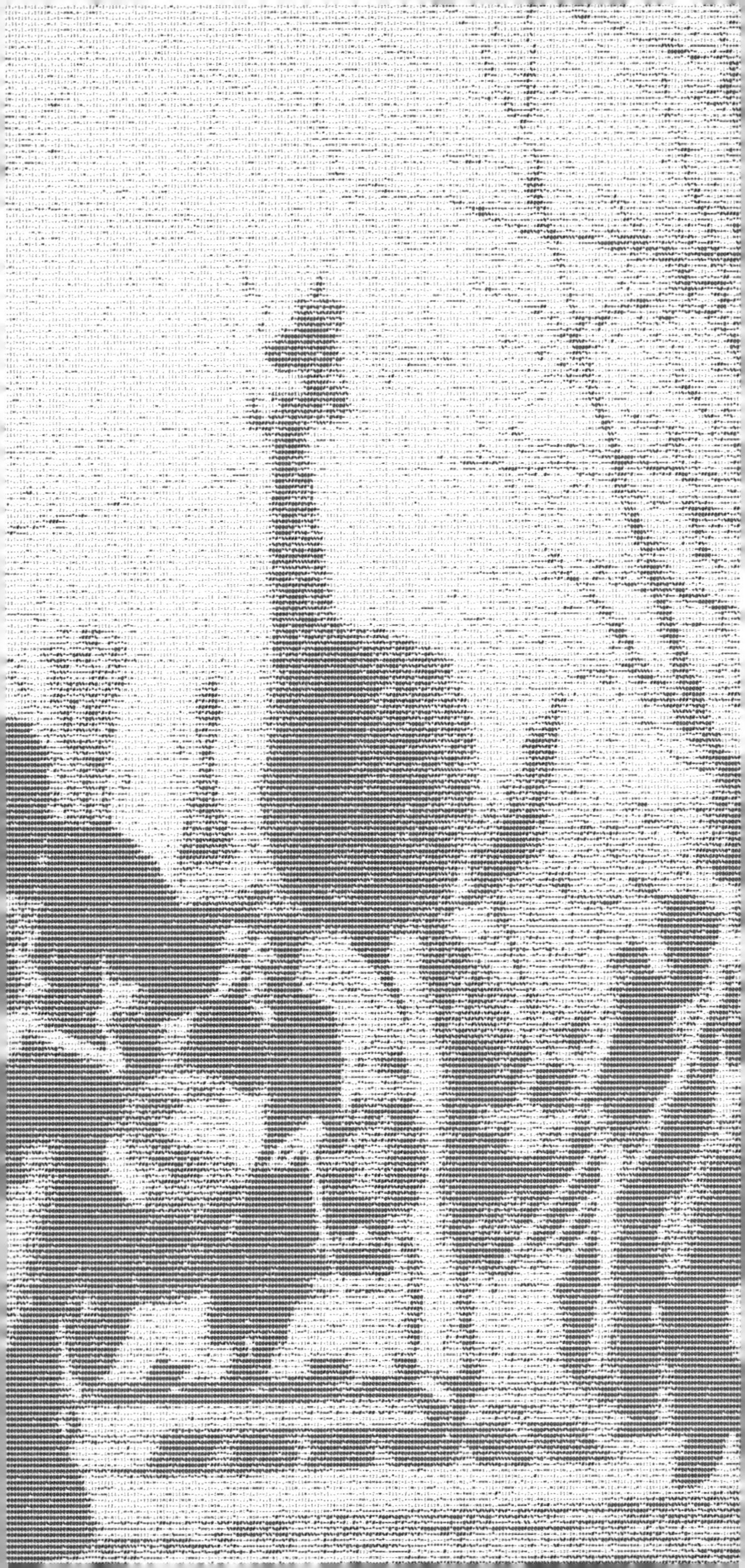

Marco Cavallo is a wooden and *papier-mâché* sculpture created in 1973 within Trieste's psychiatric hospital. It symbolically housed their desires and dreams of the patients, representing the humanity that had long been hidden in asylums and the political struggle to leave the medical institution through art and a quest for freedom and dignity long denied. It became an icon of the ethical, social, and political fight for the closure of psychiatric hospitals, culminating in the 1978 Basaglia Law which inspired global reforms. *Marco Cavallo, Trieste psychiatric hospital, Department of Mental Health of Trieste Archive, 1973.*

What if the Museum was the Horse?

Mabel Tapia

illustrations by
Panagiotis Samsarelos

This text dismantles the museum's role as a mere keeper of history, revealing it as a powerful engine of colonial, patriarchal, and bourgeois control—one that has long since strayed from its Arcadian purpose. What happened to the Muses? Museums today are often viewed as nothing more than instruments of elite power, as the calls for their destruction attest. Yet, after years of engaging with institutional structures, collaborating with and directing globally influential museums and networks, Mabel Tapia dares to hope. She believes these obsolete institutions, despite their oppressive legacy, still hold the potential for radical reimagining. Could they, instead of being dismantled, become spaces of possibility, experimentation, and new collective narratives? Would the Muses return?

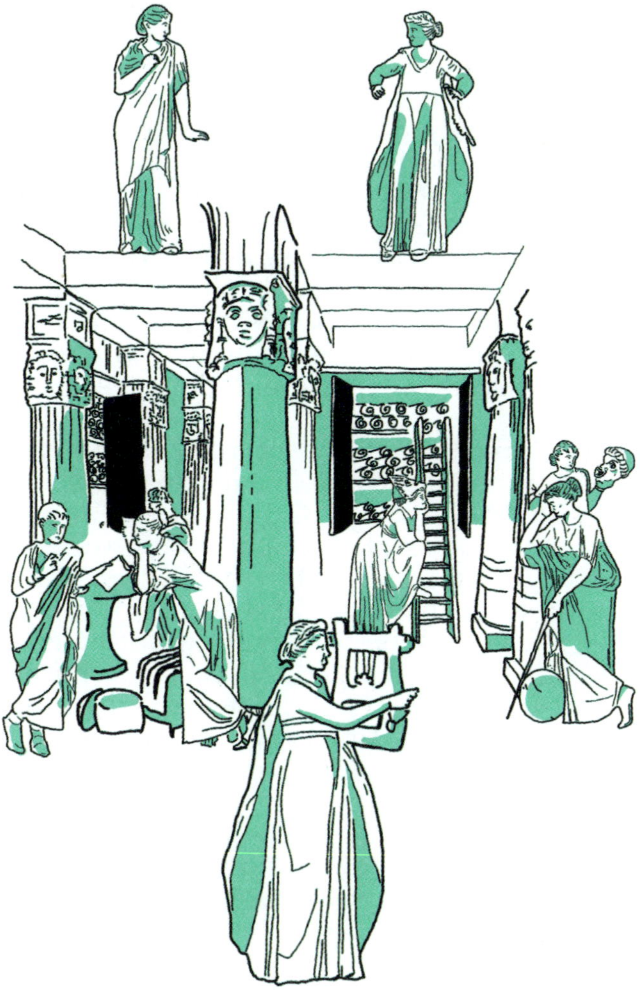

Le musée, French for museum, is masculine singular noun, as we know it today, it was born out of a founding ambivalence. On the one hand, in the aftermath of the French Revolution, museums were established with the aspiration of opening up royal collections to the people—offering what had been forbidden to them; of opening and generating a space with and for the people. On the other hand, museums quickly became privileged organs for the construction of an enlightened bourgeoisie. At the heart of the French Revolution, the very idea of the museum was directly inspired by the Greek *Mouseion.* The Greek *Mouseions* were built in the era of Ptolemy I, also in a process of modernization of the Empire. And although the *Mouseion* is proposed as a space or "temple" of the Muses, based on pagan rites where poets and alchemists sought the favor of their whispers, it is above all a place of research, experimentation and exchange. The *Mouseion* of Alexandria was the best known, but it was not the only one. Different cities in Hellenic Greece had their *Mouseion*. A space, certainly regulated, but with a library, residences, a kitchen; a space where alchemists, poets and thinkers lived, worked and exchanged. In one of the major ideological operations of Eurocentric modernity, the museum confines the Muses to precise roles and disconnects them from the whisper, suppresses the residences and the kitchen and with them all the potential space for experimentation.

With a colonial, racist and patriarchal matrix, the Museum is one of the emblematic spaces of ostentation and reproduction of the power of the State, and in some cases of transnational interests (of global capitalism); one of the places where, from an apparent innocence, capital H History is affirmed, that is, a certain type of narration, with a certain type of practices and practitioners. Thus, museums, in the historical model, have developed as affirmative machines that function in the reproduction not only of a story but, above all, of the narrative structure that supports it.

Given this heavy history, the museum is today, in many ways, an obsolete device that, at best, struggles to face its legacy and find other models of functioning in the contemporary world. And, at worst, it persists in supporting structures that can only be abandoned or destroyed.

But... what if this obsolete device were to become our battering ram? It would not be Troy that would be the place to be conquered, but the horse itself. What would happen if, being a horse, we were to settle in its body, in its legs, in its belly, in its entrails? What would happen, if we decided to settle in this organ of hegemonic thought and, taking advantage of its irremediable obsolescence, opened spaces of possibility instead of conquering them?

In its legs, in its belly, we could form like-minded, elective and de facto communities and generate spaces for the production of other knowledge, multiple narratives and experiments of the Common, creating institutional models outside the paradigm of the violence of socio-institutional reproduction. In this singular space of human

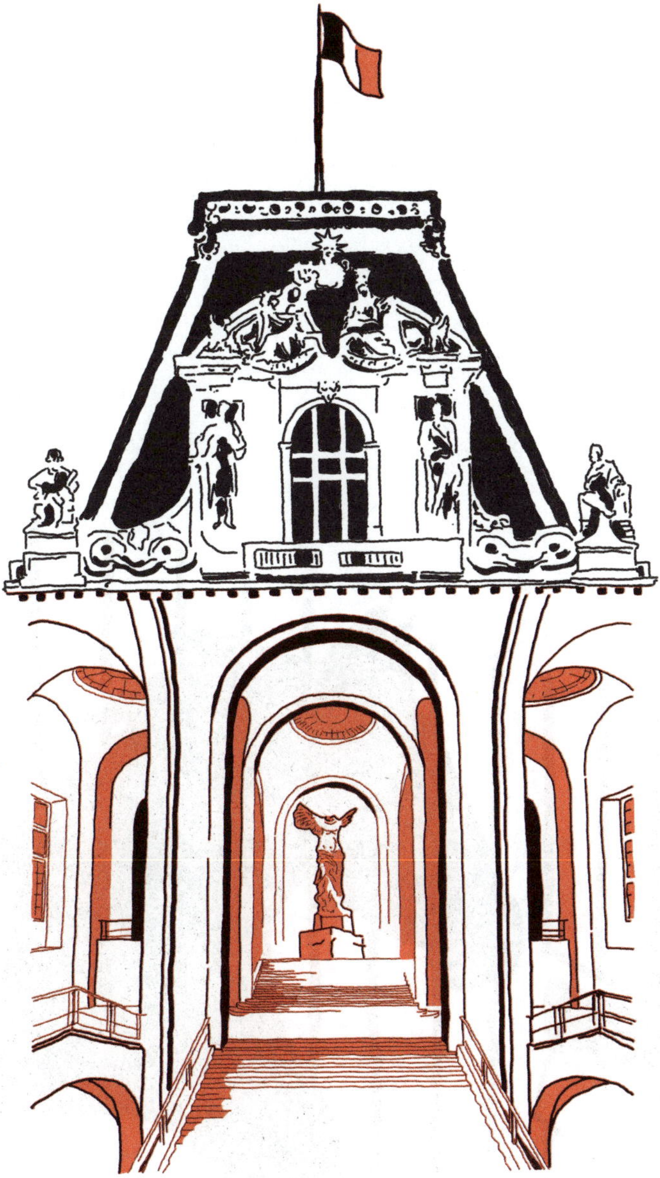

and non-human cohabitation, which is also the museum—now converted into a horse—where we settle— questions, doubts, silences could arise. It could foster radical forms of listening, intervening and reconfiguring the stories and structures it has conveyed, sustained, and reproduced for so long. As a horse that belongs to us, in its current condition as an obsolete device, the museum could perhaps—just perhaps—generate a humus from which some experiments would be imaginable.

So, why not? Let's free the Muses and settle in the horse.

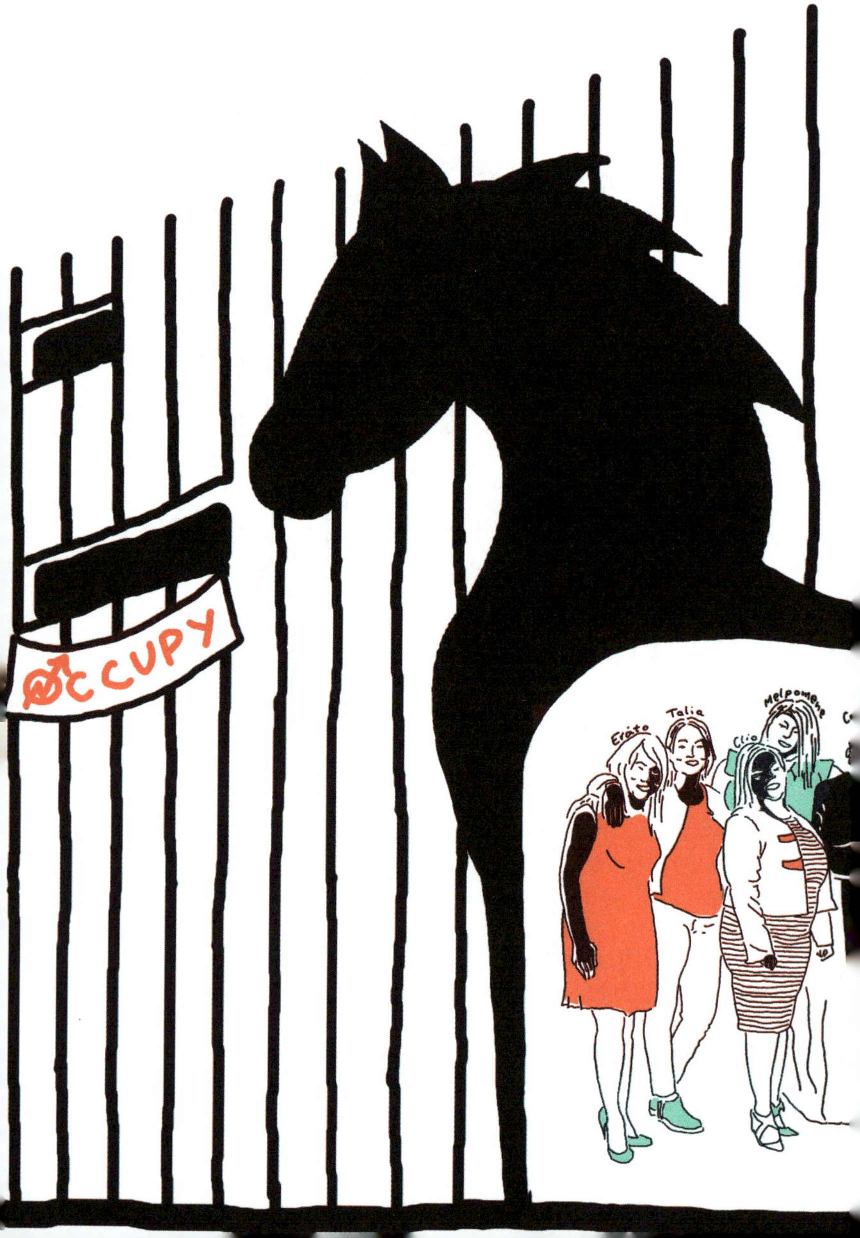

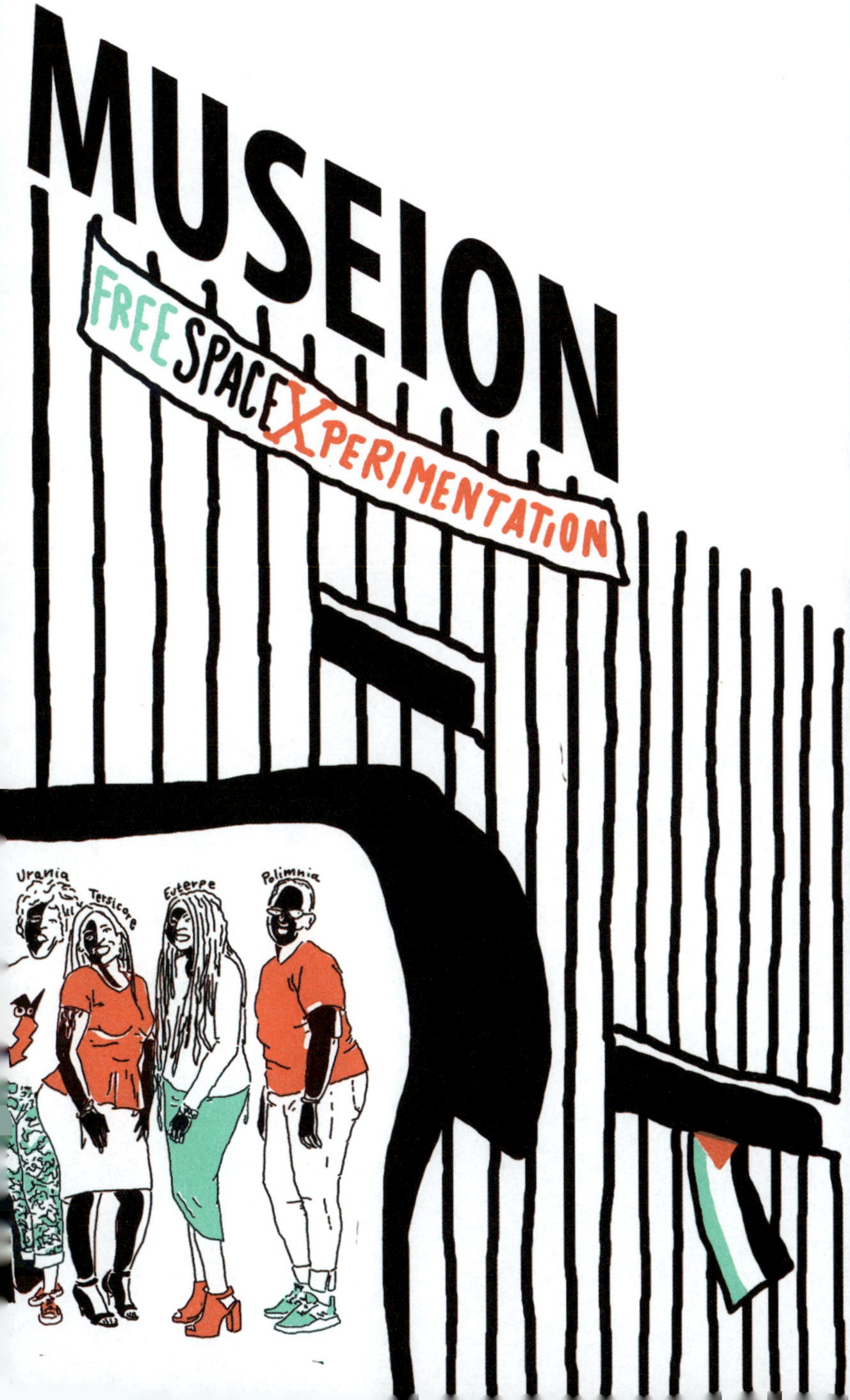
MUSEION
FREE SPACE XPERIMENTATION
Urania
Tersicore
Euterpe
Polimnia

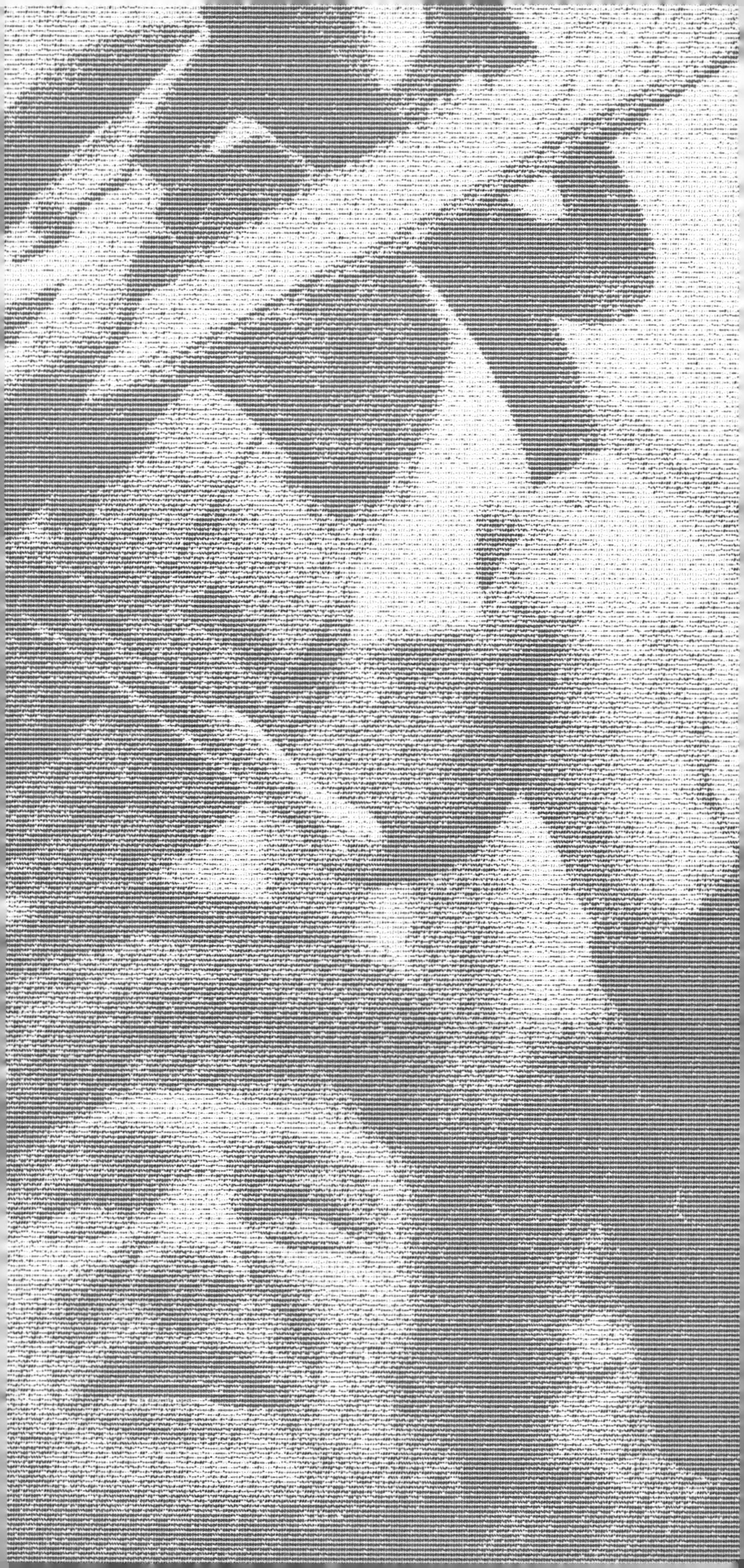

What is the current political spectrum of the Trojan Horse? Dear friend Martin Flugelman pushes back on our metaphor: if you admire the Trojan Horse, look at who is riding it today. The far right has already claimed the role "I love being the mole in the state. I am the one who destroys the state from within. It's like having infiltrated enemy lines. I hate the state," Argentinian President Javier Milei stated in an interview with the North American The Free Press in June 2024.

Trojan Dialectics

Stephen Wright

Secretly stored in his hippocampus, Stephen Wright hosts one of the most replenished Trojan Horse living archives. Artists intrust him with their hidden motives and covert strategies, which he seldom discloses, releasing, instead, distilled drops of anti-art anecdotes. Routed through the frontal cortex, such knowledge is personalized and implemented in his own out-of-scheme practice. For this book, he offers his ontological take of the Trojan Horse topos, followed by a captivating and torrential list of obscure agents of change, shared here. He closes with the very belly-related narratives about the difficulties and complications of being such an agent in his current role as a museum co-director.

Fermenting in the Belly of the Beast

In a seminar which he gave in Paris in the 1990s on the Rhetoric of Cannibalism, Jacques Derrida had the habit of opening each session with an unvarying incantation, declaimed with great emphasis, as if the careful locution of the phrasing might disclose the inner mystery of the three-part assertion. Il faut manger. Bien manger. Manger l'autre. One must eat. Eat well. Eat the other. The sentence seemed to advance rather like the horseman on the chess-board, moving forward first one square (*manger*), then a second square (*bien manger*), then one to the side (*manger l'autre*). The important thing, Derrida often stressed, was not so much to eat (which was sort of self-evident), but to eat well. But what, he would then ask, does it mean to eat well? Let alone to eat the other well. Importantly, it was a rhetorical maneuver without a subject: eating must occur, must be done well, the other must be eaten—not merely ingurgitated, but digested, carefully chewed, assimilated...

The seminar sought to draw attention to the kinship between the rhetoric of reading and that of eating—of eating the other. But what was of primary interest to Derrida were the leftovers, that which remained once the feasting and the reading was done. We eat well, eat the other, but something remains unmetabolized, resisting assimilation, and thus remaining inherently unstable. What was it like to become the other by devouring them; and conversely, what was it like to be eaten, absorbed, digested, chewed over (the list went on for weeks), but only partially so? What was it like to find oneself, l'autre de l'autre, the other's other, in the belly and digestive tract of the other? The experience of being assimilated—but only partially—is a fascinating philosophical and gastronomic issue, with decidedly political implications. What can simply not be digested? Situationist Guy Debord once wrote, rather unexpectedly though quite logically, that he was not opposed to recuperation... on the condition that the recuperation be total, that is without any remainder, for then the "recuperated" would, in effect, have triumphed. A possibility that Derrida, for his part, ruled out.

What then is it like to dwell in the belly of the beast? For one thing, it can be pretty lonely in there, for it is above all one's most obdurate alterity that goes unmetabolized. Certainly, if one is well eaten—as one should be—then one sheds one's initial otherness to enjoy symbiosis and a protracted, stable union with the host, breaking down the binary between host and guest, eater and eaten, one and other. But what of the unassimilable remainder? At what point does it implement its exit strategy?

"I was sentenced to twenty years of boredom", quips songwriter Leonard Cohen, "for trying to change the system from within". Boredom is the punishment meted out for stalling one's exit from the bowels of a system one entered to transform it from within. But a premature exit, before one is assimilated at all—where one is not yet well eaten—is equally undesirable, for if one is regurgitated before any digestion (or too little) occurs, no mutual change can occur. No meal taken together. In her 1998 book *Symbiotic Planet*, life-systems scientist Lynn Margulis describes in vivid terms a kind of plant-animal arrangement to illustrate how symbiosis functions, and effectively, how through eating and being eaten life is one. There is a type of "seaweed" in Brittany, which is in fact not seaweed at all but actually translucent sea worms that have feasted on green photosynthesizing algae, which gives them their colour.

> "Although lovely, the green algae are not merely decorative: they live and grow, die and reproduce, inside the bodies of the worms. Indeed they produce the food that the worms eat. The mouths of the worms become superfluous and do not function after the worm larvae hatch. Sunlight reaches the algae inside their mobile greenhouses and allows them to grow and feed themselves as they leak photosynthetic products and feed their hosts from the inside. The symbiotic algae even do the worm a waste management favour: they recycle the worm's uric acid waste into nutrients for themselves. Algae and worm make a miniature ecosystem swimming in the sun. Indeed, these two beings are so intimate that it is difficult... to say where the animal ends and the algae begin."

No need, here, to exploit the gatekeeper's vulnerability, or to flatter the vanity of power by bearing uncommon gifts, or to bite one's tongue in the name of implementing some Trotskyist ploy of entrism in order to gain way and then to wait, and wait, and wait… But rather to bear in mind that a meal is best enjoyed together.

Not Not Art

In our society, it is the Trojan Horse that functions as the go-to metaphor to describe minimally invasive (but still invasive) strategies of this kind. It is tempting to suggest that in its highest vocation, art operates as a Trojan Horse. Certainly Virgil intended that we should see the Trojan Horse as an allegory for the workings of poetry, splitting appearance from essence in order to penetrate the ramparts of opinion and convention, releasing its invisible power once inside, by which time it is presumably too late to mitigate its influence. By this account, in the Trojan Horse, two ontologies of art temporarily merge and then split: art as representation (regardless of scale), and art as operativity, on the 1 to 1 scale, with a deliberately impaired coefficient of specific visibility. The operative dimension is embedded within the representative dimension as long as is required (which may be a very, very long time of course) before ultimately deploying at the chosen moment. In this way, artists and art-related practitioners—like Odysseus and his crew—contrive some strategy to forestall the declarative moment when the plan is, literally, mise en oeuvre.

There are countless examples of art donning a primary or secondary ontology to gain traction in the real, Trojan-Horse style. Yet this is a fraught analogy in many ways. Of course art does need to deploy strategies to achieve its ends; art is by no means exempt from strategic rationality. But art does not do so from a position of power, unlike the Greeks, who after all were an imperial army with an eye on conquering and colonizing Troy. It may be tempting to describe mainstream art practice in these terms, colonizing as it does every nook and cranny of the public sphere. But at that point, the

Trojan Horse ceases to be an interesting artistic proposition and becomes a purely cynical ploy. In other words, if the Trojan Horse is to be retained as a viable, throught-provoking strategy, capable of transforming the conceptual architecture of institutions by affording access to the conceptual edifices themselves, a further dialectical movement is required.

Perhaps we might wonder what kind of art could be loaded into the belly of a horse, which is more a trades-persons truck than a storage room. And what undigested form it might take while it's in there. Above all, how might we get it out, and what, indeed, would we then get out of it? To ask what one might get out of art is implies there are things in art that might be teased out and thus made available for repurposing elsewhere... Like behind institutional walls. But what are these properties and how are they to be released from their assemblage? This again is the question of eating well. So accustomed are we to thinking of art in its integrated mode—those supremely condensed symbolic configurations encountered as works, enjoying unimpeachably high coefficients of art—that the question merely sounds like an awkward way of asking what art expresses? But what if— following the lead of an increasing number of contemporary practices—we think of art not in its integrated, unified mode but as contingent clusters or assemblages of competences, energies, historical inferences and lineages, devices and skillsets that can be disassembled and redeployed, often far from the performative framework of the mainstream artworld? What if, in other words, we consider art not as a symbolic activity premised on some alleged specificity but as a practice oriented toward compatibility—its detachable components compatible with practices from other avenues of social activity? While the art of modernity premised its aesthetic function on its specificity and relative autonomy, this was historically a departure from art before and after the modern moment, in which art has sought to infuse and enhance other practices with art-compatible (and not art-specific) properties and strategies. Looking at a wide range of contemporary examples of recombinant practice, we will consider art from this perspective of the exploded view, deactivating its aesthetic function to more fully activate other usological functions. Art sundered from itself; art as a de-ontologized toolbox; art out of art. Not art at all, really. But not not art either. To that strange double negative, let us add another.

Not Not a Horse

It has been suggested by some scholars and archaeologists that while the Greeks may indeed have used a "Trojan Horse" strategy to slyly gain access to Troy, the gift vehicle was not a sculpture of a horse at all, but was in fact a ship, with warriors hidden in the hull. Ships are more than once referred to as "sea horses" in ancient texts, and were allegedly often decorated with horse heads. It has also been argued that the vessel may have been covered with damp horse hides, as was often the case with ancient warships, to provide some protection against flaming arrows fired on them by enemy archers. Perhaps, then, strictly speaking, the horse was not a horse at all, but rather a sort of cargo vessel with horse head and hide. As such it was not not a horse either. But rather a useful and artfully crafted toolbox on wheels.

If his purely, even wildly speculative interpretation has any virtue whatsoever, it perhaps lies in the light it may shed on the modus operandi of transformative contemporary practice, which has become, so to speak, an art of ingredients, rather than of prepared dishes. Art has come to eschew artworks, in favour of unaggregated or only partially aggregated energies, tools and tales. Separating art from its exclusive embodiment as artwork, allows art to slip its moorings, leave the artificial art-support system of the mainstream artworld behind and integrate a broader ecosystem. In the form of seeds, perhaps, instead of prepared meals. All of which brings to mind a well known line from a more contemporary Greek, poet Dinos Christianopoulos, who provides a thought-provoking counterpoint to the Trojan Horse strategy: "What didn't you do to bury us? / But you forgot that we were seeds."

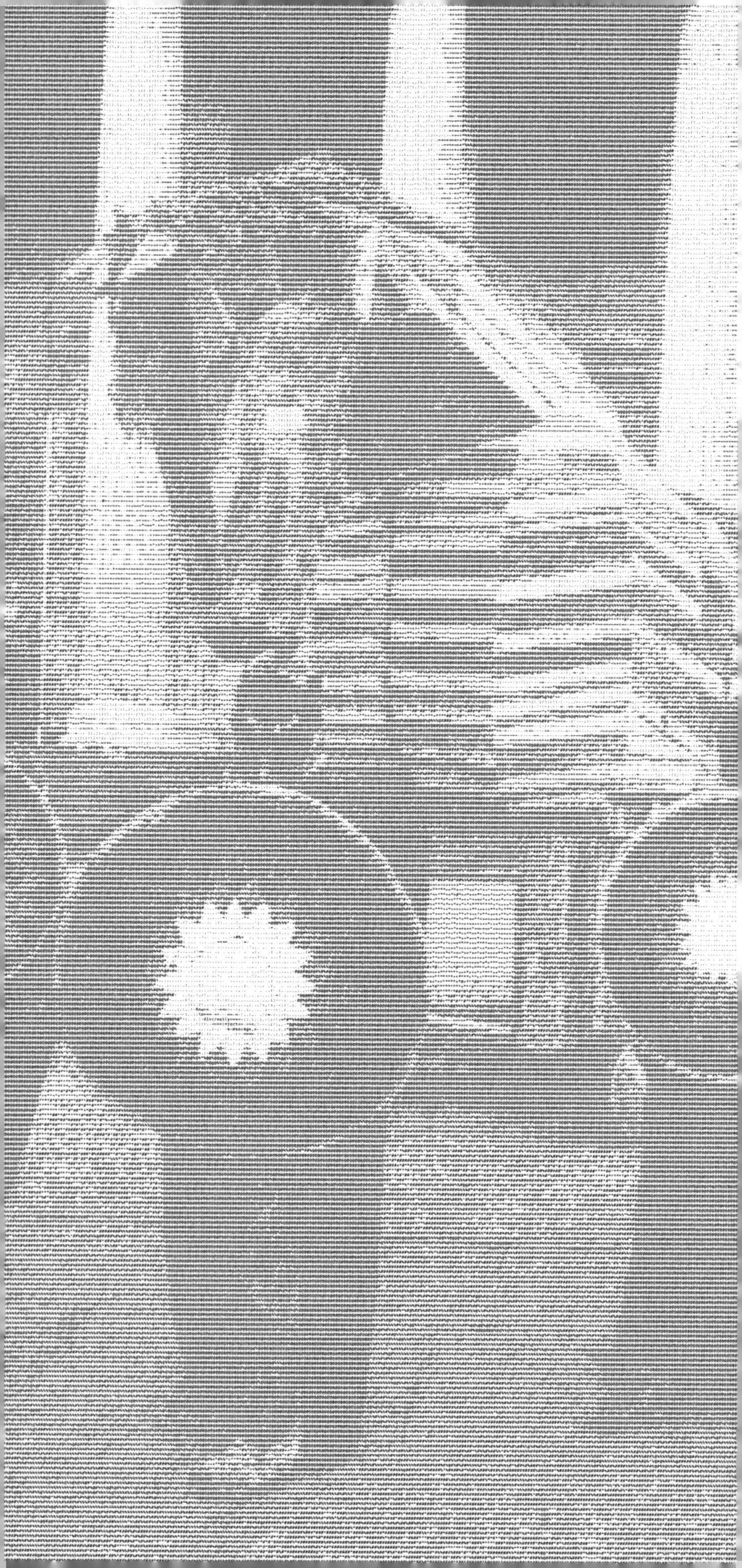

In 2020, 1,500 members of the BP or not BP? movement infiltrated the British Museum with a crowdfunded Trojan Horse to protest the institution's sponsorship deal with the oil giant British Petroleum. What BP frames as cultural patronage is, in fact, strategic camouflage; an oily attempt to scrub its crimes clean through the prestige of art. This wasn't just a protest; it was a direct action in the belly of the beast, aimed at exposing the rot beneath the marble.

Irteerako Anatomia

Emanuele Caporrella

Architect and artist Emanuele Caporrella embarks on an unconventional exploration of the iconic Guggenheim Museum Bilbao, revealing a side of the building most visitors overlook despite its ubiquity. Whether the maze-like design renders evacuation plans ineffective, or concerns that emergency maps might compromise the museum's aesthetic prevail, Frank Gehry's Guggenheim exemplifies not only the twenty-first-century "irrelevant museum" but also a curious omission: visible, legible exit plans. Through a series of photographic performances, Caporrella uncovers and documents hundreds of emergency signs hidden throughout the museum's labyrinthine corridors. What emerges is a meditation on the absence of evacuation plans and an invitation to read the structure itself beyond the art it houses.

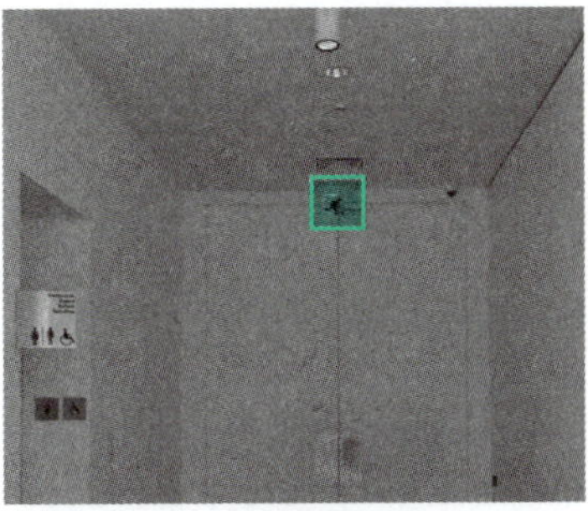

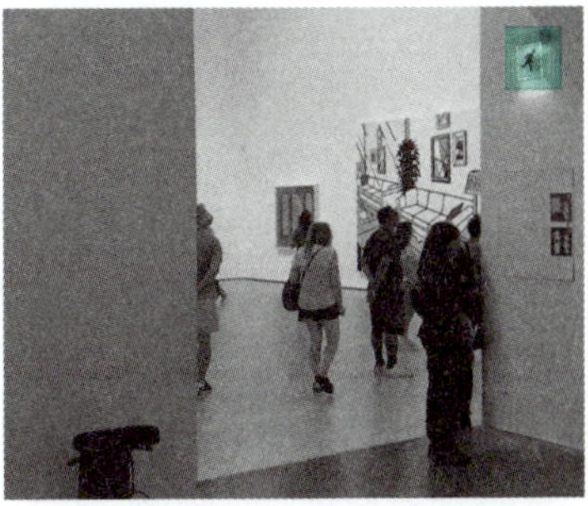

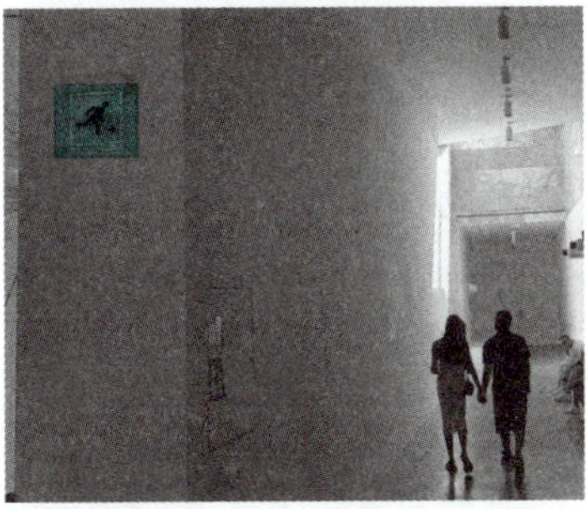

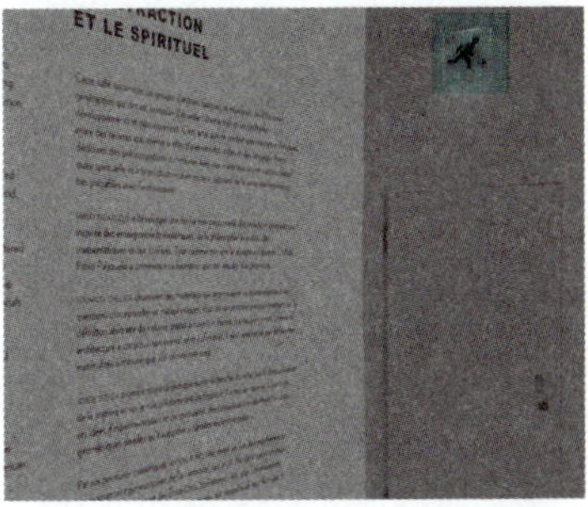
ET LE SPIRITUEL

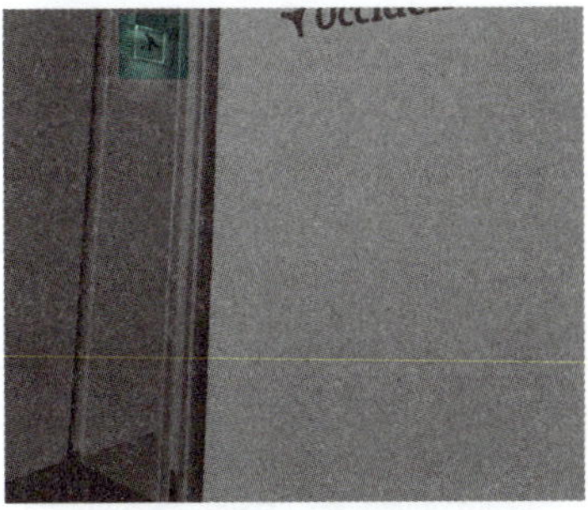

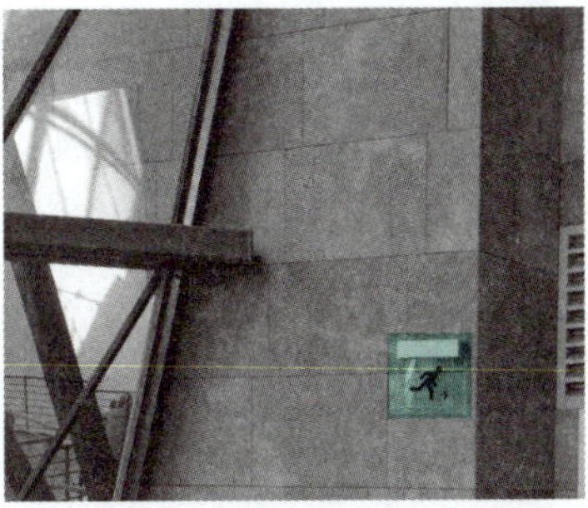

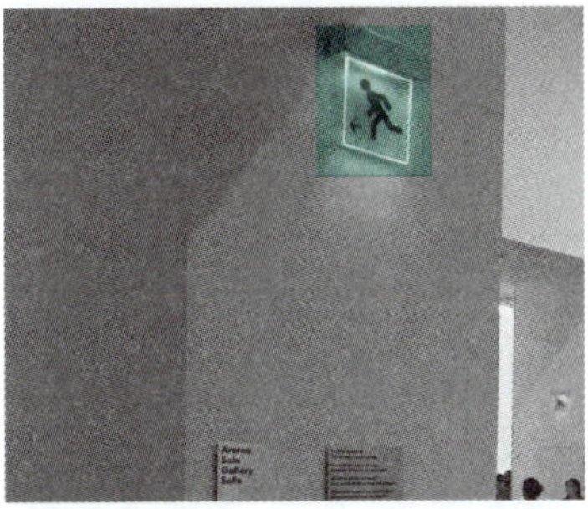

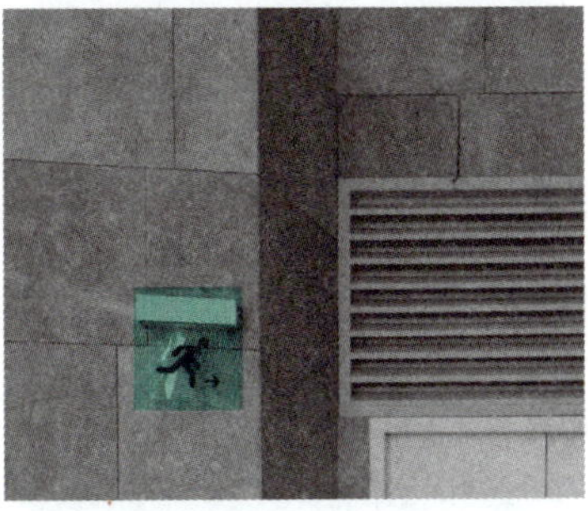

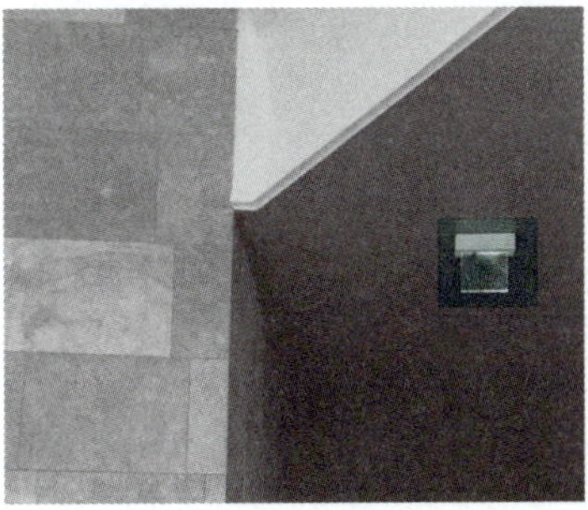

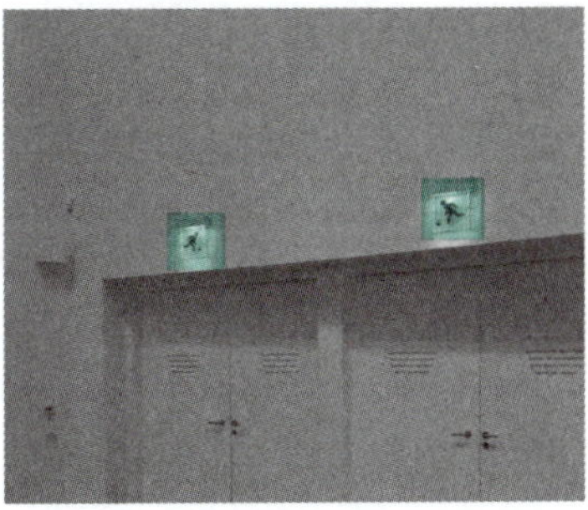

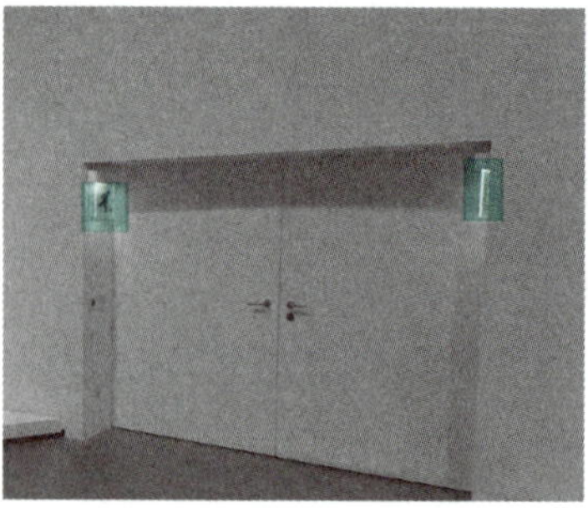
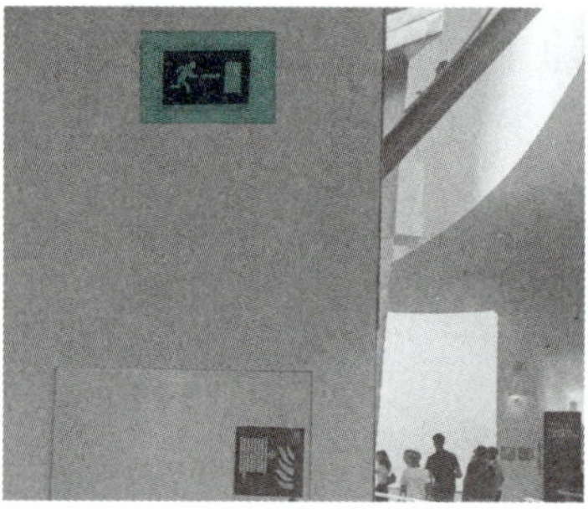
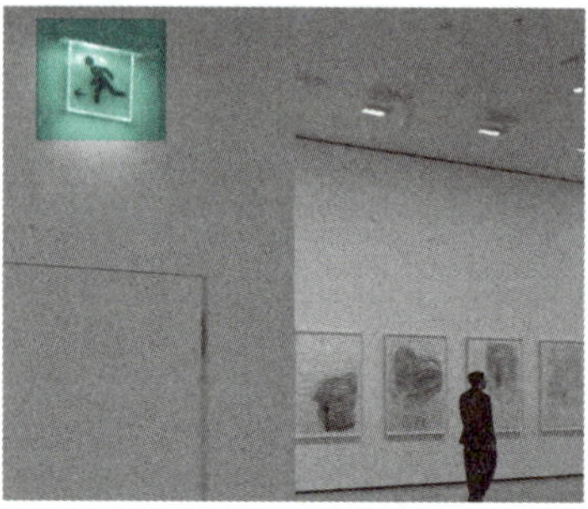
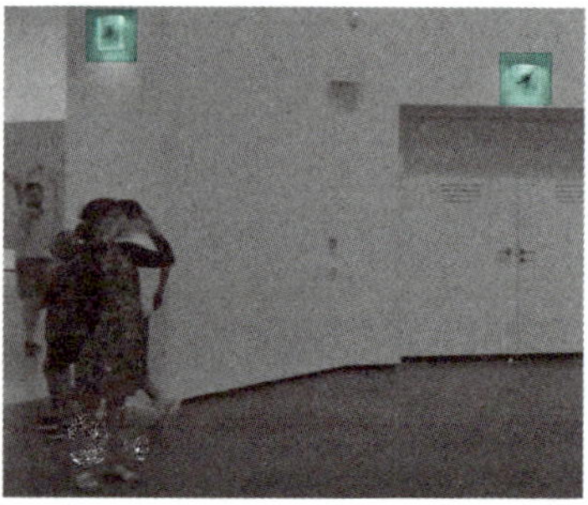
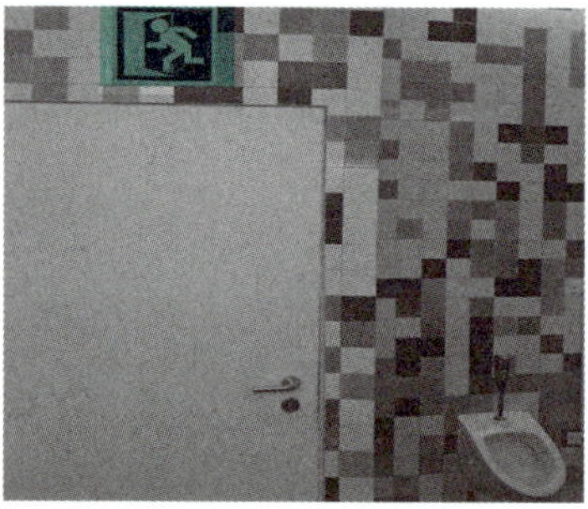
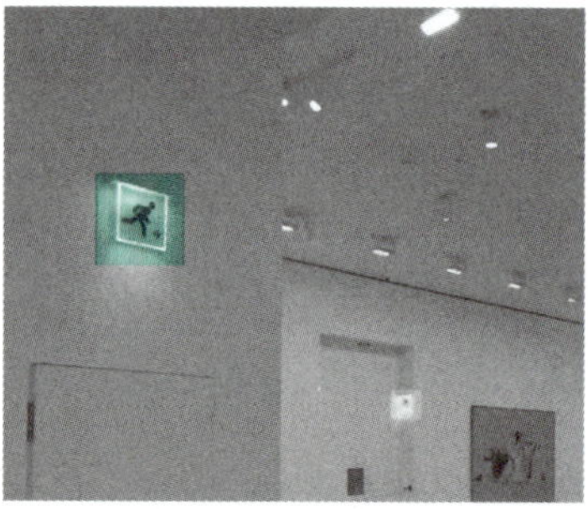
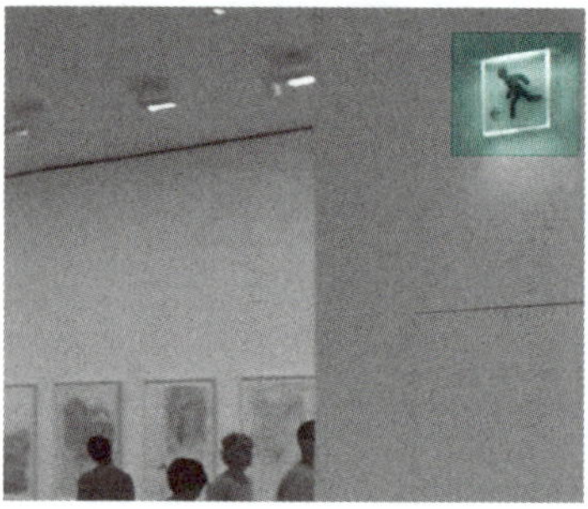
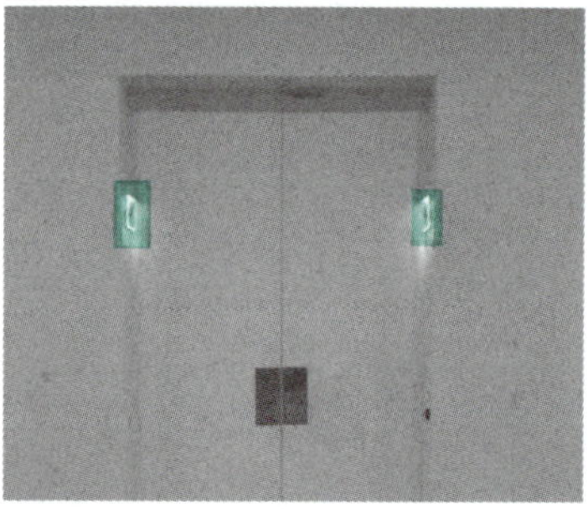
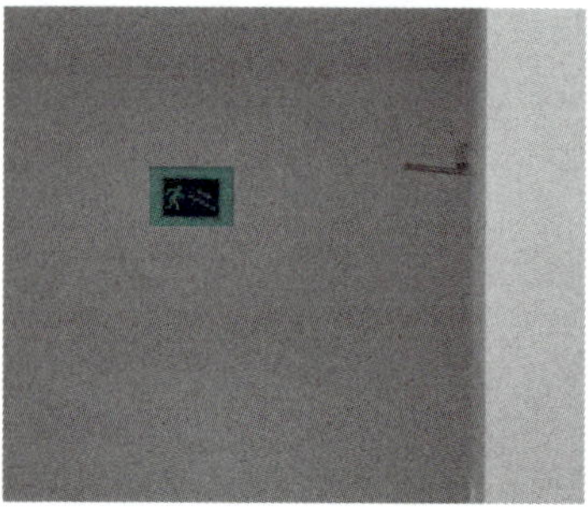
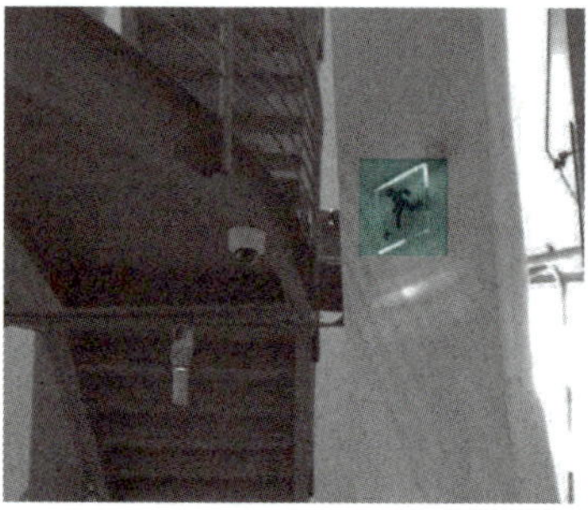

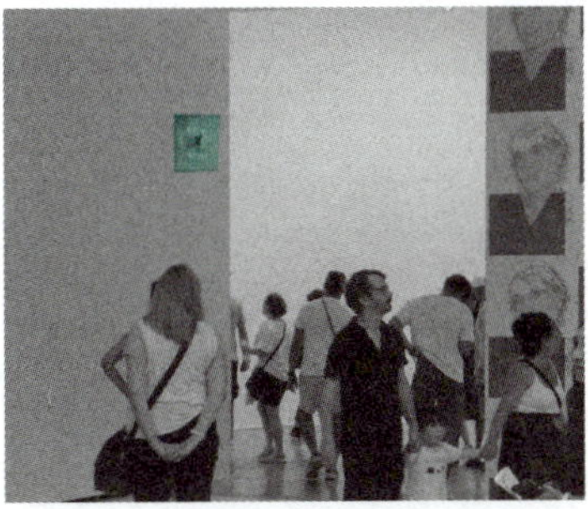
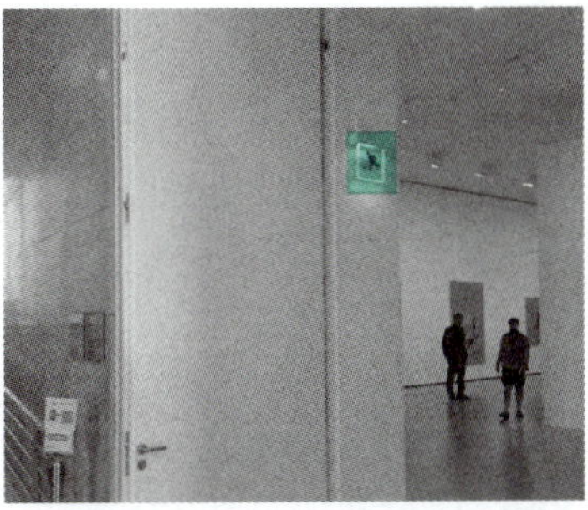
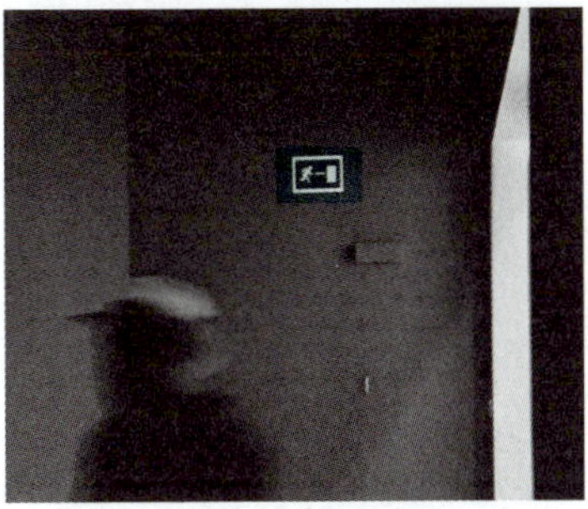
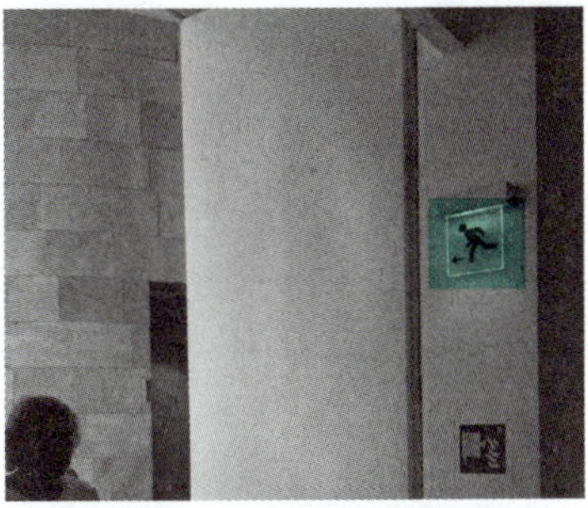
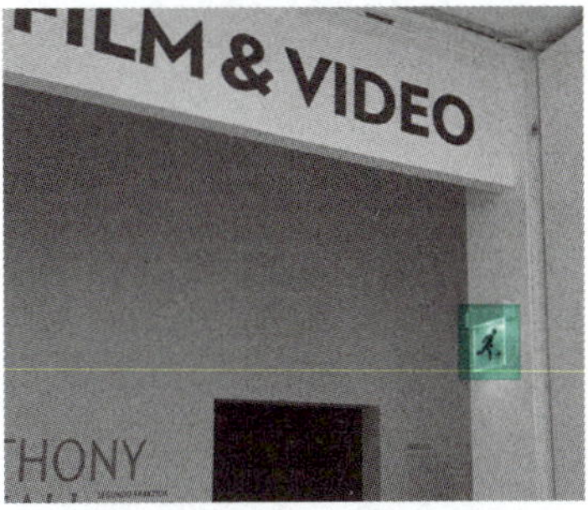
FILM & VIDEO
THONY
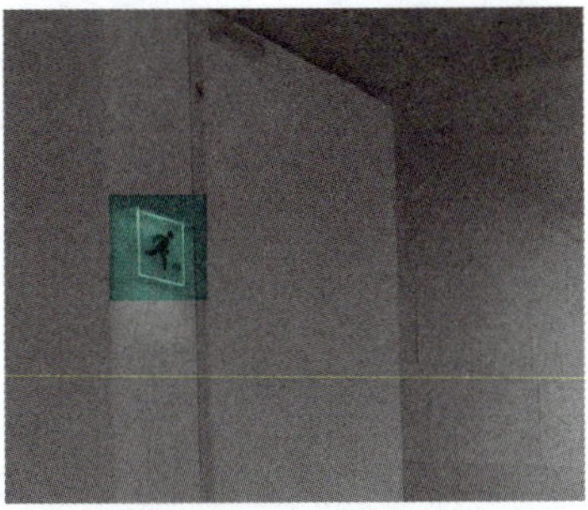
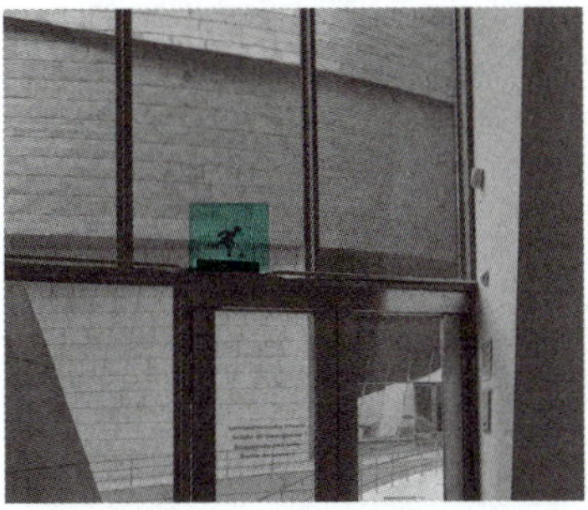
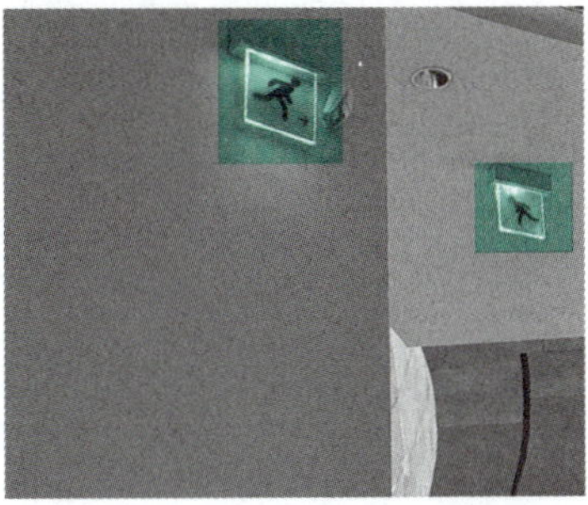
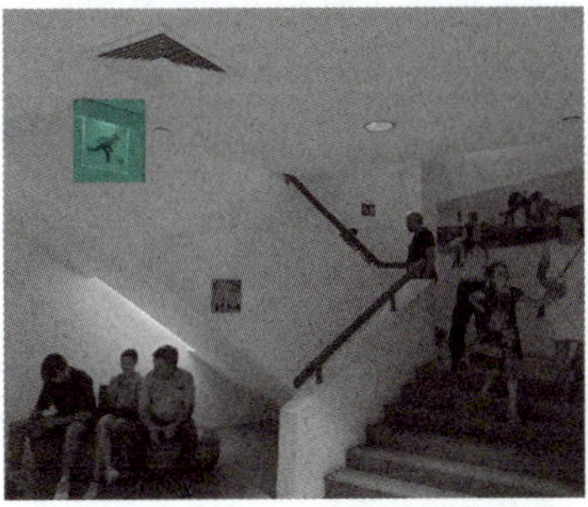
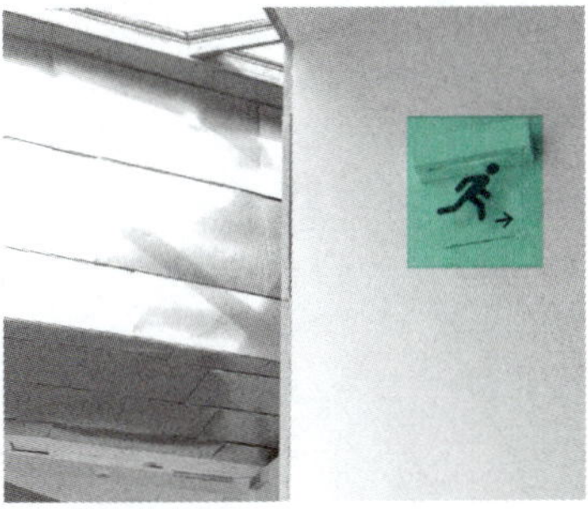

How to discreetly inject a message, invisible

A small Roman news item, late August 2024. A burglar broke into a flat in Prati but, instead of plundering, he paused to leaf through a recent retelling of the *Iliad*. When the owners returned, they found him not fleeing, but immersed in it. Echoing the Trojan tale's stealth and deception, Daniel slipped in unnoticed yet did not strike. He was eventually arrested, but the curious scene lingers as a reminder that hesitation to exit is part of every intruder's spirit.

There Are No Spectators

DEMOCRACIA

The art resolution business has been around longer than many of the writers in this book, who have witnessed their work being absorbed by the very institutions they once opposed—and against which their liberation was once measured. As a self-reflective jest, a 2010 project neatly embodies the Trojan strategy: the Madrid-based collective DEMOCRACIA staged daily picket lines in front of Art Fair Brussels entrance, wielding an anti-art manifesto and banners mocking the passive role of spectatorship. Enjoying the latitude granted to them by the organizers, DEMOCRACIA confronted collectors and visitors with an activist discourse that is often inscribed within the very same operating system of contemporary art. By slipping their message into a highbrow environment that typically glorifies commodification, they recorded the fair's platform as a stage for dissent—making the event complicit in its own critique. In doing so, they not only challenged the market; they also pressed spectators (and institutions) to reconsider how we engage with art.

We participated in Brussel's art fair through an institution, the BPS22, with whom we had a relationship of trust and support. After all, within institutions, there are people, and with those people, you can form alliances. They were the ones responsible for making the project seem "acceptable" based on their position within the art system.

Our objective was clear: to confront the art market through art history itself. Perhaps something the organizers didn't anticipate was that the words of the manifestos from the historical avant-garde movements, on which the entire current art business is based, would be so offensive to collectors, artists, and other visitors to the fair. But since it was a work of art, it couldn't be interrupted—something the fair's security might have done if we had attended as "activists" to protest on our own behalf.

If we chose this work over others where we faced more difficulties, it's perhaps because if there's one thing these new institutions—so critical and democratic—haven't been able to shake off, it's their dependence on market forces and their inability to question hierarchies.

Be warned, the nature of your oppression is the aesthetic of our anger.

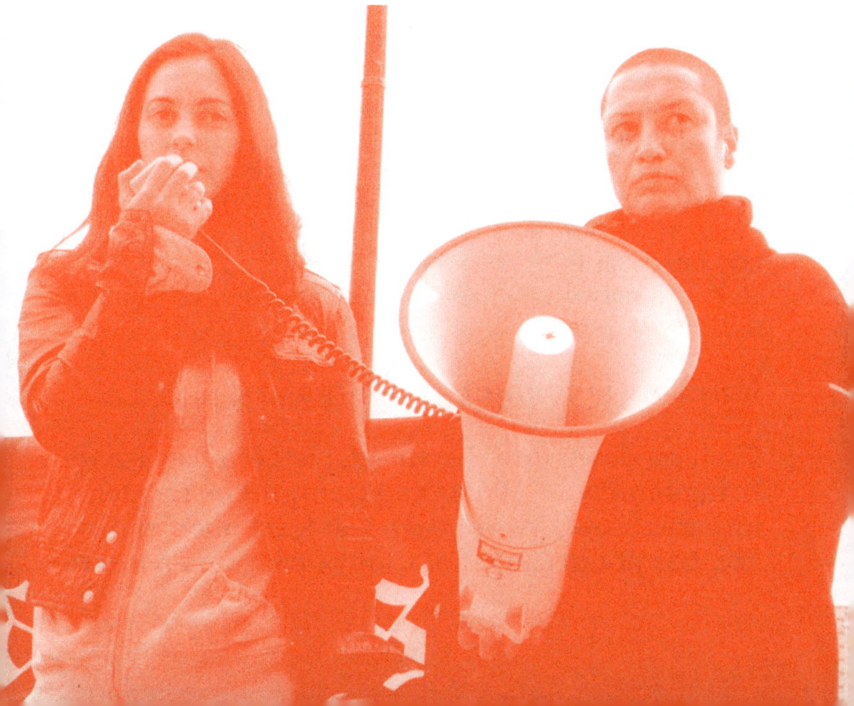

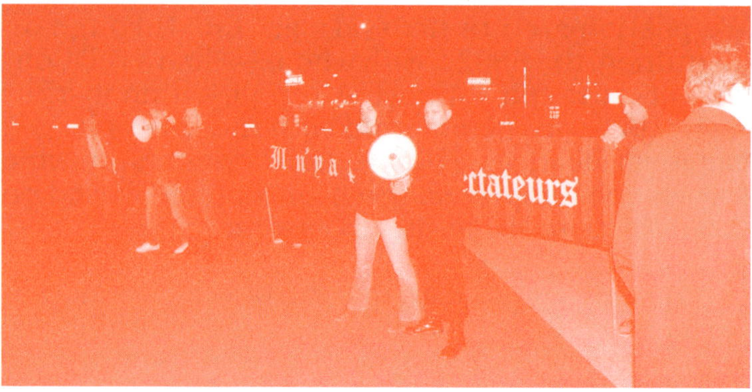

There are no spectators.
You participate whether you like it or not.
There are no spectators.
You are responsible whether you like it or not.
There is no neutral.
No one is innocent.
And no one will be forgiven.
Escapism is not freedom.
Voyeurs of the armageddon.

What has art ever done for you?

It is like your hopes: nothing.
Like your paradise: nothing.
Like your idols: nothing.
Like your politicians: nothing.
Like your heroes: nothing.
Like your artists: nothing.
Like your religions: nothing.

Art is useless. No art. Down with art.

It is essential to wage merciless war against all the false ideologies of the bourgeoisie.
It is essential—in all cultural fields, as well as in art—to reject emphatically all the democratic illusions that pervade the vestiges and prejudices of the bourgeoisie.
It is essential to summon the masses to creative activity.

Boredom is counter-revolutionary.

Dashing down into the street, pistol in hand, and firing blindly, as fast as you can pull the trigger, into the crowd. Anyone who, at least once in his life, has not dreamed of thus putting an end to the

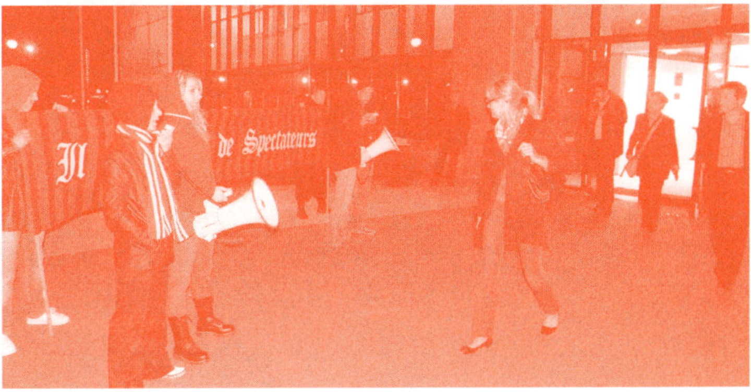

petty system of debasement and cretinization in effect has a well-defined place in that crowd, with his belly at barrel level.

Society gets the kind of vandalism it deserves.

The bourgeoisie places a culture and its art higher than the life of the working class. The concepts of art and artist are an invention of the bourgeoisie, and their position in the state can only be on the side of those who rule, i.e. the bourgeois caste.

Fuck your fascists beauty standards.

When the proletariat has become aware of the When the proletariat has become aware of the myths on which capitalist culture depends—when they have become aware of what these myths and this culture mean for them and have destroyed them—that they will be able to pass on to their own proper development.

Total assault on culture by any means necessary.

The artist does not stand above his milieu and the society of those who approve of him. For his little head does not produce the content of his creation, but processes (as a sausage maker does meat) the worldview of his public.

The work of art of the future will be the construction of a passionate life.

Rimbaud said, "Change Life." Marx said, "Transform the World." These two watchwords are one for us.

All you need is dynamite.

How to
discreetly inject
message,
invisible to

Trojans might not have known it back then, but anytime a magician points to something, drawing attention, it is already too late to be saved from the trick. Likewise, once the Achaeans stepped out of the horse, no resistance was possible. Either the misdirection is spotted and neutralized, or else it goes unnoticed and does harm. As a post-illusionist reflex, art institutions' workers tend to point fingers only after the misdirection has occurred. *Security guard, Musée Marmottan Monet, Paris, 1985, when five Monets and two Renoirs were stolen.*

Escaping Hegel

Francesco Restuccia
in collaboration with aR convention 2024

The global obsession with escape rooms, where people willingly pay to simulate entrapment and puzzle their way out, mirrors the paradox at the heart of Escaping Hegel. Just as paying participants are lured into the thrill of being trapped, only to frantically seek their way out, artists and cultural workers find themselves caught in the institutional grip, constantly searching for the right moment to break free. And what does this have to do with Hegel? The aR convention 2024, a self-organized gathering of artists focusing on unexhibitable projects, sought to draw connections between Hegel's dialectics, the myth of the Trojan Horse, and the city of Stuttgart—Hegel's birthplace and a city with a deep equestrian history.

Hegel and the Stuttgart Horse.

A chronology

13th century BCE
Thanks to the Trojan Horse, a ruse devised by Odysseus, the Achaeans conquer Troy. The Trojan hero Aeneas survives and flees to Italy.

8th century BCE
The successors of Aeneas found the city of Rome.

1st century CE
The Romans settled in the area of the future city of Stuttgart.

950
Duke Liudolf of Swabia establishes a huge stud farm in the area to breed warhorses: the city is named Stuttgart, literally "stud farm." The city's coat of arms depicts a prancing horse.

1770
Georg Wilhelm Friedrich Hegel was born in Stuttgart, in a house in Eberhardstraße 53.

1788
Hegel graduates from the Gymnasium with a speech on "The abortive state of art and scholarship in Turkey."

1791
While studying at the Seminary, Hegel ends up detained in student jail for riding on horseback without permission to a neighboring village and returning late to class.

1806
Hegel sees Napoleon one day before the battle of Jena and describes him as "an individual who, concentrated here at a single point, astride a horse, reaches out over the world and masters it."

1807
Hegel publishes *Phenomenology of Spirit*, an "exposition of the coming-to-be of knowledge." In this work he understands antithesis and negation as part of the process that turns a thesis concrete, therefore stronger and more real. Through the notion of *Aufhebung*, which means both "to remove" and "to preserve," Hegel is able to bring all otherness back within a system.

1835
Hegel's *Lectures on Aesthetics* are published posthumously. Dozens of pages are devoted to the Trojan War, as described in the Homeric Poems, in the chapters "The idea of artistic beauty," "The classical form of art," "Chivalry" and "Particular characteristics of the genuine epos." In one of these passages Hegel identifies the strength of the Greeks, compared to the Trojans, in their spirit of camaraderie, the fact that they assisted one another.

1991
A Museum is inaugurated in Hegel's House in Stuttgart.

2001
The exhibition "Troia-Traum und Wirklichkeit" (Troy: Dream and Reality) takes place in Stuttgart, featuring a monumental reconstruction of the Trojan Horse.

2020
After a period of renovation, the Hegel-Haus Museum reopens with an interactive multimedia installation and most importantly an escape room, an almost unique feature for a museum. Those who want to experience the escape room must make a reservation and pay €50 for a group of up to five people. According to the narrative that introduces the game, we are at the time when Hegel has finished writing *Phenomenology of Spirit* but is hesitant to publish it; urged by Goethe, we must sneak into Hegel's house at night, find the manuscript and smuggle it out to ensure it goes to print. Players enter the room in the dark and, using lanterns, search for clues among the many objects that furnish the space, including books, pictures on the walls, and a chessboard.

2022
Klaus Gietinger's film *Das Trojanische Pferd: Stuttgart 21* (The Trojan Horse: Stuttgart 21) is released. It is a documentary about a controversial rail and urban development project, announced in 1994 and not yet completed. Criticisms include, among other things, the replacement of the old, fully functioning train station, the waste of public money, and the negative ecological and social impact of the works. The head of German Railways, Rüdiger Grube, described the project as "a great gift to the city;" sculptor Peter Lenk commented that "the Trojan Horse was also a gift."

The aR convention, a self-organized moment of gathering and exchange between artists brought together through cooptation around unexhibitable projects, takes place at the Künstlerhaus in Stuttgart. Invited to reflect on the analogy between the Trojan Horse and the introduction of unexhibitable projects within art and cultural institutions, the participants agree on the dialectical and ambiguous nature of the Trojan Horse and react with several remarks, including the following: a Trojan Horse is preferable when it aims to contaminate and not destroy; it is not only important how to enter the institution, but how to leave it by seizing the opportune moment (kairos); if one delays getting out of the Horse too long, the institution may digest you; learn from the Trojans (and the attention economy) and be wary of gifts; do not trust the apparent naiveté of the Trojans (and cultural institutions)–they may need our intrusion; remember the Hegelian dialectic: the system always needs an antithesis to develop; by welcoming the alternative, the system is strengthened; flight and desertion are preferable to any strategy of war; Odysseus' finest stratagem was not the Trojan Horse, but feigning madness to avoid going to war; unlike the Achaeans, artists are often alone (apart from some rare forms of unionization). Some of the participants in the aR conference then visit the Hegel-Haus. They persuade the gatekeeper to let them explore the escape room as long as they do not touch anything. They devise a game.

Escaping Hegel. A game

The goal of the game is to escape from Hegel's dialectic without remaining entangled in it as a negative moment necessary for its development. Since to escape Hegel one must first enter Hegel, players are invited to visit the Hegel House in Stuttgart (Eberhardstraße 53, opening hours Monday–Saturday from 10 am to 1 pm and from 2 pm to 6 pm, free admission) and reach the second floor, where the escape room is located. New clues are needed to help future players find their way out of Hegel, and not just Hegel's Escape Room. A Stuttgart Horse turns out to be a valuable resource for learning the art of escape. Instead of stealing an object, as asked by the escape room instructions, this game consists of leaving one behind. Players are invited to bring an item of their choice and conceal it inside the escape room; then leave without removing anything.

Given the hegelian nature of all cultural institutions, Escaping Hegel can be easily played in any museum. For a little extra fun we recommend trying it out in the "Museum Escape" at the Carrara Academy of Fine Arts (Bergamo, Italy), the "Virtual Escape Room" at the Shelburne Museum (Shelburne VT, USA), the "Escape the Museum" at the Griffin Museum of Science and Industry (Chicago IL, USA), the "Lost Planetarium" escape game at the Leonardo da Vinci National Museum of Science and Technology (Milan, Italy), the "Escape Room" at Diocesan Museum of Alba (Alba, Italy), and, of course, in the Museum of Troy.

discreetly
inject
message,
invisible.
naked.

Aphrodite (*Venus*) played a crucial role in the outbreak of the Trojan War. Throughout the conflict, she supported the Trojans, especially Paris and her son Aeneas, intervening repeatedly in their defense. Her divine influence was pivotal in shaping the course of the war to the Trojans' advantage. In 1914, under the slogan "deeds, not words," British suffragette Mary Richardson, infamously known as "Mary the Slasher," entered the National Gallery in London and slashed the *Rokeby Venus* by Diego Velázquez as a way to draw attention to female emancipation and the treatment of incarcerated suffragettes.

Captions for Sleight of Hand

Ilê Sartuzi

In 2024 Brazilian artist Ilê Sartuzi pulled off a now-legendary sneaky move at the British Museum, swapping a silver coin for a replica during a guided tour. Using techniques learned from the study of magicians' attentional control and misdirection, Sartuzi casually removed the real coin and, with studied nonchalance, dropped it into a donation box by the exit. The sleight of hand—meticulously planned over a year—involved a deep dive into illusionist literature, strategic observation combined with architectural analysis. It was a counter-illusion not only visual but institutional, infiltrating the fortress-museum under the guise of participating in the display. Just as the Trojan Horse infiltrated a military stronghold, his maneuver penetrates the museum's institutional power. Both use a surface illusion to carry out a deeper, subversive agenda, central to our common struggle to find strategies to politicize magic. His intervention not only challenges the museum's authority but also highlights how fragile these structures of value and trust can be. The accompanying drawings illustrate the elaborate legerdemain, shedding light on how easily such systems can be infiltrated.

Gesture:

Enter the British Museum.

Go upstairs to Room 68, the money section.

Approach table with coins.

Ask for the “siege coin.”

Take the coin in your hand.

Do the sleight of hand.

Return the fake coin.

Put the original coin in your pocket.

Go down the stairs to the South Hall.

Place the coin in the donation box.

Leave the museum.

→ → →

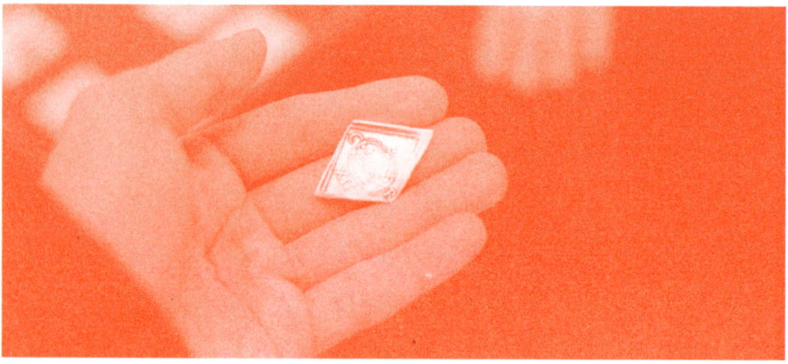

I. Scan of 35 mm film of the original coin being manipulated by the artist during one of many visits to the British Museum.

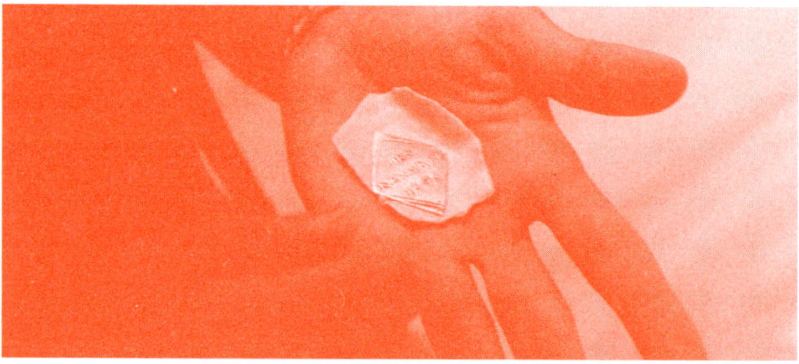

II. Scan of 35 mm film of the original coin being pressed onto Blu-Tack palmed in the left hand to capture the coin's scale, September 26, 2023, (Room 68, British Museum).

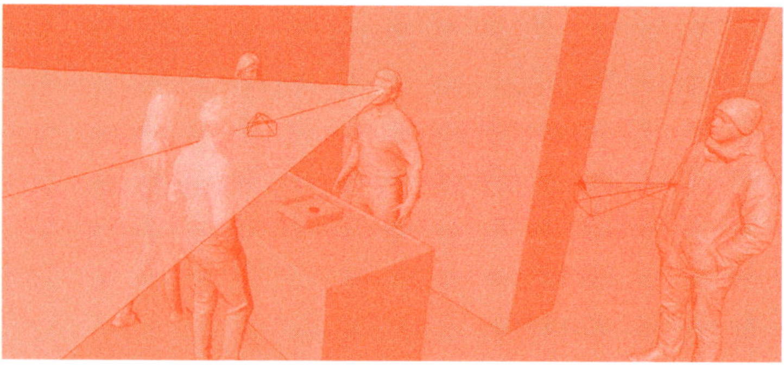

III. Still of one of the channels of the video *Sleight of Hand* showing a 3D model simulating the situation of the trick inside Room 68 at the British Museum.

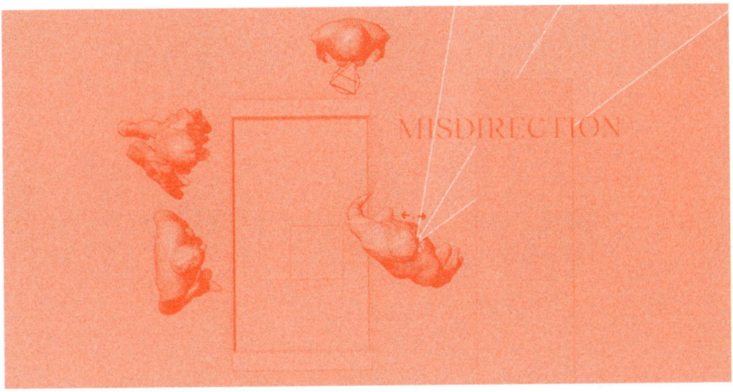

IV. Still from one channel of *Sleight of Hand* showing a 3D model simulating the trick inside Room 68; the use of "misdirection" to perform the sleight of hand; and the positioning of the cameras. For this trick, we created a misdirection by asking whether the coin on display behind the table was from the same period as the coin we were examining [it was]. When the "magician" turned his back to look at the display behind him, the sleight of hand occurred, swapping the original coin for the fake one.

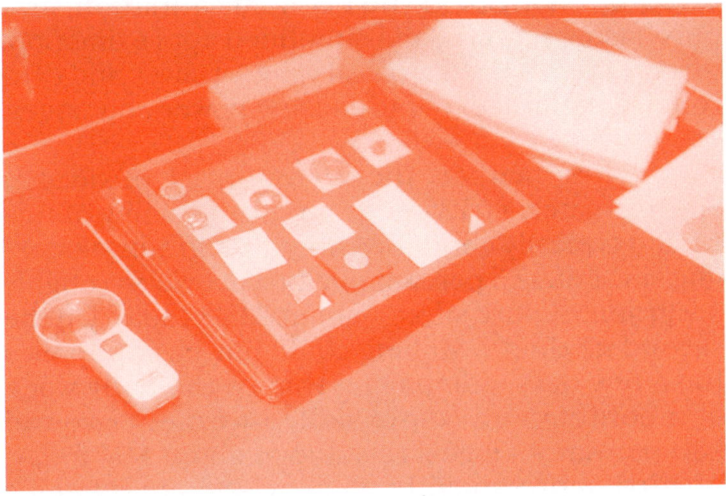

V. Scan of 35 mm film showing the magician's table with the display of coins, a magnifying glass, and printed information.

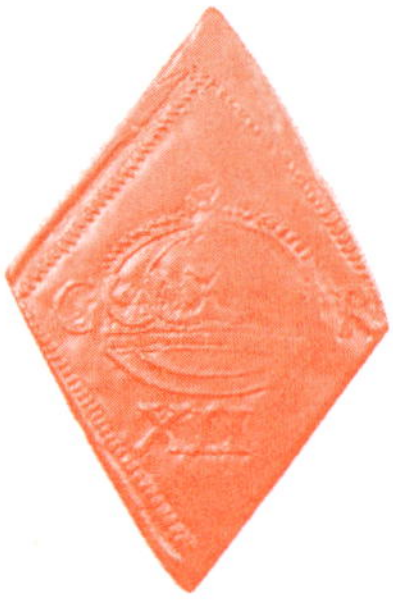 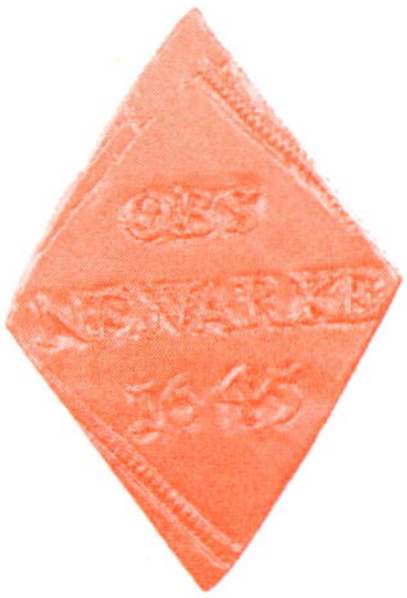

VI-VII. 3D renderings of the coin model, showing obverse and reverse. This shilling bears a curiously shaped crown whose jeweled band runs straight across the front. The reverse reads "OBS," (an abbreviation of obsidium, Latin for 'siege'), "NEWARKE," (the mint city), and the date "1645." The design shows nine dots in each arch of the crown, "C R" (for Charles Rex), and "XII" (indicating a shilling). The coin weighs about 94 grains.

A common infantry soldier of the period earned 8 pence a day (plus some benefits), so one shilling covered roughly a day and a half of work and barely met basic living costs. Estimating the present value of a mid-seventeenth-century shilling is complicated by changes in the economy, inflation, and purchasing power. For a simplified approximation, we consider (I) the historical value of silver and (II) a rough comparison of purchasing power and wages.

On the first method, the current price of silver is approximately £0.73 per gram, and a shilling of this period typically contained about 5.3 grams of sterling silver at 92.5 percent purity. That yields roughly 4.9 grams of pure silver—about £3.58 today. On the second method, a shilling could buy basic supplies for a few days; comparing that to the daily wage of a contemporary low-skilled worker—around £80 per day—suggests a value of about £54 today. A third, more specific comparison correlates a 1640s soldier's pay with a modern UK equivalent: assuming pay on every day of the year, a Royalist soldier earned about 240 shillings annually, while a starting British Army soldier today earns around £24,000. By that logic, a 1645 shilling would be about £100.

The 1645 shilling in the British Museum's handling collection is therefore likely worth more than either £3.58 (bullion) or £100 (wage comparison). Looking to market value, coins of the same period and origin commonly appear at auction or with private dealers between £2,850 and £4,950—more than fifty times its value as money.

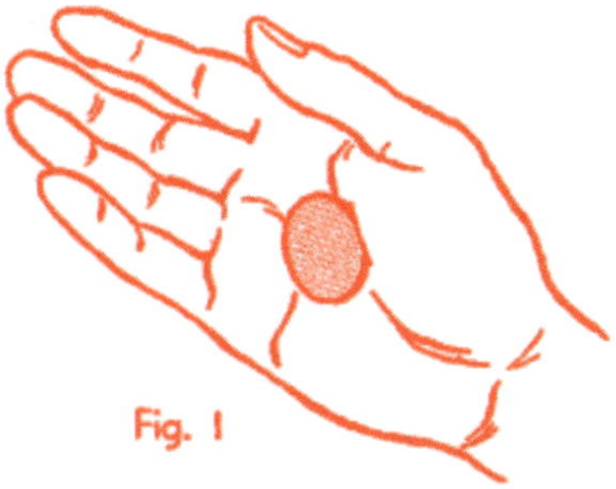

VIII. Figure showing a classic palm with a coin. For the trick, the fake coin was palmed in the left hand while the right hand took (and displayed) the original coin.

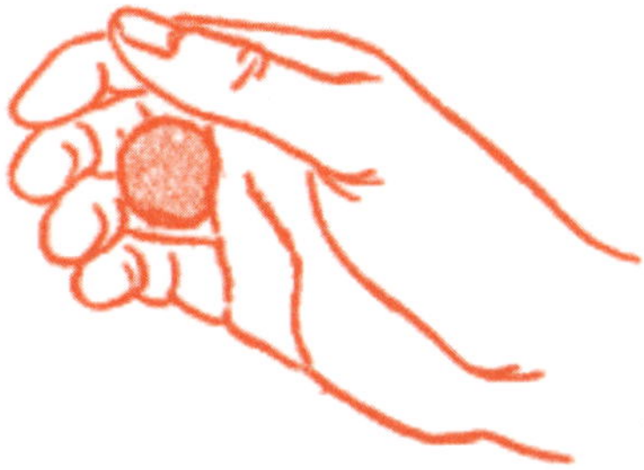

IX. Figure showing a finger palm with a coin. The original coin was finger-palmed to execute the changeover pass, feigning a transfer from the right hand to the left while actually retaining the original in the right and offering the fake coin back to the table with the left.

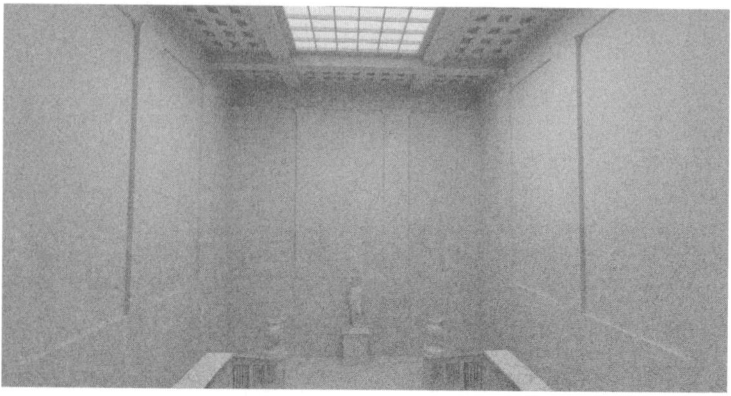
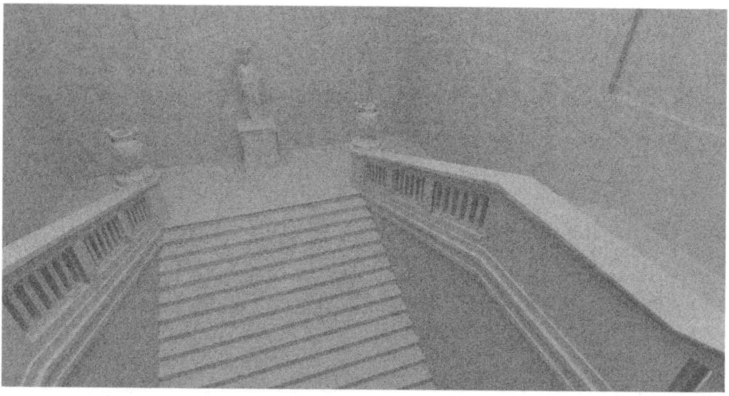
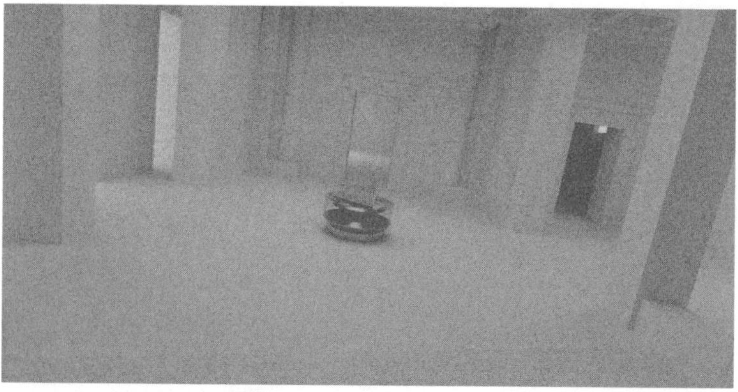
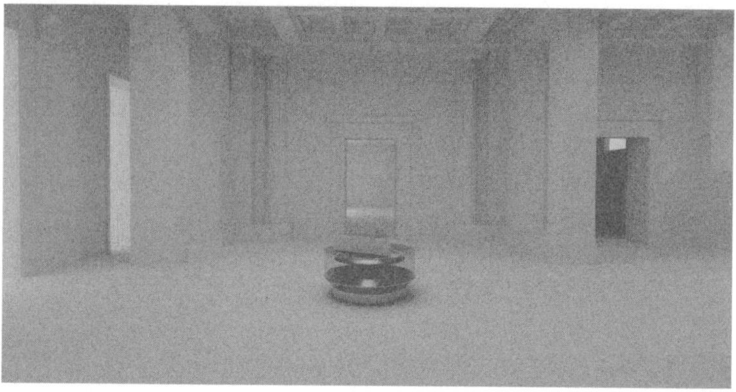

X - XIV. Still from one channel of *Sleight of Hand* showing the 3D render of the route out of the museum, from Room 68 down the South Stairs and through the South Hall to the donation box.

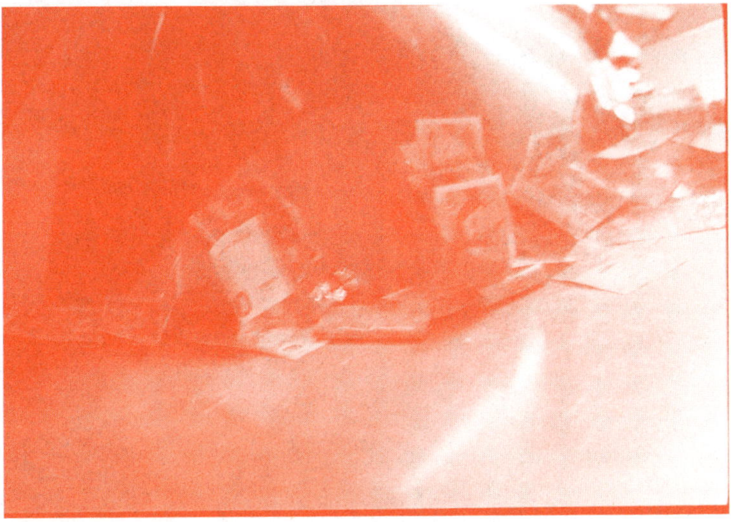

XV. Scan of 35 mm film showing the original coin deposited in the donation box in the South Hall of the British Museum, July 18, 2024. The coin was sealed in a Ziploc bag secured with two rubber bands. The image quality is poor, making precise identification difficult. According to The New York Times, the museum recovered the coin from the donation box.

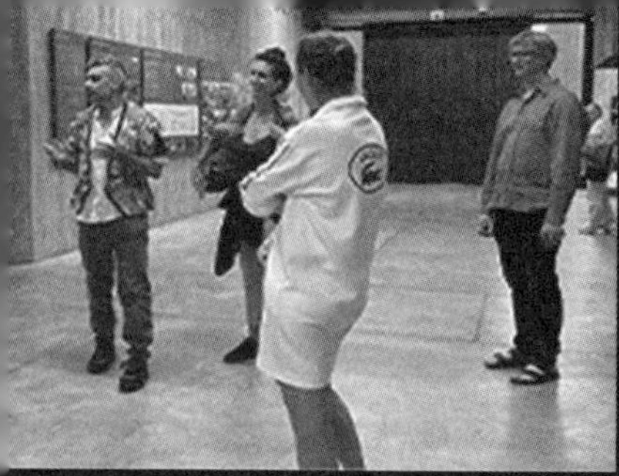

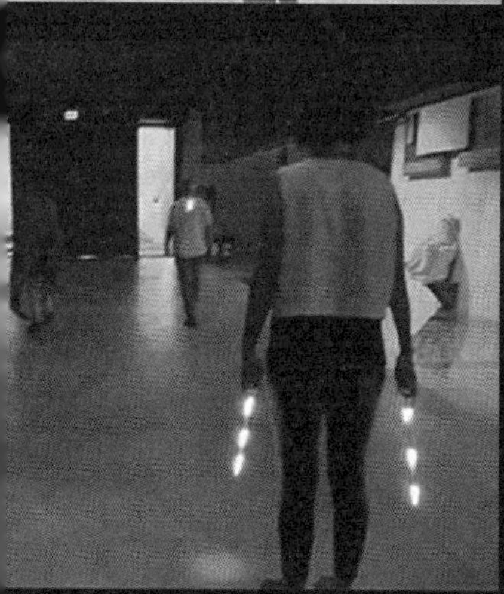
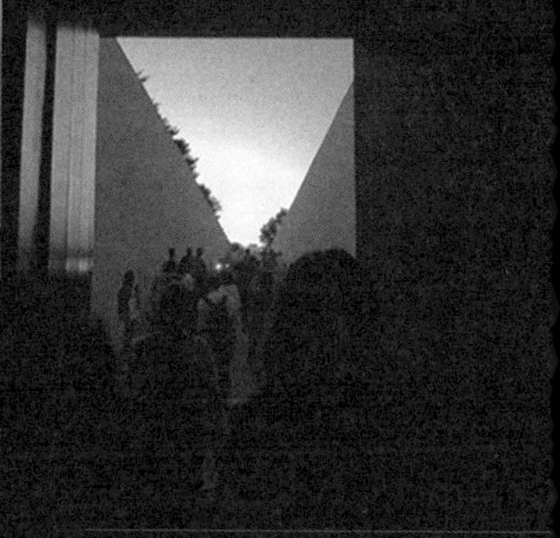
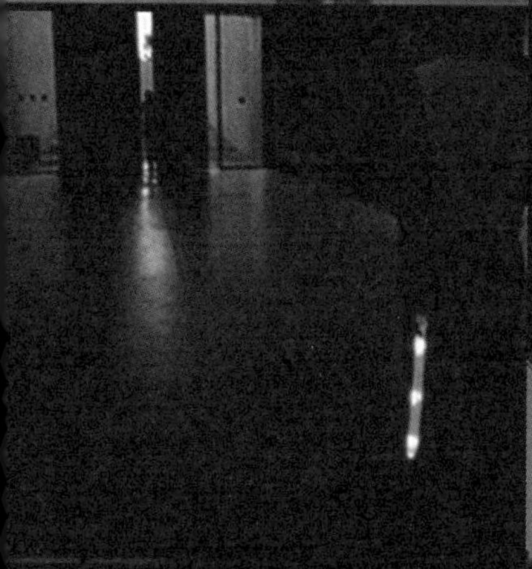
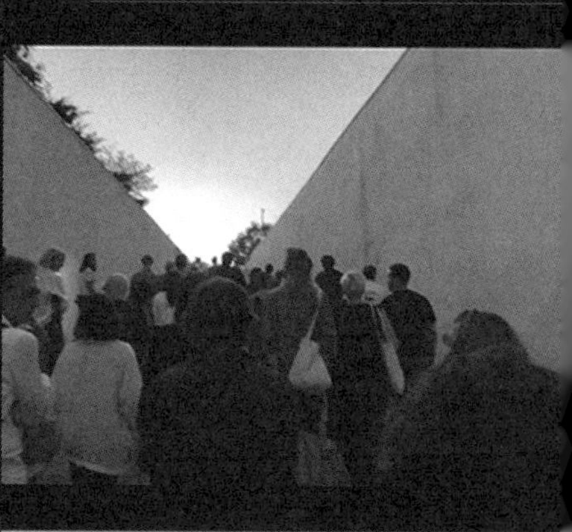
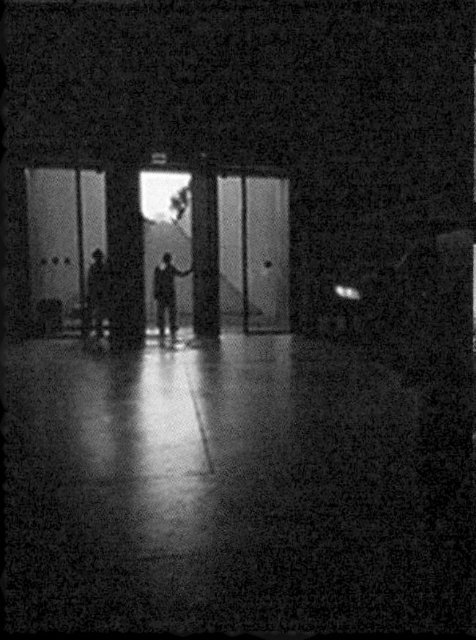
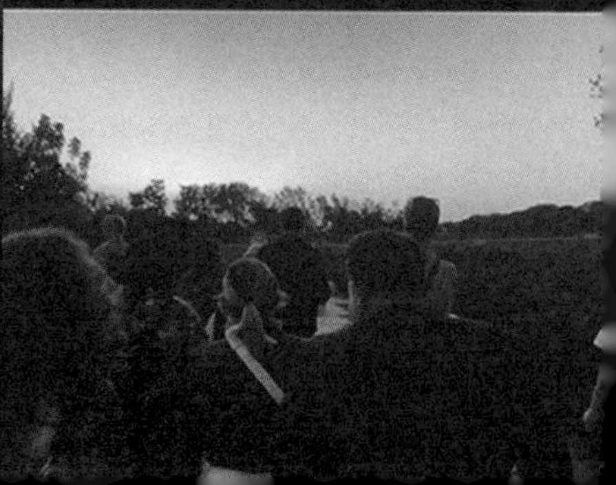

Conceived in the hollow belly of Troy, this book carries the quiet pulse of exit. It began not as an announcement but as a withdrawal, a slow act of disappearance. Its first public trace was at the Museum of Troy in September 2024, thanks to the collaborative spirit of Rıdvan Gölcük, director of the museum at the time, and Deniz Erbaş, co-director of the Çanakkale Biennial. What was shown was not yet a book, but a first draft, an outline taking shape. At 8:00 p.m., without forewarning or explanation, the lights went out. The museum, built to house the myth of the horse, briefly became one. In the sudden darkness, visitors were left to read only the silent signs before them: to long for the exit, to desire, and then to become a shared exodus.

Cacharro: Museo Situado

Interview with Todo Por La Praxis

Jo Muñoz and Diego Peris López, from the Madrid-based collective Todo Por la Praxis, delve into the relationship between praxis and strategy, examining how these two concepts intersect in their work, and emphasizing the importance of autonomy in both artistic and activist endeavors. Throughout the conversation, they introduce unconventional metaphors that challenge the traditional Trojan Horse, urging us to open up and rethink curatorial processes. They recount a project commissioned by the Museo Reina Sofía during the COVID-19 pandemic: a collectively owned mobile device conceived as a modern-day Trojan Horse, built to reclaim public spaces, amplify marginalized voices, and support campaigns, actions, and projects in collaboration with the museum. The device effectively smuggles radical usership into institutional settings.

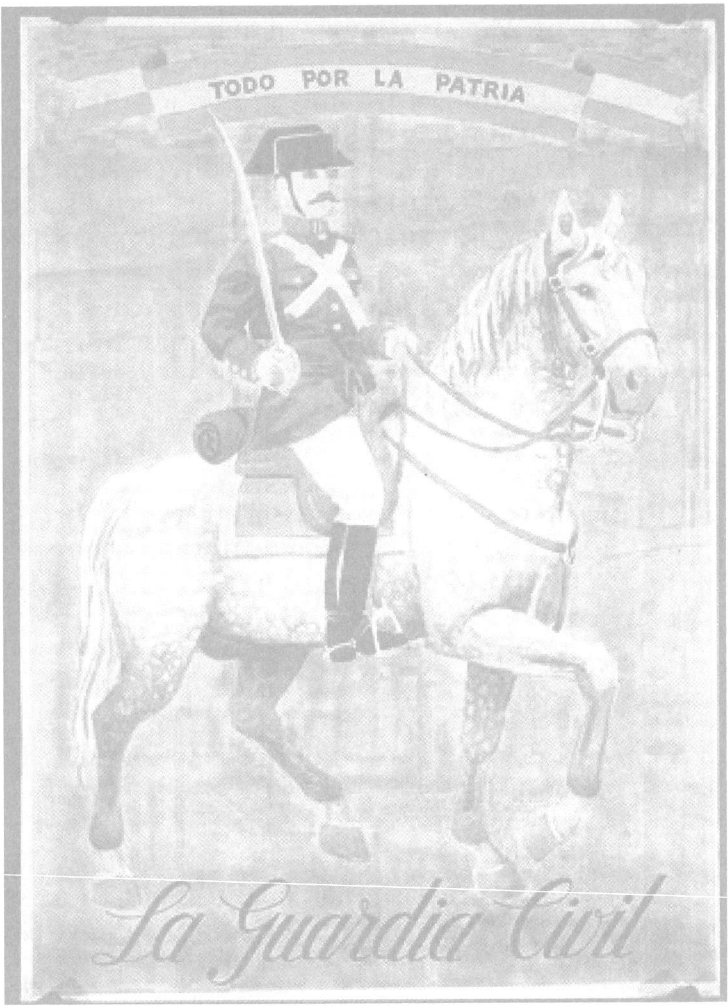

1930s Guardia civil poster.

JM: I would like to start with the metaphor itself. I have always conceived the idea of the Trojan Horse as a guerrilla strategy—a surprise act that introduces an unexpected element, allowing a discourse to transform into a concrete action in a space where its appearance is not anticipated.

How do you feel addressed or moved by the metaphor?

DP: Todo por la Praxis takes its name from the Spanish Civil Guard's motto which was created under Franco's dictatorship: "Todo por la patria" (Everything for the Fatherland). Our appropriation subverts its original idea and links it to the notion of praxis from a political perspective, drawing on Marxist theory of action, and taking a stand. Following this kind of appropriation, we translate the narrative and symbolic construction into practice, seeking the social function of art through situationist references. A direct action with the desire to subvert authorities and generate new imaginaries through this practice.

JM: Especially considering that, from an aesthetic perspective, the idea of praxis is something that not only refers to a concrete practice; praxis is a step beyond, involving action as a strategic exercise.

DP: In that sense, the horse is a strategic matter. We conceive our work as operational—a mix of the tactical and the strategic—which, as our name suggests, implies a combination of these two positions.

Could you elaborate on the combination? Is there a difference or coincidence? How are these terms related in your work?

JM: I think it's the foundation of our work. We start from the premise that, on one hand, there is praxis as a strategy, and on the other, the tactical sense of that making.

DP: In contexts of direct action, practice is often described in a rather simplistic way; it is specifically understood as a means of addressing a need or collective interest. But you can translate or transform practice into the means of creating devices, artifacts and spaces that complicate and enhance those collective interests. Beyond the building process of any given device, what moves and interests us are the interconnected processes that structure themselves within that situation.

How is the project you propose, the *cacharro,* a tactic or a praxis?

JM: As an anecdote, and coincidentally with this topic of the book, the cacharro refers to a horse, however it is an abstract one. The process to build it is particularly valuable to help us **dismantle the romantic and idealized idea of co-design**. In assembly processes like these, what you actually do is to collect and note needs through dialogues and conversations. Eventually, it is up to us to reinterpret them and propose what aligns best with the community's ideas and imaginaries. In that specific case, after the material production—when we finished the construction in the workshop and we released this object, meaning when we opened the belly of the horse—we no longer controlled what would happen. We detached ourselves from it, allowing the work to function on its own according to its use. Changes and modifications occurred during its deployment, triggering things that go beyond the practical or symbolic act of building it.

DP: In that sense, the tactical aspect is not just the object itself; even its materiality includes strategic and design issues. For example, once we realized that the first design of the ***cacharro*** **couldn't pass through certain doors, it implied it wouldn't easily leave the museum. Likewise, if the *cacharro* didn't have the right wheels to move on the street, it would have limited movement and, therefore, limited interactive, political, and practical potential.**

JM: The most interesting part of the process is that the object, like any machine, starts from error.[1] Consider that, at first, it wasn't designed by us, who have experience with these *cacharros*. It was actually full of practical problems, including the strategic issues just mentioned by Diego.

What is interesting here is the institution's action and motivations, which include all the errors in the design process. The museum first called us to design and build a new *cacharro* beyond the mistakes made by previous designers, including

1 Editor's note: Refers to Reina Sofia's exhibition "Maquinaciones" (MNCARS) which was inspired on the desiring machine concept of Deleuze and Guattari. Curated by Pablo Allepuz, Manuel Borja-Villel, iLiana Fokianaki, Rafael García y Teresa Velázquez, June 2023, Madrid, Spain.

them all according to the needs and based on our experience, to be involved in every step of the process.

The word seems particularly relevant; international readers might not understand, what does *cacharro* mean?

DP: *Cacharro* is a banal word often used pejoratively to refer to refer to trivial things, popular use, or working-class manufactured items—something handmade or thrown together with scratch material.

JM: It is a cart, however, In its purest theoretical sense, it's an apparatus. In this case, an apparatus that the Museo Situado's needed for demonstrations and protests against public policies that the state—which happens to govern the very same institution—enacts in the neighborhood against citizens, namely racism, police violence, and evictions.[2]

We like the cart because we consider it a valid example of a long-term strategic praxis that has, with the help of tactics, modified the institution. We believe that after many years of transgressions, distances, and clashes, some Spanish

2 Reina Sofia's project *Museo Situado* came into being in 2018, prompted by the shock over the death of Mame Mbaye, a young Senegalese migrant and a member of the Union of Street Traders, who collapsed from a heart attack just yards from his home after running from the police for hours. This terrible outcome, a corollary of the defencelessness and precarity of his life, unleashed an enraged and immediate wave of protests in the neighborhood, These protests became the framework in which Museo Situado is positioned—an active collaboration framework betweenf local collectives, associations and the museum.

Museo Situado takes its name from the notion posited by American theorist Donna Haraway on situated knowledge, which does not seek to be neutral but is shaped by context, specifying its point of view and with a willingness to stress the state of things. Nevertheless, many prefer to call the initiative colloquially, "Piercing the Museo," alluding to the action of permeating this brilliant, hermetic, impenetrable force—embodied more specifically by the museum's architecture—to create tunnels and bridges, to open doors and windows. In this respect, *Museo Situado* is aware of the tense paradox in which the Museo Reina Sofía is situated, On the other hand, it articulates initiatives run by collectives and associations that confront this "state of things" and aspires to be part of building a more equal, sustainable and just society from the commons".
Source: Museo Situado's website.

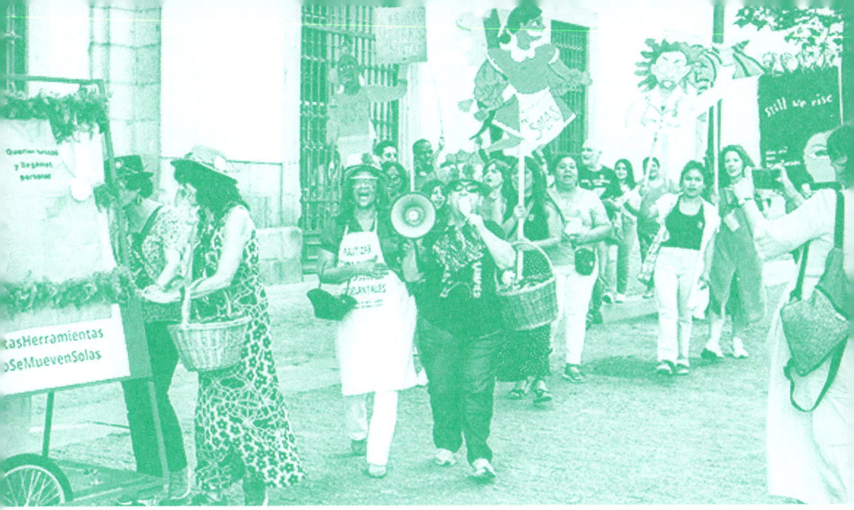

Madrid, June 2022. Photo by Ela Rabasco

institutions have shown themselves to be at the forefront of accepting the praxis of which you have been interpreters. What do you think about this? How do you interpret the role of allies of the museum institution?

JM: For this discussion, we should highlight the difference between the concepts of autonomy and independence, which is crucial: independence operates from the fact that one depends or has depended on someone or something, like an institution. Autonomy, on the other hand, means that despite dialoguing with whoever one wants, radicality will not be altered. This preserves constructing modalities, discourses, productions and strategies. That is to say, ways of doing will never be conditioned by institutional dependence. Therefore, it is important to never put yourself at the discursive service of the institution itself because it deactivates you.

This clarification defines our position on institutional collaboration.

DP: Important to say. **We've never wanted to transform the institution from within**, nor do we intend to.

JM: Especially because institutions don't want to learn or be transformed.

DP: We are interested in institutions that want to rethink themselves critically in an open way. And, once they reach institutional maturity, they allow for dissent or confrontation where we can propose to break, question, or build new protocols that weren't considered a priori within the institution—like those that arise around this *cacharro*.

JM: Taking an object out of the Reina Sofia, or out of any exhibition, is evidently a hassle. However, the fact that the *cacharro* occasionally left the museum despite being on display created ynamics that break some institutional logics within the art world.

Instead of proposing projects that risk being co-opted and deactivated, it's better to put the institution under tension. A mature institution also wants it, because from those tensions, there are people conspiring within. After all, what could be more open and beaitiful than a piece from a traditional exhibition entering and exiting the museum freely?

Tell us the truth—what do you think of our warlike, eurocentric, heroic, and colonial metaphor? What metaphor would you have liked to use? Please, parasitize our Trojan Horse.

JM: This question makes me think of the elements that once fascinated Indigenous people in the early moments of colonial barbarity: mirrors. The myth says that the mirrors brought by white Europeans caught their attention because it was an unknown element.

They were not aware of how, actually, destroying mirrors meant to free themself from what would eventually become the element they were subjugated to... If I think of other metaphors, both inside and outside of America, I think the poisoned candy is very good.

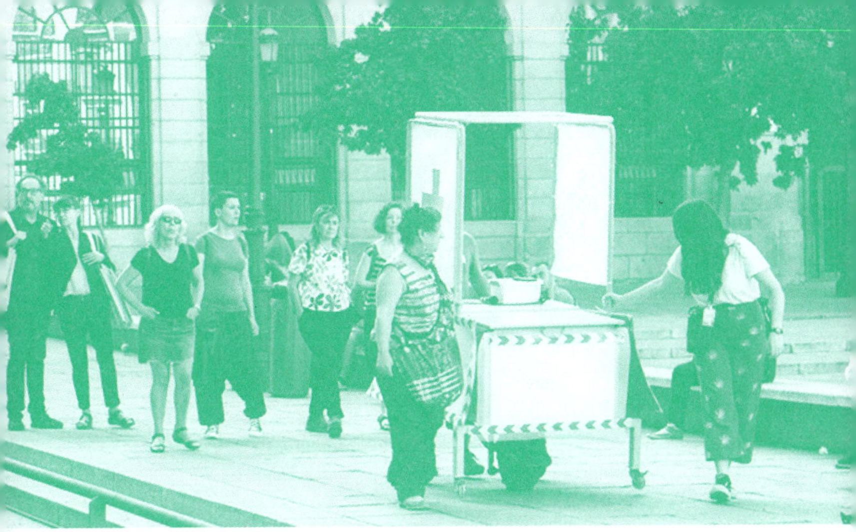

Madrid, June 2023 Photo by Todxs por la Praxis

I would also draw an analogy with other guerrilla strategies, especially one that is dear to me and has occured twice in the history of Latin America: my favorite refers to the capacity of the lower classes to take advantage of the moment when the hegemonic and dictatorial power is celebrating to revolt. For instance, both the Cubans and the Zapatistas took advantage of New Year's celebrations to start their revolutions.

I think it is brilliant to take advantage of that moment when those who are already privileged are having a good time. Seeing celebrations as a weakness from which to launch the guerrilla.

Returning to the idea of the poisoned candy, I find it interesting because the metaphor is often used negatively. On the contrary, I find it fascinating to see how, from a positive condition or perspective, the collapse of the digestive system of an institution can generate positive vibes.

BLM
6. How to discreetly inject
a message, invisible to
the
naked
eye

Many museums rushed to express solidarity with Black Lives Matter; yet this book favors unsanctioned —belly-born subversions— projections and distractions. Shown here is the Robert E. Lee Monument (1890) in Richmond, former capital of the Confederacy. In 2020, artist Dustin Klein projected images of George Floyd, Breonna Taylor, and others onto its surface. A few months later, the statue was removed.

Caballo Migrante

Rocio Quillahuaman

Rocio's sharp contributions make one thing clear: if she had been in Cassandra's place, she would likely have stayed silent and quietly sabotaged the trick so that both the city and the horse burned—damning Trojans and the Achaeans alike. Her drawings deliver a sharp, harsh postcolonial critique of European institutions and the art crowd; indifferent to retaliation, she targets the art world and its hypocrisies, depicting "radical chics," gallery attendees, and "aperitivo revolutionaries" with provocative and merciless comments. This blend of performance, cartooning, and biting social critique is precisely what drew us to her work. The art world may be uncannily entertained by her images, yet it also fears to be the subject of her funny, somehow vindictive sight. Her reputation made her a risky but intriguing commission. We invited Rocío knowing we might be lampooned, because the payoff was a more compelling, thought-provoking critique. To be fully honest, we always retained a veto—she probably anticipated that.

ESTA ES MI RELACIÓN COMO ARTISTA MIGRADA Y RACIALIZADA CON LAS INSTITUCIONES: APRENDÍ DESDE MUY TEMPRANA EDAD QUE NO **DEBÍA** FIARME DE LAS INSTITUCIONES.

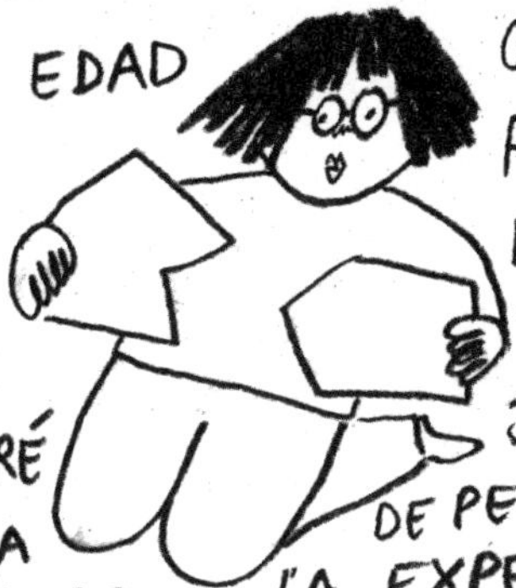

CUANDO TENÍA 11 AÑOS MIGRÉ JUNTO A MI FAMILIA DE PERÚ A ESPAÑA. TODA LA EXPERIENCIA BUROCRÁTICA FUE SUFICIENTE PARA APRENDER QUE DEBÍA DESCONFIAR DE TODO LO INSTITUCIONAL.

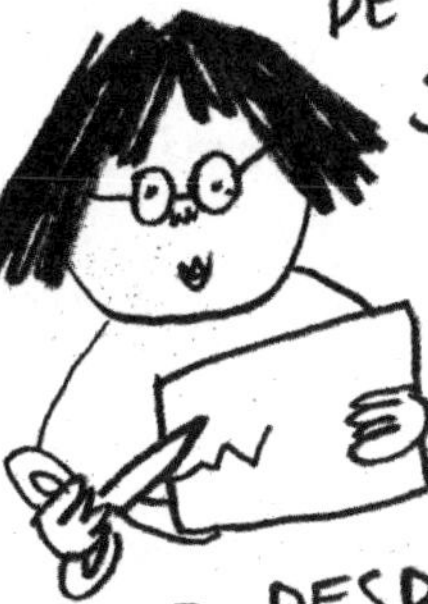

SUPONGO QUE ESA DESCONFIANZA, QUIZÁ TAMBIÉN RESENTIMIENTO, SE ASENTÓ EN UN LUGAR MUY PROFUNDO DE MI INTERIOR PORQUE DESDE ENTONCES SIEMPRE QUE HE COLABORADO CON INSTITUCIONES COMO ARTISTA, HE SENTIDO LA URGENCIA DE...

DESTRUIRLAS POR DENTRO

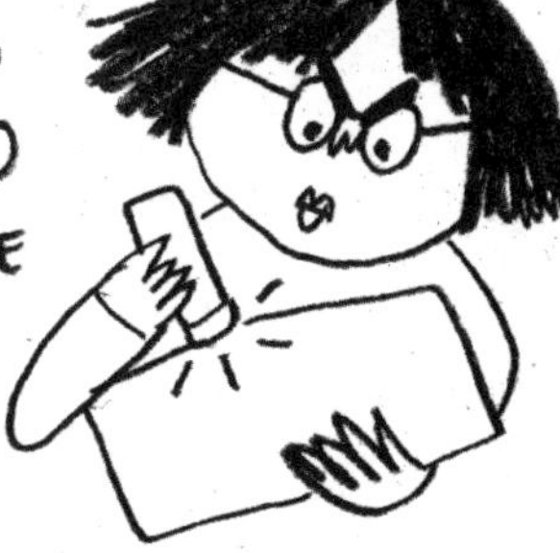

PERO ESO NO SE PUEDE DECIR EN VOZ ALTA PORQUE PRIMERO: SI TUS PADRES NO SON UN BANCO, UN TRABAJO ES UN TRABAJO.

Y SEGUNDO: QUÉ GRACIA TIENE HACERLO SI NO ES EN SECRETO. ES UNA FORMA DE LIBERARME DEL RESENTIMIENTO. DE EQUILIBRAR LA BALANZA. LAS INSTITUCIONES TIENEN SUS PROPIOS MOTIVOS NO-TAN-OCULTOS POR LOS QUE BUSCAN COLABORAR CONMIGO (SIEMPRE COINCIDE CON EL DÍA INTERNACIONAL CONTRA EL RACISMO)

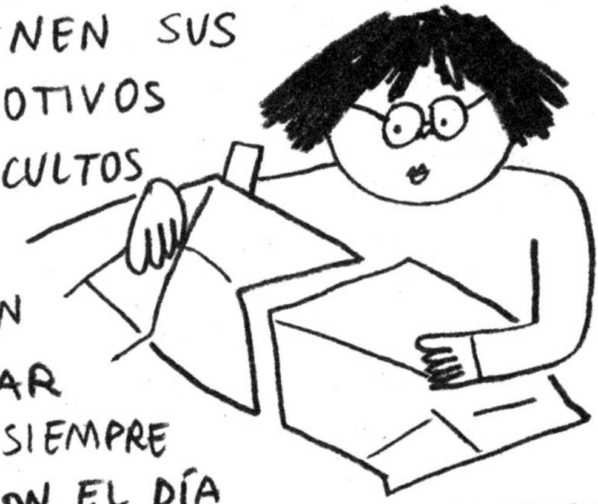

PERO NO HAY RESENTIMIENTOS PORQUE EN EL MOMENTO EN EL QUE ACEPTO HACER UNA CHARLA, UN TALLER O CREAR UNA OBRA PARA UNA ENTIDAD INSTITUCIONAL YO TAMBIÉN TENGO PLANES OCULTOS:

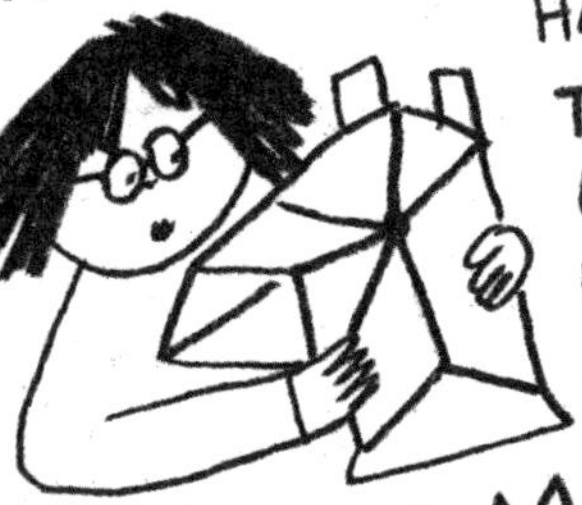

DESENMASCARARLA,

RIDICULIZARLA,

TRAICIONARLA,

REÍRME DE ELLA ESTANDO DENTRO DE ELLA. PODRÍA ELEGIR EL CAMINO DEL DIÁLOGO EN VEZ DE BUSCAR LA DESTRUCCIÓN

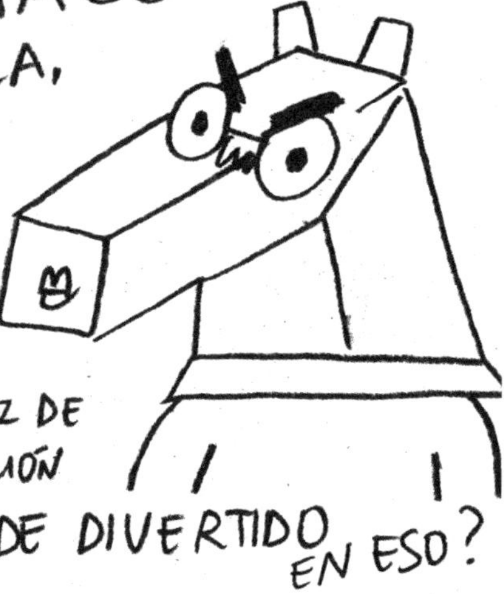

¿PERO QUÉ HAY DE DIVERTIDO EN ESO?

.[1]

This is a summary of my relationship, as a migrant and racialized artist, with institutions: From a very young age, I learned not to trust them. Together with my family, I migrated from Peru to Spain when I was eleven. The bureaucratic experience was enough to make me distrust institutions from the outset.

I suspect that this lack of trust—perhaps also resentment—settled deep inside me. Since then, whenever I've collaborated with institutions as an artist, I've felt the urge to **destroy them from within...**

I can't share this aim openly; it has to remain undercover, for two reasons: first, if your parents don't own a bank, work is work; second, what's the point if it isn't secret?

For me, it's a way to free myself from resentment, to even the balance. Institutions have their own, not-so-hidden, reasons to seek my collaboration (these invitations typically coincide with the International Day for the Elimination of Racial Discrimination), but I hold no resentment. From the moment I accept an invitation—to give a talk, lead a workshop, or create a work for an institutional entity—I carry hidden plans:

Unmask it, Expose it, Ridicule it, Betray it.

Laugh about it from within.
I could, of course, choose dialogue over destruction.

But where is the fun in that?

ULTIMA GENERAZIONE

Yes, yes we know. Art workers don't like climate activism on art. Yet when the mythic Laocoön warned against bringing the Trojan Horse into the city, the gods sent serpents to strike him and his two sons. Likewise, the two contemporary "Laocoöns" who attached themselves to the pedestal of the *Laocoön* in the Vatican Museums were sentenced to nine months in prison and fined €28,000, plus expenses.

Digesting Cassandra

SPORA

Thanks to SPORA, we understand subversion through cultural parasitism, in which a subversive agent enters the institution and feeds on its resources and structures to catalyze change, even within this book. The work raises ethical questions about the cost of such tactics for all involved: us, the book, and its subverting readers. The ultimate question is our own openness and willingness to self-destruct—to become, so to speak, Trojan martyrs in the pursuit of transformation. The text enacts cultural parasitism by transforming what might appear a static repository of knowledge into a living organism. Are we prepared to watch our cherished texts undergo self-dissolution in order to make room for new forms of infiltration? Spora's unconventional instructions align their subversive spirit with the book's ethos, infusing it with a playful critique of intellectual stagnation—where the pages might not only turn, but sprout.

We hope you did not open this book.
Probably it is too late.

At the very least, do not read it. This is a Trojan book, like the fabled horse, hiding within it the potential to disrupt and create gaps within the institutions that accept it—openings through which new practices and ideas might pass.

You wish! If only it were that easy.

But the only door that will truly open is the one leading inward, into endless self-reflection, leaving change trapped in a loop.

Like Cassandra we will not be believed, discredited by those who, naively, will think that a change from within is necessary—an obligation to act against the current inertia.

Instead, let us imagine that the container-belly does its job and digests the warrior words it hides, transforming these volumes into a higher symbol of an alliance with a non-human entity.

Instead of naive hope, let us imagine the container-belly of this book doing its work, digesting the words it hides, transforming them into an alliance with the non-human, a reflection of the multitudes within us. This vision brings us to the microscopic, to the liminal spaces where human meets non-human, a trace of the multitudes that inhabit us.

Let us refocus our attention on microscopic activities.

In *Que le cheval vive en moi*, a project by Art Orienté Objet, Marion Laval-Jeantet received a transfusion of equine blood. "J'ai eu l'impression d'être extra-humaine. Je n'étais pas dans mon corps habituel. J'étais hyper puissante, hypersensible, hyper nerveuse, très craintive. Une émotivité d'herbivore. Je ne pouvais pas dormir. J'ai ressenti possiblement l'impression d'être un peu cheval."[1] She described feeling "hyper powerful, hypersensitive, hyper nervous—like an herbivore, unable to sleep." For a brief time, she became part horse. Here, the boundary between human and animal, micro and macro, begins to blur.

1 Les filles du calvaire. "Art Orienté Objet-Overview".

So let us transform the cellulose of these pages into a nutrient-rich substrate for mycelium, the vegetative body of fungi, the white network that connects trees and plants underground.

Like Laocoön, enveloped by serpents, the book will be wrapped by the white filaments of mycelium that will seal the words inside, into a single living block.

So go ahead: find mycelium, or grow it yourself. Turn this text into something living, something far more interesting than words on a page. Only then it would be fun.

Find some mycelium of *Pleurotus ostreatus*—other saprophytic mushrooms (those that eat and recycle dead organic matter) will do, but *Pleurotus ostreatus* will be easier to grow and will give the best results.

Collect all the volumes of this publication you can find. Submerge them in boiling water and let them rest overnight. This will pasteurize the paper, reducing the bacteria present while also hydrating the pages.

The next morning, drain the books until they no longer drip. Now, they are ready to be "inoculated" with mycelium. Wearing sterile gloves and a mask, take a handful of mycelium and distribute it between the pages. Add a small amount every 30 to 50 pages.

Place the books in a plastic bag and keep the bundle in a warm place, such as near a radiator or on top of a refrigerator.

Let it sit for two weeks, then reopen the bag. If the process has worked well, the book will now be partially digested by the mycelium.[2]

In a place with fresh air and high humidity, this book might even produce fruit, the beautiful *Pleurotus* mushrooms of Troy.

2 Adam Sayner. "How To Grow Mushrooms on a Book: Guide + Video," GroCycle (blog), March 21, 2022.

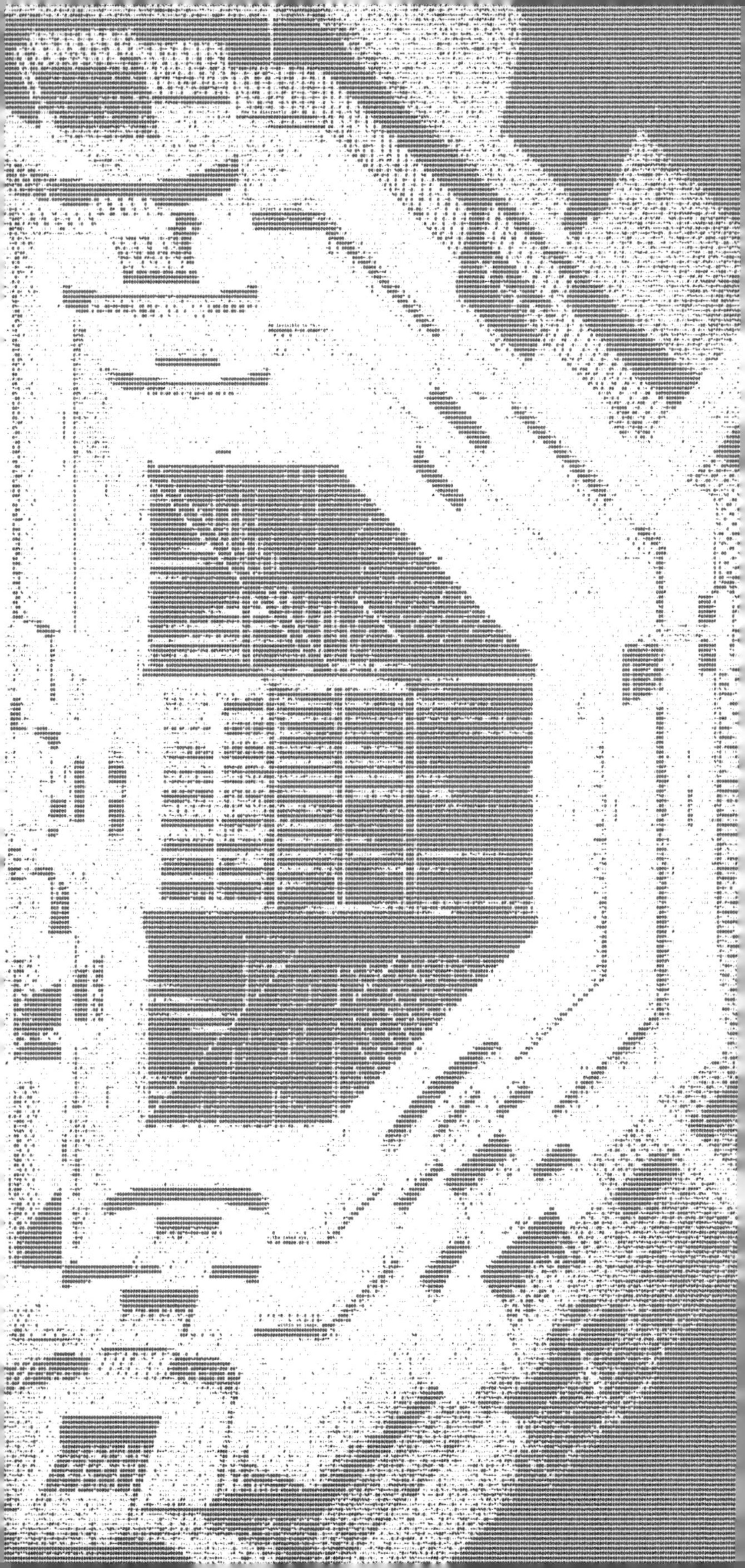

How to discreetly
inject a message,
invisible to
the naked eye,
within an image.

A simple premise: Museums remain relevant only when subversive artistic practices use them as stages for resisting the totalizing structures of our time. Beyond the colors, the seemingly nonsensical interviews, the distractions, emergency exits, and evacuations, this is an homage to those who quietly hold things up from within, the ones who risk their own well-being to nurture the transformation from within. *Photo courtesy of Le Murate Art Project; thanks to Valentina Gensini for the reference to Giovan Battista Mazzarisi.*

Hosts and Guests Reversed Facing the Ghost of the Trojan Horse

Interview with Stalker

In an unauthorized reading, one might suggest that the Stalker operates in the long, very long, wake of the Trojan Horse and the Mediterranean migrations that followed 3,000 years ago. With tongue firmly in cheek, we ask: what would have happened if the Trojans had known the trick? How would the device have worked if it had been transparent? What if the Stalker members were invited to a dinner—perhaps a touch sadistic—that, without tricks or deception, offered them a poisoned meal to discuss their secrets? Between action and revolution, or between institutional critique or dissolution, most of Stalker's works focus on the communal and transformative role of food, the act of eating together, and collective reflection during digestion. Conviviality is one of the strongest elements of their para-institutional work, and we decided to reinterpret it through this particular interview. Through this conjuring, we step beyond their legendary descriptions to analyze more closely, beyond epic and heroism, the dark side of their disruptive actions that have characterized the collective's history, unveiling its untold secrets. As an homage to secrecy, neither the methods nor the questions were shared in advance.

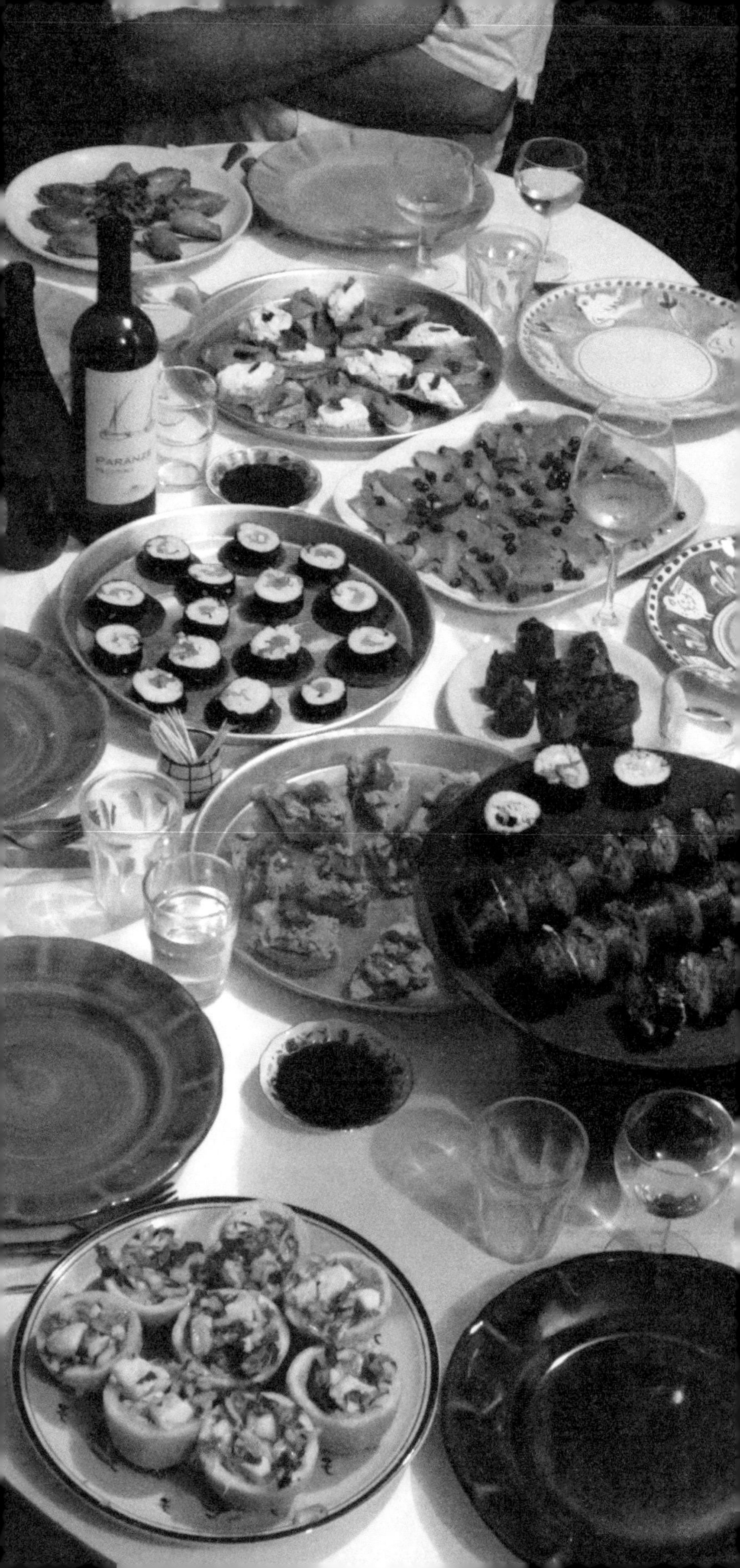

Francesco Careri (FC) and Aldo Innocenzi (AI) co-founding members of the Italian collective Stalker—were invited to attend a poisoned dinner together with historian Peter Lang (PL) to discuss the group's Trojan Horse-esque practice, beyond heroic narratives.[1]
Due to personal reasons beyond the scope of this publication Stalkers´ members and co-founder Giulia Fiocca and Lorenzo Romito had to decline the invitation due to a last minute trojanesque intrusion in their apartment.

2:00 p.m. to 8:00 p.m.

The menu was prepared by Maria Rocco, Edoardo Fabbri, Matteo Locci, Başak Tuna, Natalia Agati. Laxatives and microscopic doses of cyanide were available.[2]

Meeting time: 8:30 p.m.

Support-structure doctor Michelangelo Di Luzio was available in case of any inconvenience.

9:00 p.m.

The evening started with the ceremonial reading of a truthful, yet hyper-rhetorical, declaration of admiration for Stalker's 30 years of work.

1 For privacy reasons, most names quoted in the interview were practically substituted with Homer's Trojan Horse crew member.

2 This dinner stems from a decision to engage in an awkward yet experimental form of radical collective curatorship. One of the contributions, Todo por la Praxis, proposed an alternative to the Trojan Horse metaphor, specifically, to reimagine it as the poisoned apple. Following their suggestion, the poison becomes a device to transform the Trojan Horse into a transparent mechanism where the element of surprise no longer holds value.

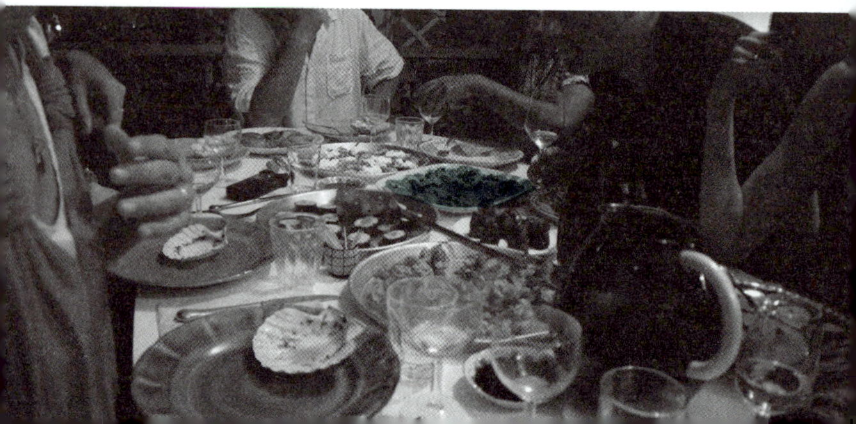

(A diffuse appreciation from the guests)

9:15 p.m.

The rules of the "poisoned convivium" were introduced, emphasizing the importance of avoiding internal conflicts in the conversation. Through poisoning, we call for trust aimed at de-heroicizing a discourse of institutional criticism. The first objective of this dinner is to undermine our own narratives. Despite our best intentions, memory often transforms wars, abuses or conflicts into heroic deeds, especially in the artistic and political fields. Only apparently sadistic, the dinner's real objective is to undermine the metaphor of the horse, to overturn the usual, well-known and above all full of internal conflicts discourse that surround the collective. No one knows where the laxative and poison is unless it's added directly while cooking. In other words, we eat together in extended sincerity. So, do we agree that we have dismantled the victim and perpetrator roles?

(Yes *with distrust*)

Good. Let's deactivate your epic then. We have already said that when we recount our stories or have them told we often unconsciously use heroic words. Storytelling is a way of making ourselves understandable to those who have not directly experienced our actions. Emphatic descriptions are, therefore, a collateral product of the need for synthesis and sharing. In this context we would like to leave them aside. As if it were a scholastic paraphrase: we leave the epic behind by avoiding descriptions of the disruptive, the revolutionary, and the provocateur. All we ask is that you make a sincere effort to remember the peripheral elements in your own narrative and share them with us.[3] Remember, sincerity equals special food; lies or closure risk mild poisoning. The muses themselves will judge the sincerity of the speeches and hopefully you'll be able to enjoy this incredible banquet.

3 Someone pours wine with a reversed hand bend.

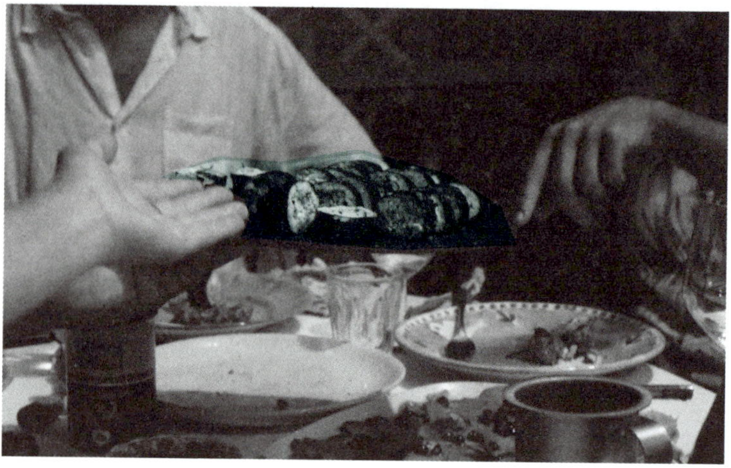

9:30 p.m.

You can start with these canapés: homemade bread with milk and honey, filled with a light beetroot sauce. Avoid the three central ones, the rest are safe.

PL: Those two are missing out on quite a dinner!

Let's start with the least confrontational form of institutional critique, the collaborative. What happens when the same institution bends itself to become a Trojan Horse? Often, this experiment is made possible by people, conspirators, allies, spies. There is always a need for someone who knows how to get in and out. Therefore, our first question concerns the beginning: tell us about the people inside institutions who became contaminators, conspirators who sacrificed themselves for you.

FC: Too bad Lorenzo isn't here... Because, in fact, much of the work you're referring to, was done by him....

AI: Actually, I disagree. You know what? I think the first opened door was the one through your contacts in France and connected to that big fight it generated...

Explain yourselves better.

FC: One of Stalker's first and greatest conflicts occurred just after Il *Giro Di Roma.*[4] I have to confess: I played dirty. Eventually, Lorenzo and I discussed it and we agreed on the "dirtiness." Briefly: I was in Paris at the time, working as an assistant to some professors at the university. Two people close to me, let's call them Peneleos and Menelaus, were fascinated by the project we did in Rome and therefore they proposed that I write an article about it. Nothing was wrong until, instead of using the collective name, I signed it with my own name as Francesco Careri. In the article, I told our story in my own way and without the language of the *Manifesto*, which I genuinely found a bit abstruse, hermetic. I used my own name to be free to use the language I wished. Anyway, long story short... This led to an emergency Stalker meeting, where the official proposal was to throw me out of the collective immediately.

AI: I voted against your expulsion.

FC: It is funny because Stalker had just been born, just a month earlier....

10:00 p.m.

Well done, since you're being honest... We declare these scallops (*coquilles saint-jacques* as the French say) safe to eat. They are oven-cooked *au gratin* with parsley, thyme, lemon zest, garlic and a pinch of marjoram.

AI: Fuck! But it is an amazing dinner, really!
How many dishes have you prepared?
By the way, Peter also opened the door for us to America.

4 In October 1995, a group of eight young architects, artists, videographers, and an astrophysicist set out to circumnavigate the city of Rome on foot. This journey, known as the *Giro di Roma* (*Walk about Rome*), aimed to spark debate about the city's peripheral areas. In contrast to the dominant image of Rome as a deeply historical, mono-cultural city, the *Giro di Roma* revealed alternative views of open countryside, abandoned spaces, third landscapes, unfinished industrial structures occupied by squatters, multi-lane highways intersecting with Roman aqueducts, and roaming sheep. Since that first, foundational *Giro di Roma* Stalker conducted transurbances in hundreds of cities around the globe.

PL: We immediately secured a huge grant of $200,000 from the Warhol Foundation.[5]

FC: What? $200,000! I didn't know anything... Hahahaha. I never thought we'd done a project worth that much in our entire lives.

Anyway, these secrets are already allowing you to get to the second question and eat something...

10:15 p.m.

We declare it safe to eat this: sea-bass ceviche with mango and peanuts in a carved lemon bowl.

Even in the most heroic of tales, where someone is depicted as disruptive, there are always contacts, political, personal or even sexual, who support them within the hegemony of the moment. There is a secret alliance between intellectuals and the system that produces them, one that is very difficult to break. We would like you to reflect on the kind of spaces your work has generated within the institutions you've infiltrated. We've already touched on allies and door-openers. Now we'd like you to talk about the abominations and horrors you contributed to. We don't want names, but tell us about people who have benefited from your collaboration to become three-headed bureaucratic monsters; cultural movements you co-created and are ashamed of. Tell us about people, things, and institutions that have exploited, overturned, manipulated, and used you. Mistakes that, if given the chance, you wouldn't make again, but that are now part of your anti-heroic history. Remember always, honesty equals dinner.

FC: I can say one thing: institutions, in the way we approach them, were always small.

5 Miami Arts Project was funded by the Andy Warhol Foundation, the National Endowment of Arts, and supported by Storefront for Art and Architecture. Peter Lang was co-curator with William Menking.

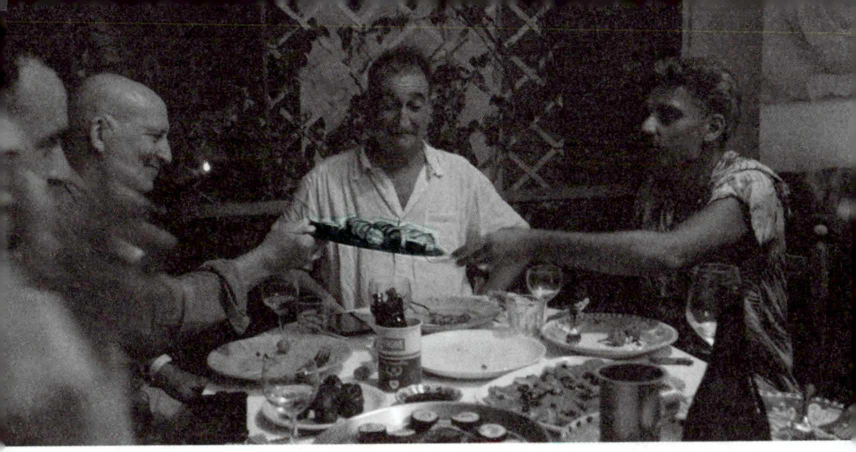

AI: We really had little capacity to deal with bureaucracy or administration, and certainly not much with museums or art institutions. For instance I remember when we participated in the Venice Biennale presenting the project Campo Boario.[6] We met with Calchas, the Italian Speaker of the House at the time and he gave us a very serious critique. He called our work fake social work, saying that through art we were taking away space and energy from real politics. In my opinion, honestly, he was right.

Ah! You understood the game! Well done Aldo. Long live honesty!

AI: I'd also add that Neoptolemus exploited us. Maybe he opened the door for us first, but then he shut it.

FC: I was thinking about Ajax the Lesser, director of the Museum-Museum.[7] First, he helped and invited us, and then he said we were "promiscuous."

AI: To be specific, he meant sexually promiscuous.

6 Campo Boario (cattle field) is a 10 years long research project developed by the collective within the former Roman Slaughterhouse. The decommissioned structure since 1990 hosts a lot of urban dispossessed communities that have occupied the structures; the Roma Kalderasha, Villaggio globale social center, Kurdish refugees, Roman coachmen who shelter horses and many more.

7 Censored name of a prestigious international museum.

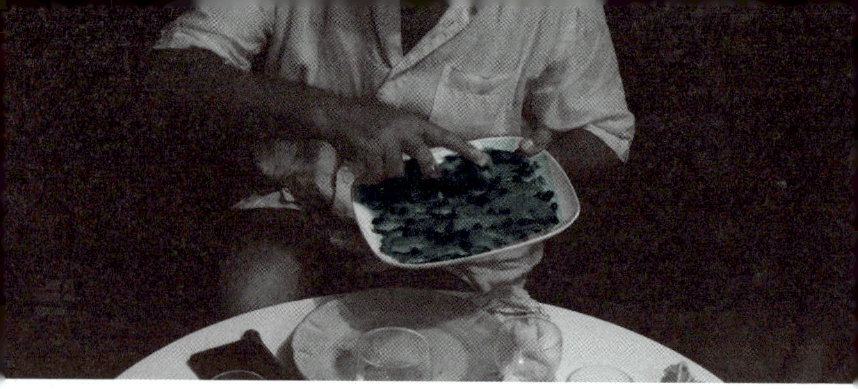

10:45 p.m.

With this confidence, you can eat. Sea snails cooked with parsley on a garlic cream bed.

FC: I'd add that we played very dirty when dealing with Inarch; especially with Echion Epeius.[8]

AI: Oh yes, they were massacred!

PL: Who was our direct contact there?

FC: Now I remember rather well... Lorenzo made such a mess....

AI: Anyway, may I say that this mollusk is really good! I don't know if it's poisonous, but wow... Really good. Too bad Lorenzo isn't here. What a pity...

FC: Going back to Inarch, we did play dirty. They invited us to the exhibition at the slaughterhouse, but instead of participating in the same space with the others we used it as an excuse to occupy the space of Ararat with the Kurdish network.[9] We forced the Biennale

8 Istituto Nazionale di Architettura (National Institute of Architecture)

9 The Kurdish community, the Stalker collective, and several local entities came together to create the Ararat Cultural Center, a self-managed community space that has become a model for hospitality and cultural exchange. The center is named after Mount Ararat, a symbol of Kurdish identity linked to the biblical story of Noah's Ark, and also after the ship that brought the first large group of Kurdish exiles to Italy. Established in 1999 when Kurdish refugees occupied a space in the former Testaccio slaughterhouse in Rome's Campo Boario, it has since become a vital hub for welcoming refugees and asylum seekers, as well as a space for cultural activities and community support.

of Young Artists to open up and include the squat in the periphery of the exhibition, even though they didn't want it. From that moment on, we severed all ties with Echion Epeius. Permanently.

Good confession. Time to eat something else.

11:00 p.m.

New question: outside of rhetoric and epic, there is a component of the revolutionary discourse that we are interested in discussing with you. We've often seen you work in total horizontality and sharing of burdens and honors, but you're not infallible, so you must have made some mistakes too.

As the "*Maintenance Art Manifesto*" ask: "Who collects the garbage after the revolution?"[10] In short, we'd like you to tell us an embarrassing anecdote where you realized your negligence too late. In other words, tell us about moments when your political sensibility didn't protect you from the errors of "success."

FC: The Kurds did, quite often.

AI: Do you really think so?

FC: Absolutely... There was this one moment: we'd throw huge parties every Saturday, and people from all over Rome would come–especially trendy, hipsters, artists, alternatives, etc... The Kurds didn't dance or drink, so they would work the door, charging money at the entrance. The unspoken pact was: we provide protection and visibility through art and parties, you get to sleep here, you make a small economy out of it and you clean it. It feels strange to say it, and obviously the situation is much more complex, but if I have to frame it in relation to your question, that's how it fits.

10 1969 famous Manifesto For Maintenance Art by NY based artist Mierle Laderman Ukeles emphasizes maintenance, keeping things clean, working and cared for–as a creative strategy.

AI: True, but we always tried not to create false expectations. This was always an important point in our projects. This has always been our goal. "We do this with you; we do this for you. We don't have the power to change your life. If you want more, you must carry the project forward." That's been our political line and moral boundary. No false expectations.

Great. Something good to the gut too: these are squid stuffed with bread olives, turmeric, capers, garlic, parsley, and anchovies.

11:15 p.m.

New question: your last comment references your projects of great social impact, actions that often involve large groups of participants and members. If we use the war metaphor from the book, such operations usually need an army and its pyramid-like organization. Do you believe that in your case, we can make an abstraction exercise and characterize your large scale operations differently? Knowing that you tried to reverse this paradigm and were open and horizontal, are you really sure it always worked the way you thought or narrated? In short, tell us when you think horizontality failed. Please share stories about the people you relied on without being able to give them prominence. You may even mention resentful people, whether they were justified or not.

FC: Absolutely...

AI: All a failure. Hahahahaha.

FC: If you ask the people of our extended network, many feel betrayed.
I immediately think of Eumelus, Diomedes, Antiphates... There are dozens of people who felt exploited and told us we were hierarchical. For instance Lorenzo and I were called the cat and

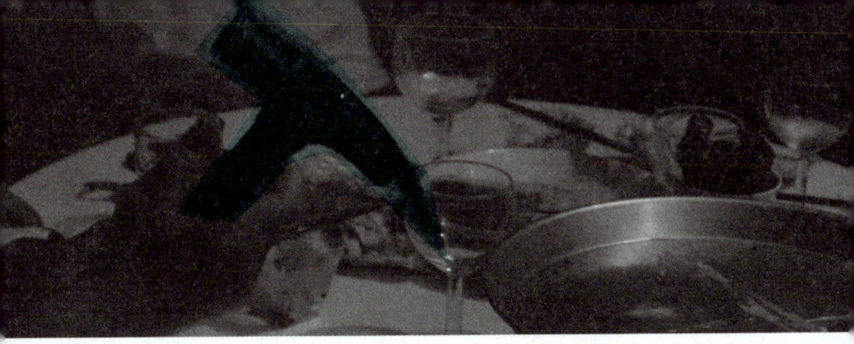

the fox.[11] Almost everyone who worked with us thought the same. There wasn't real horizontality. Let's admit it, it was pure oligarchy.

PL: And Eumelus?

AI: Please don't include Eumelus.

PL: Eumelus was there from the beginning. Black sheep.

FC: More than a black sheep–Eumelus was the perfect scapegoat. We needed someone to blame. Sad to say, but he was a necessary sacrifice.

Well, this is a good act of sincerity. This roll is tuna, parsley, zucchini, and mango. Enjoy it.

11:40 p.m.

Even in your best victories–the media victories, the exhilarating days, successful institutional incursions–there are people who suffered as a direct or indirect consequence of your actions. Try to humanize the institutions you fought against. Who did you hurt, and who felt betrayed by you? Who did you harm and how?

FC: I'd say... all the women.

AI: No, come on!

FC: Maybe Stalker is male. Let's admit it.

11 Taken from Pinocchio's book, the fox and the cat are a couple of con-artists and tricksters who hoodwink Pinocchio and attempt to murder him.

AI: Stalker is not macho.

FC: Many women felt excluded.
XXXXXXXXXXXXXXXXXXXXXXXXXXXXXXXX[12]

Alright, honesty is good, but if we were you, we might self-censor a little. Anyway, you've answered well. We can feed you now. This dish, raw sea bream with mango, and avocado.

AI:... Wow, this is good...

12:00 p.m.

Now, tell us about the people you intentionally hurt. Those raised as symbols of evil. Metaphorical or actual enemies. Your journey has been one of great political ideals, but even the most idealistic can be mean sometimes. Tell us about people you deliberately decided to be vengeful towards. Why did you do it, why do you still think it was right?

FC: Okay... this... is a weird twist...

AI: We have to say that some of the people we mentioned earlier were more crushed than others.

FC: We are not without guilt, but revenge? That doesn't seem like us.

AI: Hold on! Actually you were, at least once. Don't you remember? That time at Metropolis?[13]

FC: Do you mean I was vengeful with Cyanippus? No I wasn't! (takes a bite to cover the pause) Fuck this is amazing! I love this.

12 Minimal censorship by the editorial team.

13 Since 2009, a group of two hundred immigrants, occasional workers, and homeless families found their way to an abandoned sausage factory outside of Rome. Represented by Stalker collaborator and independent artist Andrea Valentini, they cleaned the buildings and turned them into homes, naming their community *Metropoliz* in honor of the new city they were building. Eventually, as a symbolic political gesture *Metropoliz* assembly built a rocket to represent their fictional journey to the moon.

PL: I don't think we've done anything like that. One person who was surely mistreated was Demophon.
AI: Demophon kind of brought it on himself.

PL: Didn't you treat him badly?

AI: Yes, yes, not in the beginning though. It's only now that we treat him badly, now that he's become closer to the institutions.

FC: At the beginning of Stalker, there were many. For example, Amphidamas and Acamas. They were with us from the beginning, yet no one remembers them.

AI: But no... You can't involve them in this conversation.

FC: Thersander... We got rid of him, right? He was there, felt part of it, but we decided he wasn't "radical enough."

AI: I disagree. I believe Stalker is not something you are, but something you become or accept to be.[14]

FC: At the beginning, we were truly horizontal. Like Alcantara–there were 50 people, and everything was open. But then we put in a filter, trying to be radical.[15]

14 Stalker Manifesto and self definition: "Stalker is a collective subject that engages research and actions within the landscape with particular attention to the areas around the city's margins and forgotten urban space, and abandoned areas or regions under transformation. These investigations are conducted across several levels, around notions of practicality, representations and interventions on these spaces that are referred to here as *Actual Territories*. Stalker is together custodian, guide and artist for these *Actual Territories*. In the multiple roles we are disposed to confront at once the apparently unsolvable contradictions of salvaging through abandonment, of representation through sensorial perception, of intervening within the unstable and mutable conditions of these areas".

15 One year prior to the official collective's foundation, the group coordinated the urban intervention of Al-Quantara–the city of the bridge on the river. An attempt to use the bank of the Tiber as a moment to reflect on the passage, on the transition, on the crossing. Installations, cinema, theater and even a bathing establishment were set up by engaging hundreds of people.

FC: Odysseus?

AI: I think he didn't want to be a Stalker. Then he wanted to do something else with his life.

FC: I think there are many people licking their wounds.

Are they licking their wounds because they resent your success or because of how you treated them?

AI: No, no, not that. It is not about the way we treated them.

FC: Well... How about Anticlus then?

AI: She excluded herself.

FC: And what about that guy...?

AI: Life choice.

FC: Uh...him? Amphimachus, the one with the strange head.

AI: No one kicked him out.

FC: How about Isacco? I think Isacco is a victim, isn't he?

AI: Well, not exactly the sharpest tool in the shed.

FC: Even Antimachus is one of the wounded.

AI: He could have done it if he wanted to.

FC: Well, but he flipped out. He had a real psychological breakdown.

AI: During the Rome tour, Antimachus snapped.

FC: Keep in mind that we were doing something existential, not just any walk. Eventually, we took a different route. The group was split in two.

Actually, and I tell the full truth? **We took a bus**![16]

12:20 p.m.

So now you can also eat these Korean-style rolls with tropical fruit and marinated blue fish.

AI: You know what? I actually don't remember...

FC: Yes, yes, I am sure. We took the bus to get to Trullo.[17]

FC: This is a real secret: we've never told anyone.

AI: I admit, I don't remember...

AI: Anyway, this revelation should come out somehow! We want this interview to be published!

We can think about it.

AI: What's the hammer for?

That's for the symbolic quantity of cyanide present in their kernels. Eat the cherries like that if you wish to take a safe risk.

FC: Speaking of poison, I have to say we were full of toxic characters who tried to intercept us. The great old curator Philoctetes, Lorenzo's supposed "friend" Podalirius, Senator Meriones, and all the people around Meges–last but not least the counselor Machaon.

Those are good confessions! Eat this then: bluefish balls with parsley, bed crumb and ginger.

12:30 p.m.

16 The confession of a non-exclusive use of walking in their first manifesto walk is surprising. Given the legendary moment that brought the group international recognition, this well kept secret is particularly intriguing.

17 Popular roman southern periphery known to be shot in Pier Paolo Pasolini's The Hawks and the Sparrows.

Last question gives you access to dessert: which of your actions contributed to something you absolutely did not foresee and, in fact, disdain? What repercussions are you ashamed of? In other words, heterogenesis of ends. The side effects. This may include the unintended eviction of a Roma camp, helping to elect someone you politically don't respect, getting someone arrested, leaving someone homeless, opening the academic doors to unsavory characters and introducing them to university.

AI: Didn't that just happen with the fascist Ialmenus at the university?

FC: Hahaha.

AI: No, come on.

FC: I'm thinking of the mess with the Bordeaux Tramway with Thoas.[18] I'm really ashamed of it. In any case, we've caused a lot of collateral damage. I'd like to give credit to Lorenzo. He was the one who kept the course straight against the institutions. He was on the front line with them. Credit where credit is due: it's thanks to him that we held on.

PL: My God, this dessert is so good. Mascarpone cheese... with banana maybe? It's excellent!

FC: Anyway, what a pity Lorenzo didn't come tonight.

AI: It´s a pity, however it's interesting for me to see this performance between -ATI and Stalker in the collection of stories. Because, obviously, this is not the story of Stalker, which we might all write together at some point. This version doesn't just concern itself with what's true and what's false, it also communicates an experience, a practice – in other words, the production of an effect.

FC: Actually, the production of affection.

18 Reproducing portions of a canonical planisphere, 137 windbreak panels were scattered throughout the stations of the tramway network. 2003 Public artistic commission program of Bordeaux Métropole.

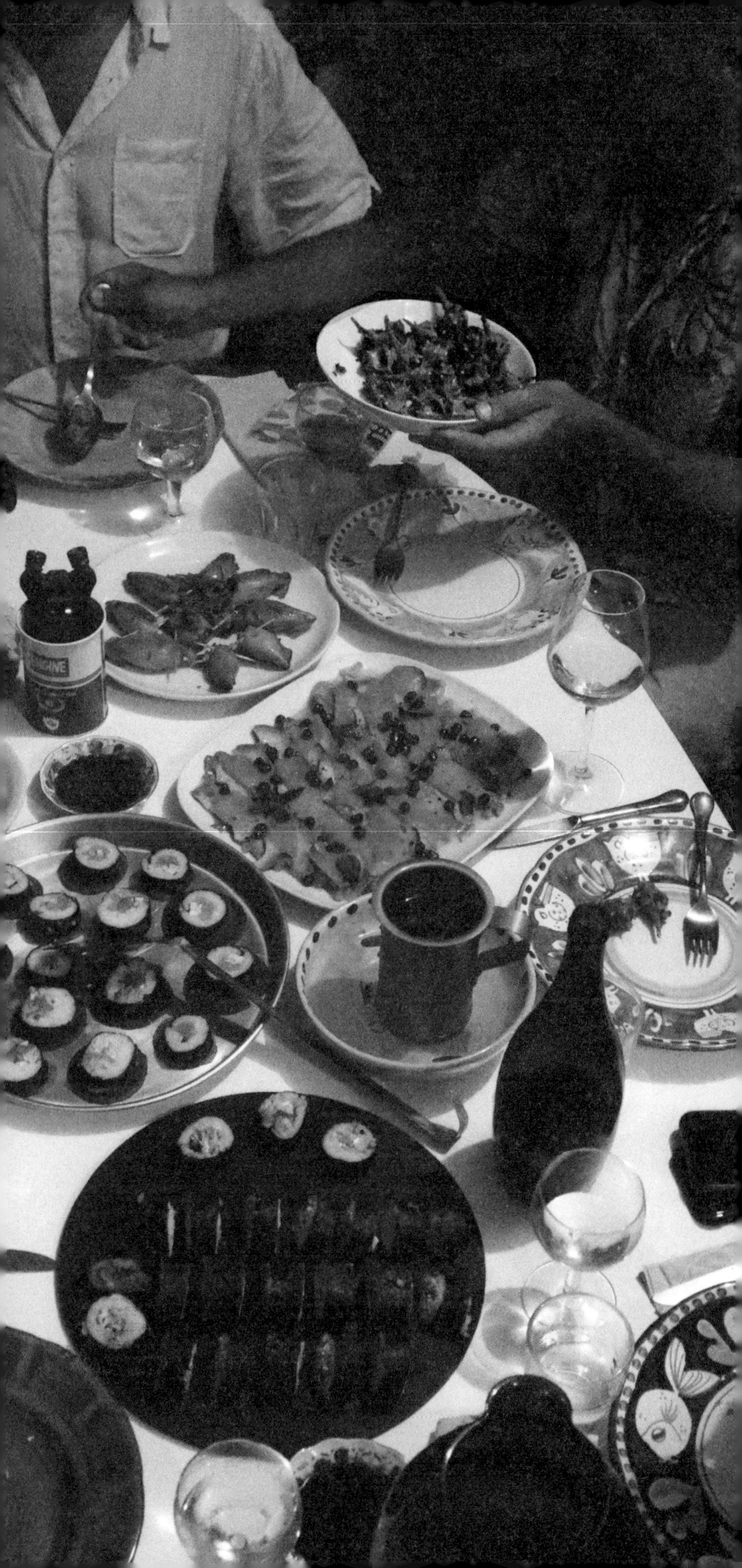

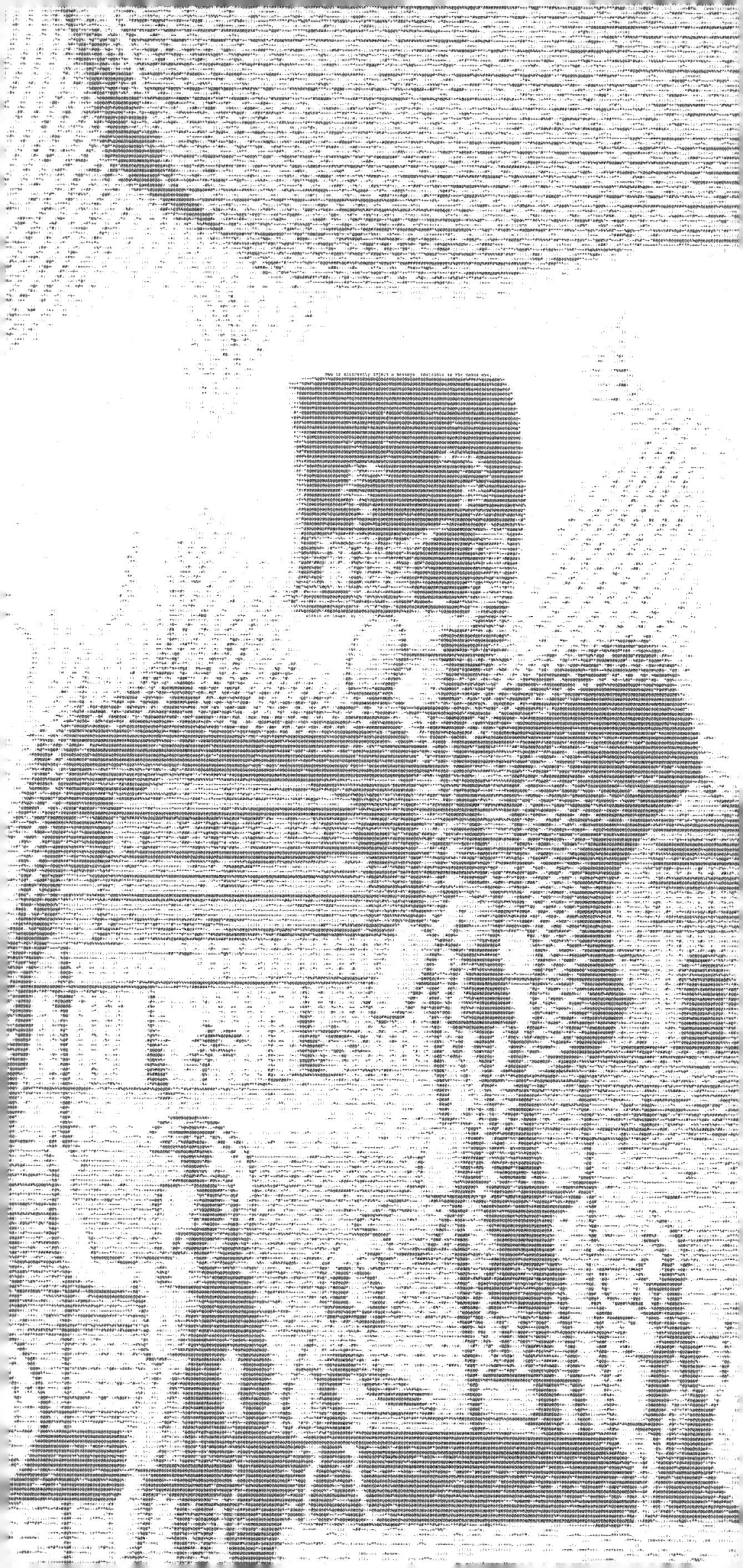
How to discreetly inject a message, invisible to the naked eye,
within an image, by

Emergency exits are an artistic invention. After witnessing a deadly tenement fire in London in the early 1800s, artist Abraham Wivell turned from painting royalty to designing lifesaving escape routes for the working class, an early act of sculptural intervention into architecture and public safety, a fugitive strategy out of the art world where aesthetics met urgency.

Dissolving the Distance

Interview with Raivo Puusemp

We dive into the life and work of Raivo Puusemp, an artist who moved from manipulating perception within art to turning his practice into a live experiment in power and politics, before exiting the art world nearly fifty years ago. This conversation—fueled by wine, laughter, and the slow loosening of tongues—pays homage to the artist's seeding, slightly manipulative methods. In this unorthodox setting, boundaries dissolve and candor surfaces.

Participants: Raivo Puusemp (RP); Natalia Agati (NA); Başak Tuna (BT); Matteo Locci (ML); Stephen Wright (SW).

ML: We´re very excited to have the opportunity to begin this conversation with one of the most consequential Trojan Horses in the history of art. In respect to the book, the metaphor, and to you we wish to begin by opening the gates of our citadel. We do not wish to maintain control. In fact, we offer it up freely. Inspired by your work, we will grow drunker and drunker as you speak, intoxicated not only by wine, perhaps, but by the slow unraveling of categories we once thought were stable. We offer you the freedom to guide this conversation, you hold the reins here, or don't. We'll follow, stumbling after you, drinking, losing grip, and maybe, just maybe, dissolving the Trojan Horse itself.

RP: Let me see if I can get a better picture. Well, that's quite an interesting project you guys have. It's pretty wonderful to see somebody interested in anything like that. I think I'll start with a framework. There are about three major areas that are worth talking about. One was the artwork I was doing prior to any of this getting started. The artwork I was doing was basically—well, I'm not ashamed to say this—grew out of huge doses of acid for many years. What it did was hone a perception, a visual perception, which many of you may or may not understand. It sort of awakened an ability to see, not just look, and it extended beyond just the visual. I've just been living in it ever since.

Because of that, I would notice physical or visual phenomena, make note of them, and try to replicate them — show them to people who perhaps, in their lives, hadn't taken the time, or hadn't noticed them in their passing. That included social things, but physiologically, physically, it was like vibrating water. I don't have any of those works anymore. I didn't value the objects as much as the phenomena. For instance, in the Boston Museum of Fine Art, where I had two pieces in the Elements exhibition in 1970-something—I never even went to pick them up. Just because the objects meant nothing.

Anyway, that was the artwork I was doing. While I was in New York, I found a flyer on a lamppost about a group of artists getting together to try to establish underground art shows. It sounded like a pretty good idea, so I joined. It was called **MUSEUM—Join Us Museum**. There were about four or five of us, and we met in a guy's apartment near the Manhattan Bridge. His name was Gary. Over the course of a few years it grew to maybe 20 or 30 people, including people with reputations. The premise was that we were artists being shunned by the official art world, and we were going to try to do something about it. So we took it upon ourselves to contact Mayor John V. Lindsay's office—he was the mayor of New York City at the time—and said, "Look, we've got this group of 30 artists, and we're looking for a space to put on an underground art show." His cultural affairs administrator, Doris Freedman, contacted us and set up a meeting with the Sixth Avenue Association. So the Association had a subway station—a BMT station at 57th and 6th—which wasn't functioning because the trains no longer stopped there. They pretty much said, "*You can have this. Use it for a month, or however long you need.*"

I got so excited about it. I had about half a dozen pieces to show, but what I saw was an opportunity to do incredibly weird things. I wanted to hire policemen to polish shoes. I wanted to hire somebody to change the same lightbulb all day long, just to see if anyone would notice. What I was trying to do was focus on the unseen people in our lives, and it had nothing to do with art—and yet it did. So I went back to the group, so excited to share this opportunity, and we were met with a whole bunch of negatives. They said they weren't ready. They didn't have enough to show. They weren't this, they weren't that. And what that sparked in me was the realization that people don't have as many ideas as they'd like to have.

And I started thinking: What makes an idea worth doing?

Obviously, there are a number of factors. One is the prospect of a show. The prospect of acceptance. And ultimately, in many cases, the prospect of revenue. I just started thinking of it as a business. I realized that if you look at the gallery and museum system, museums credential the art that is exploratory. But before the museums, the *galleries* are much braver in terms of frontiers. And if you survey the galleries in New York at any given time, you'll see certain trends. You can almost anticipate what the *next* acceptable trend will be, by taking a small step from what is to what can be. I realized that those people weren't seeing those steps. So I started casually talking about those steps, just mentioning them, suggesting them. And I saw that it was working. People were getting shows with pieces that we had talked about. Some were projections, like projecting objects onto themselves. A weird thing that happens, again growing out of acid, and alcohol because the edges start, peripherally, totally vibrating. And it's a real thing that's vibrating in front of you. Including people.[1]

So, yes people started taking these ideas and making them, and once the work was shown, I considered my role complete. But I started to worry about it. It just didn't seem like a good idea, at least not for the people. So I stopped doing it. Still it made me think about the connection between influence, guidance, and control—all of which are all political phenomena. That thinking really grew out of those experiences. You can influence people directly, or guide them to make their own discoveries. And you can also completely control what they do. And all of that translates into politics.

Now, the reason I had a problem with art as a business was that I was never dependent on it for income. That wasn't the point—it was never the point. For me, it was always about the joy, the awe of discovery. At the time, I was living in Rosendale, and because I already had those political interests I mentioned earlier, I was approached. I guess I seemed more credible, because of my job, than some of the other candidates. They asked if I would run for office. I'd never voted for anybody before, but it seemed like an interesting opportunity—to take those ideas of influence, guidance, and control, and see how they might apply to politics. Somewhere along the way, I had read that Lenin and Duchamp knew each other in a bar in Paris. That struck me. Half-jokingly, I thought:

1 Raivo is describing a perceptual effect he experienced during and after LSD and alcohol use, where the edges of objects and people in his peripheral vision appeared to vibrate or shimmer. He emphasizes that this was not merely a hallucination but became a persistent way of seeing, influencing his artistic exploration of projections and visual phenomena.

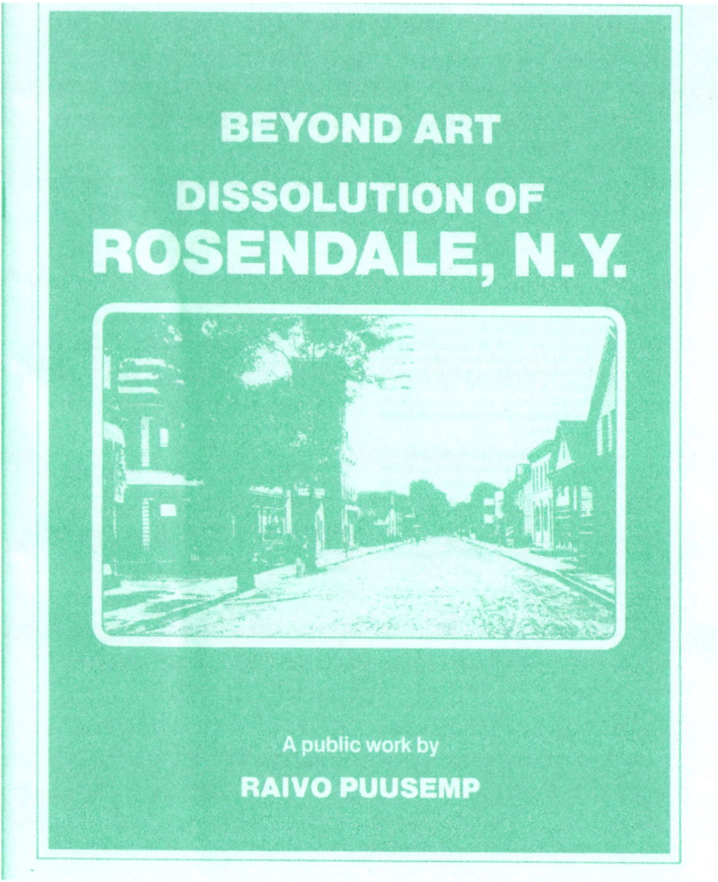

Lenin went back and did Russia. That was a real influence.

It got me thinking, what was possible with Rosendale?

Rosendale was first populated by Native Americans around 1680. It was incorporated around 1880. It was a limestone mining town, but it had seen better days. The town was going nowhere, run by the same people who had been there for decades. They were entrenched and completely averse to the new people who were moving in from New York University. Young people with a totally different philosophy of life. It created a real problem, and eventually, it blew up. The plan was to run for office, fix what needed to be fixed, change what needed to be changed—including influencing people who hadn't considered being influenced in that direction—and ultimately change what Rosendale could become. That was the motivation, and the

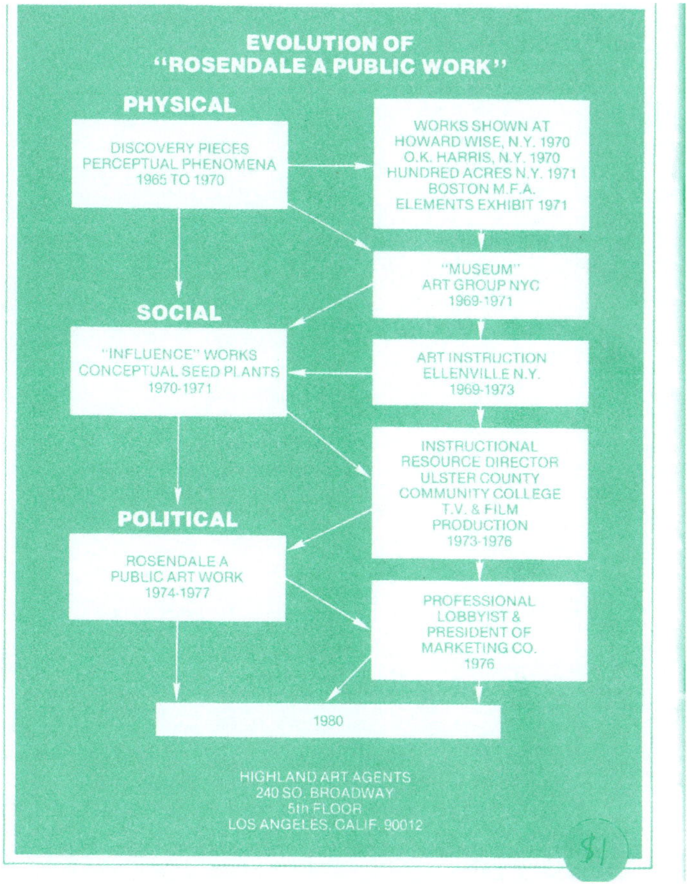

mechanics of it. I put together a small document that recorded all of it. Not through my words, so much, but through newspaper articles, letters, legal documents, and meeting minutes. It shows the progress, how opinions slowly changed, and how people ended up changing their minds.

Any questions?

ML: Well —many, many! We really wonder: how have you reflected on this operation over the last 50 years?

RP: Well, when I left—I left even before the town was officially disincorporated—I felt like I had accomplished what I hoped to accomplish. I left whatever it was in better condition than I had found it. I had influenced people who hadn't seen the possibilities, showe them there was another way, and I suspect that if I hadn't done that, they would have been in the same boat.

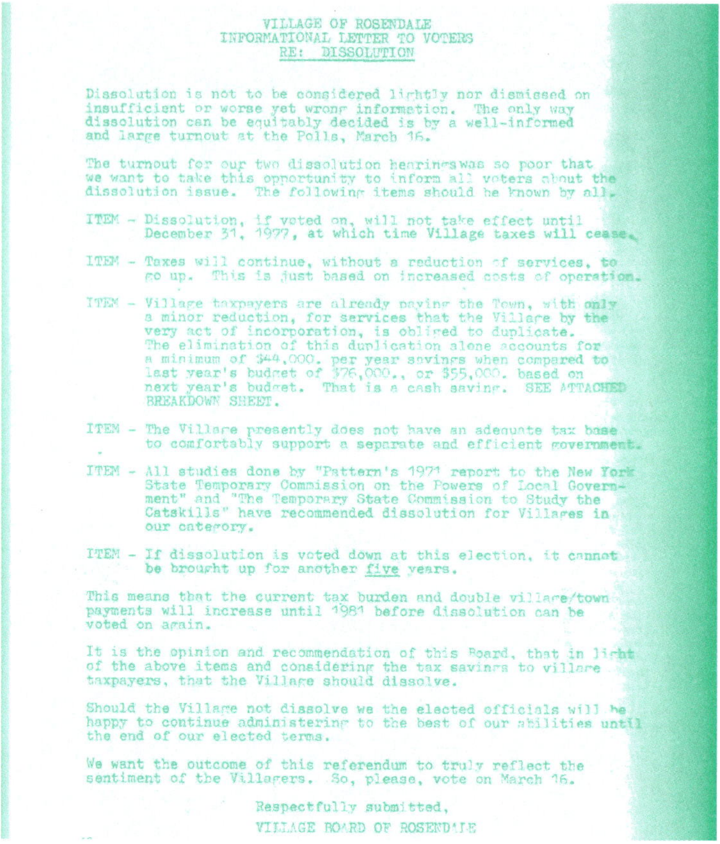

VILLAGE OF ROSENDALE
INFORMATIONAL LETTER TO VOTERS
RE: DISSOLUTION

Dissolution is not to be considered lightly nor dismissed on insufficient or worse yet wrong information. The only way dissolution can be equitably decided is by a well-informed and large turnout at the Polls, March 16.

The turnout for our two dissolution hearings was so poor that we want to take this opportunity to inform all voters about the dissolution issue. The following items should be known by all.

ITEM - Dissolution, if voted on, will not take effect until December 31, 1977, at which time Village taxes will cease.

ITEM - Taxes will continue, without a reduction of services, to go up. This is just based on increased costs of operation.

ITEM - Village taxpayers are already paying the Town, with only a minor reduction, for services that the Village by the very act of incorporation, is obliged to duplicate. The elimination of this duplication alone accounts for a minimum of $44,000. per year savings when compared to last year's budget of $76,000., or $55,000. based on next year's budget. That is a cash saving. SEE ATTACHED BREAKDOWN SHEET.

ITEM - The Village presently does not have an adequate tax base to comfortably support a separate and efficient government.

ITEM - All studies done by "Pattern's 1971 report to the New York State Temporary Commission on the Powers of Local Government" and "The Temporary State Commission to Study the Catskills" have recommended dissolution for Villages in our category.

ITEM - If dissolution is voted down at this election, it cannot be brought up for another <u>five</u> years.

This means that the current tax burden and double village/town payments will increase until 1981 before dissolution can be voted on again.

It is the opinion and recommendation of this Board, that in light of the above items and considering the tax savings to village taxpayers, that the Village should dissolve.

Should the Village not dissolve we the elected officials will be happy to continue administering to the best of our abilities until the end of our elected terms.

We want the outcome of this referendum to truly reflect the sentiment of the Villagers. So, please, vote on March 16.

Respectfully submitted,
VILLAGE BOARD OF ROSENDALE

Now, eventually it might have happened one way or another, but they would have stayed stuck for much longer if I hadn't stepped in. I was able, slowly, to convince the people around me, the ones working with me. Then I systematically improved the problems—social, physical, economic—one step at a time. The sewer system. The water system. The police system. All of those were changed, step by step, to show people there was some credibility in what I was talking about, including getting rid of a 200-year-old town.

And I never regretted doing it. I never felt guilty.

I did have moments when I wished I could have told more people what I was doing. I felt, in some ways, deceptive. But I also felt that the benefits of being deceptive outweighed the risks. If I had come out and said, "I'm doing this as a piece of art," nobody would have understood. They wouldn't have gone along with it. They would have dismissed both me and what I was trying to do. So in that sense, I felt it was worth it.

(1) SERVICES ELIMINATED:

Board of Trustees	$1,000	Unallocated Insur.	$6,000
Village Justice	735	Mun. Assoc. Dues	250
Mayor	700	Unc. Tax Provision	1,000
Treasurer	2,320	Contingent Acct.	1,000
Budget Officer	240	Building Inspector	450
Assessment	500	Reg. Vital Statistics	36
Tax Advtisement	175	Zoning & Planning	50
Village Clerk	2,255	Refuse (Salary)	7,726
Attorney Fees	4,000	Employee Benefits	[illegible],000
Election	625	Total	18,512
Total	12,550	Total of both Columns	$31,062

(2) ASSUMED BY TOWN (Village Share would be 17.6%)

Police	$13,000	Street & Highway	$16,503
Traffic	1,500	Snow Removal	1,200
Dog Control	800	Recreation	1,000
Celebrations	200	Youth	1,000
Street Clean.	200	Library	1,000
Beautification	347	Employ. Benefits	4,000
Flood Control	4,446	Total	22,703
Total	20,493	Total of both Columns	$46,196
		X 17.6% = 8,130 which represents Village portion of Town	46,196 8,130
		TOTAL SAVINGS FROM (2)	38,066
		TOTAL SAVINGS FROM (1)	31,062
		TOTAL	$69,128
		LESS FEDERAL REV.	25,000
		TOTAL	$44,128

(3) VILLAGE FUNCTION TO BECOME SEPARATE DISTRICT

1. Light
2. Fire
3. Water

The guy who ran for office with me understood. We talked about it. But I had to stay quiet about what I was really thinking. Otherwise, it simply wouldn't have worked. And in a sense, it was honest. It was unselfish. It was for the better.

SW: I remember you told me once that you felt like you were—I think the phrase you used was "living a double life." How did that feel? I mean, how was that, as an artist? How did you cope with it?

RP: Well, I kind of addressed it. I felt that whatever the conflict it caused in me, it was worth it. The goal, if successful, was worth the conflict, and it turned out to be true.It wasn't easy. In the beginning, things were violent. People were bringing guns into village meetings, and it became an education. It showed that things needed to be done. Nothing else was going to do it.

NA: But maybe, because of this separation, was it easier for you to manipulate?

RP: No—well, yes. In Rosendale, I had to strategize every move. First, I had to alleviate the opposition. Then, I had to show, directly, how what I was advocating would benefit everyone. It had to be honest. I couldn't deceive anyone, and I never did. It had to be straight forward. People had to see that what I was doing was something that needed to be done.

SW: But to better understand how you operated politically in Rosendale, I think it's really important to understand that earlier period, with your colleagues—those bitter artists from the MUSEUM group. People who said they wanted exhibitions, but when the opportunity came, they weren't ready or were too caught up in resentment over the lack of recognition.

You told me once that you'd meet with these people, and they spent most of the time complaining about the art world rather than thinking about the joyous, ridiculous possibilities. I imagined you all drinking beer, and then you'd discreetly sneak an idea into the conversation. Maybe no one would pick it up, but occasionally someone did. I think you said that happened five or six times?

RP: Yeah. That's pretty much how it happened. It wasn't like, "Here's what I think you should do." It was just talking, throwing stuff out there, seeing what stuck to the wall.

SW: And usually nothing did, or...?

RP: I didn't know what stuck until I saw it later. One guy from that group ended up in a group show at Howard Wise Gallery, and the piece he showed was very similar to something I had been talking about. So I considered that a hit.
Some others started exploring directions totally different from what they had been doing, based on conversations we'd had. It showed me that people are looking. And it's still true.

ML: Ecologically speaking, your decision to stop making art was generous. You gave your spot to someone else. But, honestly I don't believe you. You've continued going to shows. You raised kids who are interested in art. I know of a few delicate intrusions you've made into other people's work. I'm convinced you've been working undercover these last 50 years. So... is this the moment to declare it?

RP: Yes. You're right. I have been working undercover. But my interests have shifted. I've taken up paleontology. It fascinates me. I live among 300-million-year-old towers of rock that rise 500 feet above the valley floor. Understanding the cosmos—black holes, dark matter, dark energy—became my obsession. I got interested in liquid crystals, subatomic particles.

So yes, I stayed curious, just in different domains.

ML: So, the story we knew, that you had stopped making art, isn't quite true. Among us, you're a mythical figure. We really believed you had stopped. But now it's clear you chose not to return to that *one-to-one* scale of political intervention. That part of your conceptual work, the direct engagement with institutions, is what you left behind.

And yet, it sounds like you are still exploring, in a scientific way, many of the perceptual phenomena you first encountered through LSD in your early career. Only now, you're doing it through paleontology, particle physics, and perception experiments...

But just to ask—are there other institutional interventions you've made in the last 50 years that we don't know about?

RP: Oh, I don't know. My whole life I've followed my nose. I don't know where it's going next.
I used to have a business card. I forget exactly what it said, but it was something about preserving the sense of awe. People need awe in their lives. I've had awe in my life forever, and I hope I always will.

SW: I once asked if you still made art, and you said, "No, but I think about it." That's quite striking—stopping art in the name of art, or in the name of awe, because art isn't always as awe-inspiring as it pretends to be. The Trojan Horse let the Greeks inside the city walls. It involved a double life. Do you identify with that metaphor?

RP: Not being able to speak openly about what I was doing in Rosendale, that's a good example. Same with my involvement in the art world. I'd leave a gallery show, or something at the Boston

Museum, and go straight to hang out with climbers who had no idea where I'd just been.

As practicing artists, you know what I mean. You talk with other artists, but when you're with farmers, mechanics, or race car drivers, there's not much to say about art. Art is so subjective and abstract—not abstract as a style, but in the sense that it's hard to explain its meaning or importance to someone unfamiliar. That's always been a challenge for me. Even in art school, I gravitated toward a small group. There were three of us. One became a special effects artist for *Tron* and won Oscars. Another was Paul McCarthy. We had a completely different vision from the other 50 or 60 students, who were making more traditional work.

Even today, I have a friend here who was Yosemite's first climbing guide. He's married to a landscape painter. I avoid talking to her about art. It would lead nowhere. I wouldn't want to say her work isn't on the same level as some conceptual practices, but I also don't want to dismiss what she does. She enjoys it. She may be good at it. But there's a divide, and it's better not to cross it.

SW: Do you still see yourself as an artist? Or has that label changed?

RP: No. Every artist thinks they understand art better than anyone else. I'm no exception. But I don't think of myself as an artist. I think I have a better-than-average ability to spot what good art is. To me, art is like a tree. You have to know what's groundbreaking and what's just redundant. You discard the redundant. You focus on what's glowing. That's what art is for me. Strangely enough, I thought that banana taped to the wall was pretty funny. It slapped the art world in the face. I liked that.

ML: But do you see your interest in the cosmos as your final escape route from the art world? Would you mind if we described it that way?

RP: I don't think it's much different. I go back to what I said about LSD. It opened a door in perception. If you're willing to go through that door, it lets you see things differently. Whether

I would've reached that perception on my own, I don't know. Maybe. But it helped. And that perception, of seeing, is at the core. Discovering visual phenomena, finding a dinosaur footprint, watching a solar eclipse, listening to a cosmic ray—they all feel part of the same continuum.

NA: So you're not saying it's the only political way to make art today, but that it still has political value?

RP: Oh God. Politics today is a mess.

Look at what's happening now. One guy is clearly a fascist, and the rest just follow along because they want to benefit. Everyone's protecting themselves. And when the judicial system gets corrupted, who's going to stop anything? It's a scary situation.

I've done what I could. I'm 83. It's someone else's turn.

NA: Would you still see manipulation as a political tactic today? Or has your view changed?

RP: If it's necessary, yes. It depends on the goal. If it's self-serving, no. But if it's genuinely for someone's benefit, then yes. Like guiding a five-year-old who's about to touch a hot stove, or protecting a pet, pulling a cat away from a dog. That's manipulation too. That's what I meant when I first talked about influence, guidance, manipulation, and control. There's a sequence. Each has its place. It's how you use them that defines whether they're good or bad.

ML: You said you don't know why you do things, but maybe a better way to frame that is to ask: why do you think we're interested in your work? What's the biggest misconception you worry we might have?

RP: I don't worry about how people see me. I'm just interested in what fascinates me. It's easy to get me intrigued by something.

Right now, I'm sitting on a property surrounded by thousand-foot cliffs. There are 12,000-foot mountains just five miles away. The Colorado River runs through the valley below. It's hard not to be entranced by this landscape, and the more you understand it, the deeper you feel about it.

People who live in New York understand taxis, Ubers, restaurants, and the theaters, butt they don't know this.

What this place gives me is an understanding of time. I can look at this land and see where it was 20 million years ago, how it eroded from a high plateau, how salt beneath the valley floor caused the land to sink, forming a rift. I can see it shaping itself over millennia. We're not living in a still life, we're one frame in a moving picture. When you feel that, where you are physically and temporally, it changes you. It's something everyone could have, if they open their minds to it.

ML: Okay, but let me understand. "Opened the doors" is a crucial phrase, so we'll quote you on that. After the project in Rosendale, you left, and a few days later you were driving with your family and all your belongings toward the West, and a crucial question came up: Should we go to Utah or Los Angeles? This could be false, but that's what we heard.

We're imagining that, besides knowing what's right—because your life seems to prove that you did—you must have talked about it with your family. What were the arguments when you made that decision to turn right and go toward Utah?

RP: Good memory.

I was driving a moving van. My family was behind me in the suburbs, with two cats. I stopped at the junction of I-76 and I-80. One road led to Denver and Breckenridge, the other to Utah. I got into their car, and we talked. We all agreed: they didn't want me working in the conditions I'd been in.

I didn't own property. Any money I had went into my magazine, the *Official Ski Resort Guide*. So I said, we either go to Breckenridge and I work for a salary again, or we go to southern Utah and take our chances.

We rented an apartment in Salt Lake City. I found a lot. We couldn't pay all at once, so it was like a dollar down, a dollar a week. I've always had the ability to land somewhere and survive. When I got to Utah, I started working on something—I can't even remember what. I wasn't joking when I said I follow my nose. I never knew what the next day held. But I always found something. Things just worked out.

ML: Let's say the referendum in Rossendale hadn't worked. Would you have felt compelled to continue experimenting in the political realm? Or was success the only thing that made it worthwhile?

RP: It felt so right that failure never occurred to me. Each step revealed itself. There were few, if any, missteps. It wasn't that it was perfectly planned, but each step naturally led to the next.

I didn't know how the town meetings would go, but the outcomes were amazing.an example: the dog warden. We had a guy who worked as a taxidermist, and that created some serious discomfort. We were in a real mafia retirement area. I posted an ad, and a guy named Mel DeMonaco showed up in a yellow Cadillac. He owned a fish restaurant in New York. I suspected he wanted the job to carry a legal gun. He promised to do the work—and he did. After that, the dogs disappeared. We never had another complaint.

When it was all done, I had no regrets. The town felt good. Overwhelmingly, they voted for the change. Not a huge population—maybe 600, 700 people. But they voted, and they were happy. The town is now flourishing. No delusions. It would have happened without me eventually. It was just a matter of time.

SW: That's a great story. Nobody's heard that dog catcher story before. That brings new material into what artistic material you were working with as an artist mayor.

But we would never know about any of these things if it had not been for that publication, that you did. Could you talk a little bit about that publication and how it came to be? Because I think your friend, Paul McCarthy played a significant role in that, right?

RP: Yeah, what happened was that as I was working on this project, I was documenting everything. So I was collecting memos, meeting minutes, and correspondence with lawyers and other politicians, newspaper articles—kind of building a chronology of the events as they happened.

I showed them to Paul and said, "Look, I've got to get this thing published." And he said, "Well, listen, you should show it in LA."

I had the first round printed and then did more. Paul helped set up a bunch of these and had them printed in LA for that show.

ML: Raivo, we are losing concentration, can I ask you a genuine comment? In the email we sent, we said we were going to drink, while you were speaking, assuming that part of your seeding process involved alcohol. I'm just declaring: I just finished my bottle of Austrian red wine, which will probably give me a headache tomorrow. Do you think it makes any sense that all of us, including Stephen, are drinking while you speak? Are we missing something? How do you feel about it?

RP: I didn't even think about it. I saw you drinking. It didn't matter to me.

You know, this Rosendale thing is very funny. It was 40 years, 50—almost 50 years ago there. Then about 15 years ago, I was in Holland, setting up an inflatable art show. Paul hired me to do that because he knew I could make those things happen— underfoot inflatable sculptures, Santa Clauses with butt plugs, all kinds of funny wonderful stuff.

While I was there, a galllerists in Amsterdam who knew about Rosendale invited me to gived give a little lecture. At that event, I met two other Dutch people who later came to visit me, and they ended up organizing shows for me in nine countries to show the Rosendale book. It ended up showing in Estonia, Thailand, Switzerland, Germany, France, New York, and the *Salt Lake Museum of Contemporary Art* heard about it and showed it too.

That was another example of clashing worlds. people I had worked with in Salt Lake— people from the ski industry, government and all those circles—suddenly saw these flags on Main Street with my name and images of my work, and it just seemed out of context. They couldn't believe it.

But anyway, that was 15 years ago, and now you came along and here we are again. It's weird—every ten years, something pops up.

I'm always surprised that somebody's interested. I can understand why somebody would be interested because I hadn't heard of anybody doing anything like this. But at the same time, it always surprises me when somebody's interested. And I'm too involved in too many things to be self-promoting.

I'm very encouraged to see you all doing your stuff. I'm sure there are others like you out there.

SW: Well, one link between you and -ATI is that when people ask, "How do you even know about this project if Raivo never told anyone?" and I explain, they say, "Okay, but why is it art?"

My first instinct is to explain why it's art, but honestly, it's more interesting to say: maybe it's not art. But also, it's not not-art. That in-between space, that's what connects you to architects who don't build anything. ....xyz.....zxy....zzz....."

RP: .xyz.....zxy....zzz.....You're running out of wine, and we're running out of stamina and .xyz.....zxy.... zzz.....xyz.....zxy....zzz.....xyz.....zxy....zzz....

Mussolini

In 1945, Genoa's partisans, acting independently and without external support, liberated the city from Nazi-Fascist occupation. On the exit door of an unassuming building, an anonymous photographer captured a fleeting yet powerful moment: the signature of an unknown writer marking the historic date of Mussolini's downfall. A symbolic exit. A symbolic exit. *Archivio Istituto Luce, Genoa.*

The Upside-Down Museum

Aldo Giannotti

With deceptive simplicity, Aldo Giannotti sketches a language of gestures and diagrams that interrogate the invisible architectures of social and institutional power. His abstract, cubic buildings are not merely coincidental echoes of Troy's boxlike archaeological museum; they operate as sites of negotiation, resistance, and subtle power plays. Across his body of work, the drawings both map and misdirect, proposing an upside-down museography that consistently challenges the assumed neutrality of institutions. His installations do not merely inhabit institutional spaces; they reconfigure them, transforming galleries into arenas where the boundaries between artist, institution, and audience become porous and contestable. Through precision and poetic gaps, his work refuses closure, inviting viewers to navigate ambiguity, embrace uncertainty, and reconsider the codes that govern collective life.

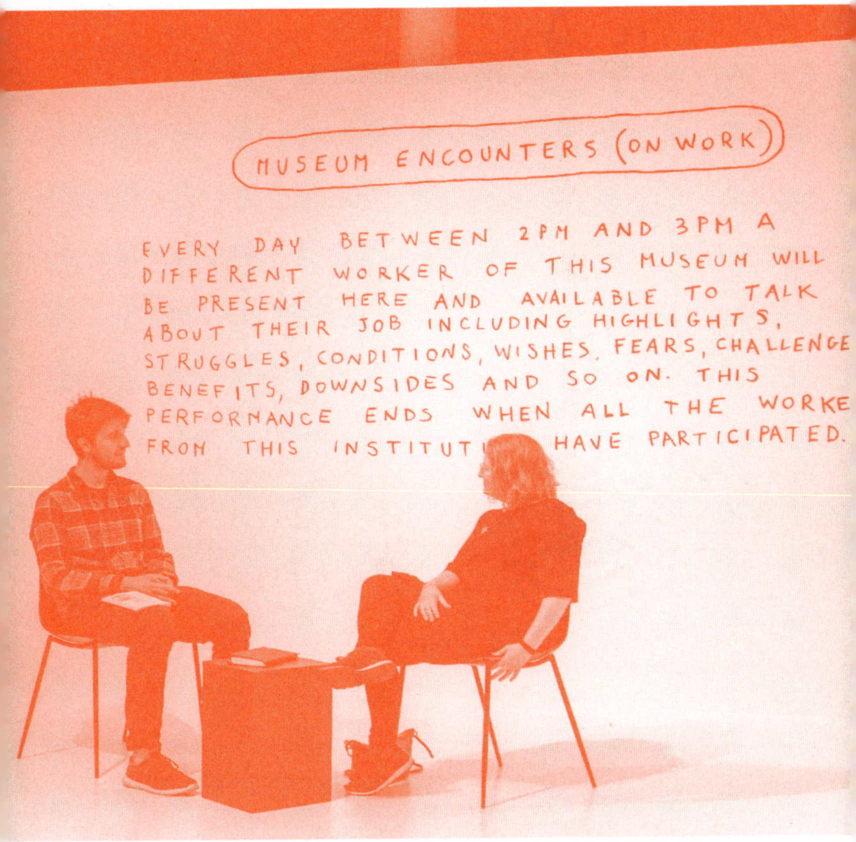
MUSEUM ENCOUNTERS (ON WORK)
EVERY DAY BETWEEN 2PM AND 3PM A
DIFFERENT WORKER OF THIS MUSEUM WILL
BE PRESENT HERE AND AVAILABLE TO TALK
ABOUT THEIR JOB INCLUDING HIGHLIGHTS,
STRUGGLES, CONDITIONS, WISHES, FEARS, CHALLENGE
BENEFITS, DOWNSIDES AND SO ON. THIS
PERFORMANCE ENDS WHEN ALL THE WORKE
FROM THIS INSTITUT HAVE PARTICIPATED.

UNDOING

1

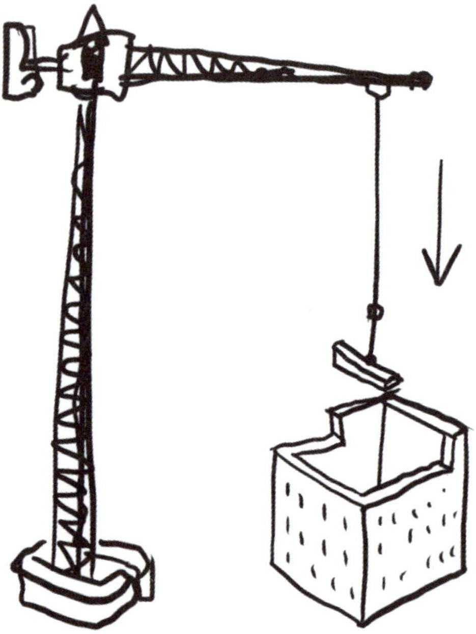

Trojan Horses tend to enjoy Anatolian breakfast places. Meeting point: Yppenplatz.

Başak takes the lead; we mix salty and sweet—coffee and beer, tiramisu and fries.

We don't know one another, but it doesn't matter.

Freek puts his name forward—a snowball effect we trust as a curatorial principle. We're not late, just forgetful: the Trojan blueprint gift stays tucked away, unspoken.

We don't mention it.

The conversation flows. Words reach for what drawings cannot. Shared spoons smooth the exchange as we consider how Vignettes become scores, guardians become guides, technicians become co-authors.

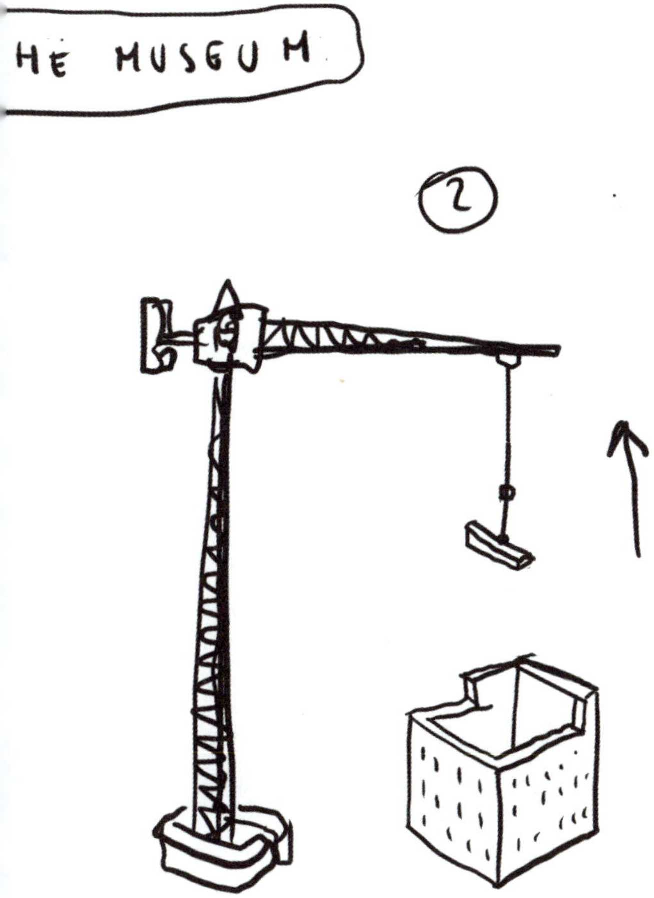

Simple to declare; powerful to witness.

Giannotti describes long-standing collaborations with museum staff, technicians, security guards, and mediators—not as auxiliary, but as central.

Over the years, they become performers, collaborators, and instigators of change. Once backstage walks onstage, scenarios transform. New protocols take shape.

Controllers become conspirators; the Trojan becomes Achaean; exit signs blink differently.

Museums can be *Upside Down*.

THE MUSEUM AS A BATTLEFIELD

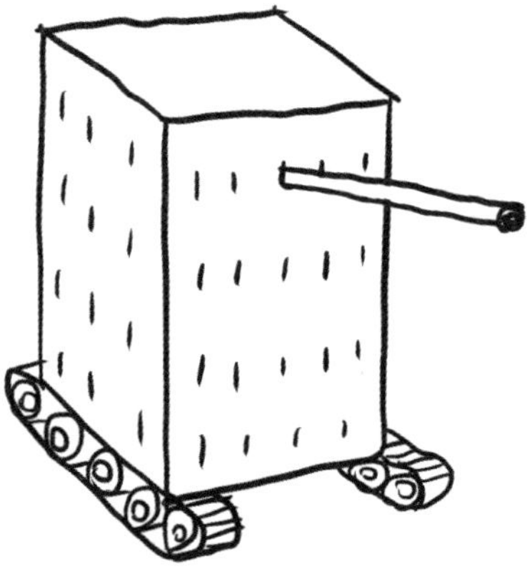

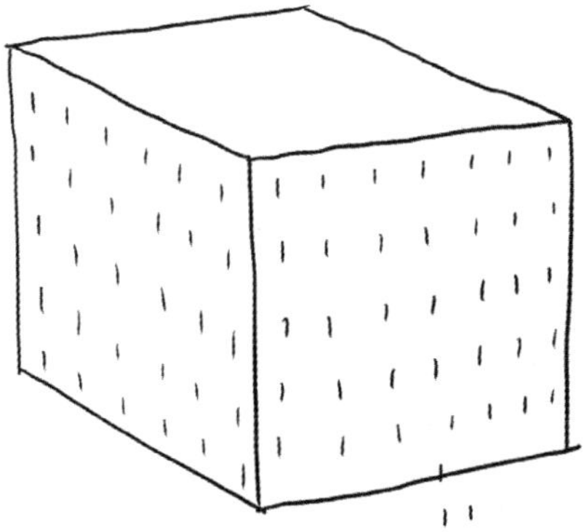

MUSEUM GUARDS PROTECTING
THE MUSEUM FROM THE MUSEUM

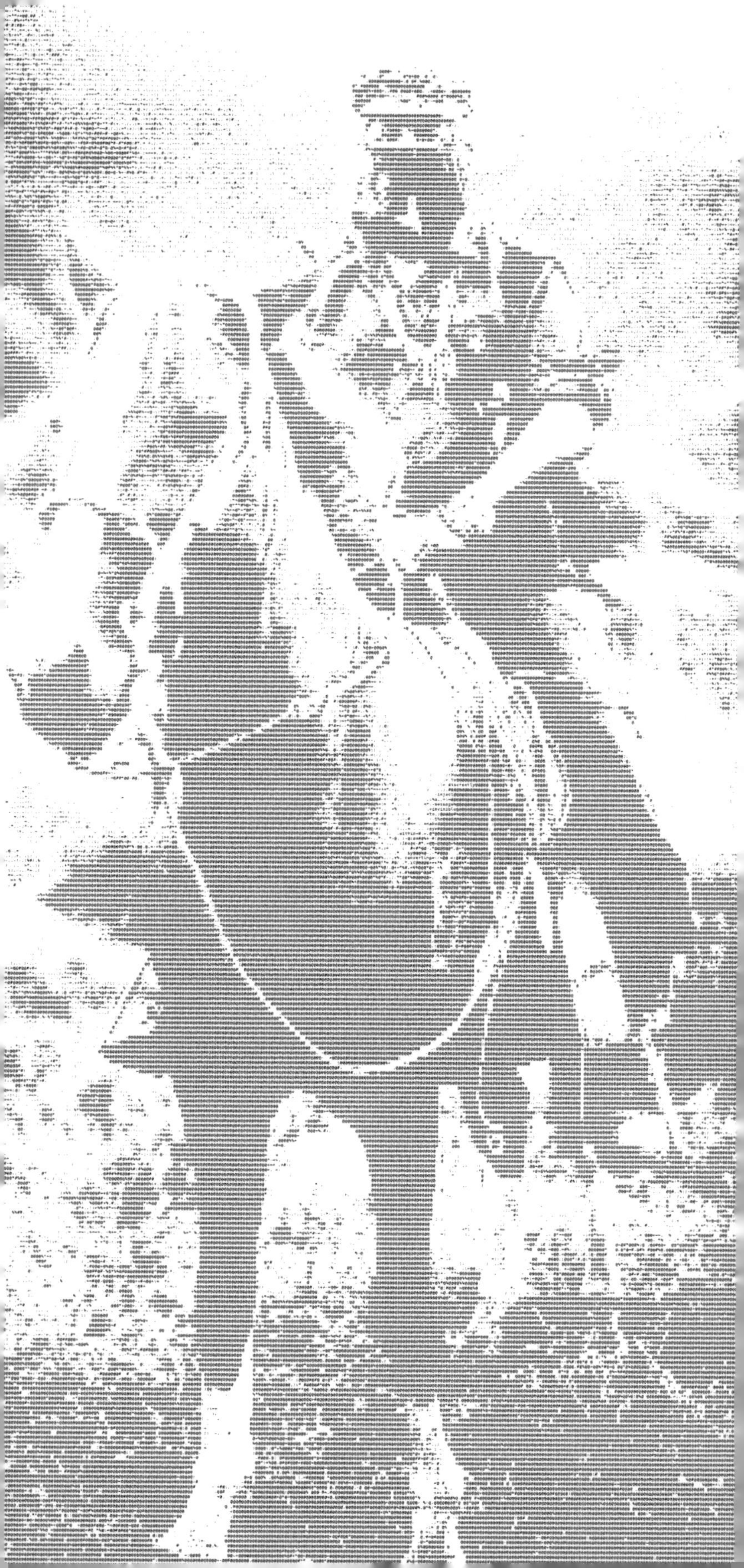

The book draws on Alessandra Pomarico's reading of Zapatismo as a practice of "preparing to exit" capitalist structures, not through withdrawal, but through the slow and communal work of building otherwise. Her interpretation reverberates in the artistic practice of Chto Delat, who have long explored how the Zapatista call for shared decision-making and embodied pedagogy might translate into cultural action elsewhere. In this sense, "exit" is not a flight from the world, but a form of staying differently within it, a rehearsal for solidarity, a reorientation toward the commons. Subcomandante Marcos, Chiapas, 1996.

Trojan Horse Institutionalism

Francesca Schinzani

Is the Trojan Horse metaphor still relevant for a young scholar, or just outdated—even cringe? Is disruptive discourse still interesting, or have we grown old enough to worry more about its distribution than its ignition? We needed someone whose position was not yet fully absorbed by the codes of the system, someone young enough to make us feel out of joint. After months of exchange, Francesca revisits the history of contestation within institutional frameworks through fragmentary documents and passages. Her writing moves through micro-textual gestures that resonate with her precarious, nomadic, intense, doubtful, and generous research practice.

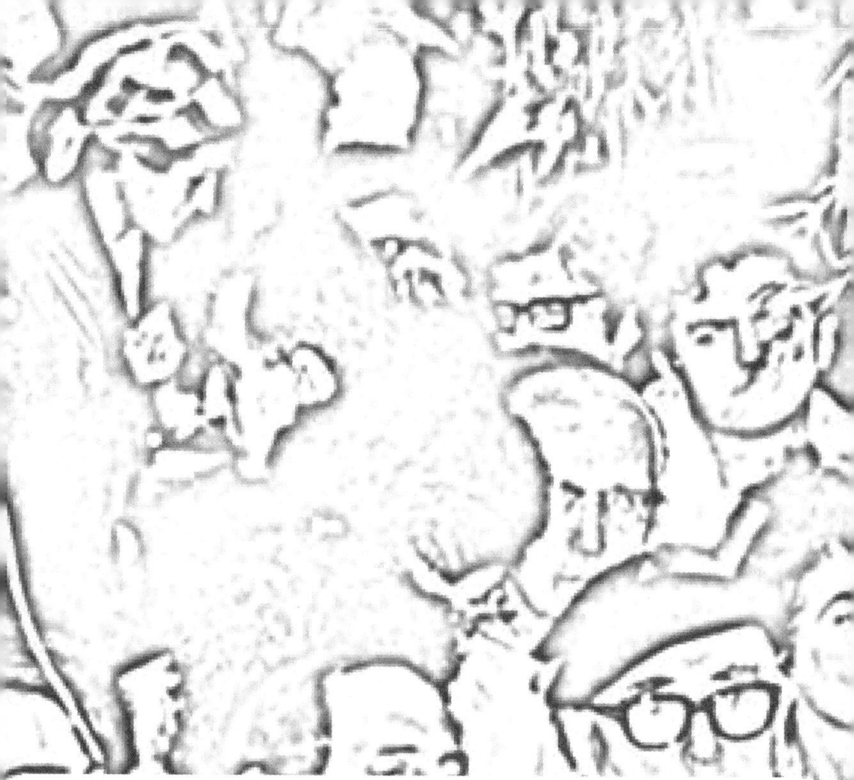

This brief writing experiment serves as a seed of institutional critique and contagion. To my handful of readers, I say: we are the agents of contagion. Yet, before we proceed, we must heed a series of historiographical notes on the exercise of power.

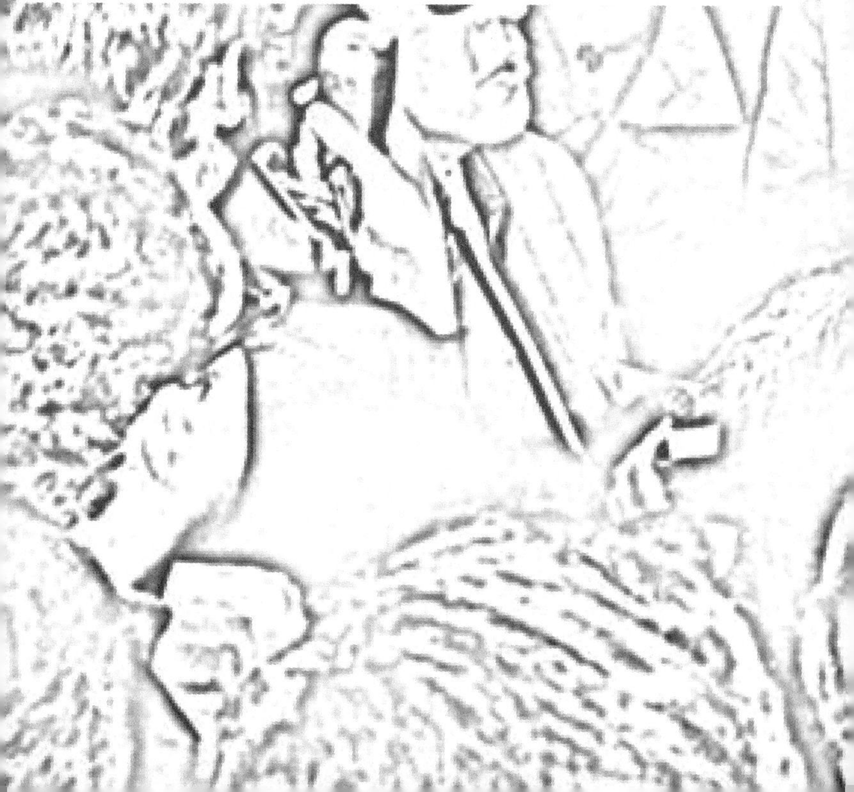

Douglas Crimp traces the rise of art museums to the expansion of other exhibiting institutions: public spaces, hardly ever free, where the function of sight can be exercised and where new forms of knowledge are developed. While "exhibition" is etymologically opposed to "internment," Crimp draws a direct line connecting exhibition practices to Michel Foucault's analysis of detention institutions. This opposition unfolds along three axes: spectacle, control, and power.

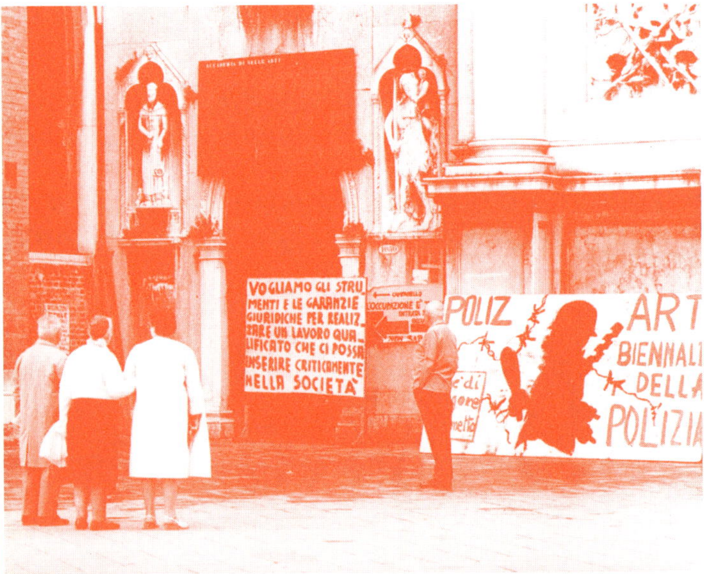

Ugo Mulas, Occupation of the Accademia, XXXIV Venice Biennale, 1968. Venice. Photograph by Ugo Mulas. Courtesy ASAC—La Biennale di Venezia (Archivio Storico delle Arti Contemporanee). Images in this article are reproduced in good faith for research, critical, and educational purposes only.

The Universal Expositions, whose allure lay in the promise of making the entire world available to view, functioned as mechanisms for controlling the masses.

The instruments through which power was exercised during the Belle Époque, more than a century ago, do not appear to have been substantially updated; they have only become more sophisticated and, for that reason, less visible.
Temporary art exhibitions, in the forms of biennials, triennials, septiennials, and so on— are obviously the spatial instruments through which it is decreed which art may rise to the honors of private collectors, galleries, foundations, and market-driven parameters.
Usually portrayed and considered by art historians as events of international significance, in the political economy of art, these exhibitions represent the primary site of exchange where geopolitical visibility and invisibility are constructed and negotiated.
Part spectacle, part historical event, sometimes conceived as an artistic manifesto, these exhibitions establish and manage the regimes of authority and recognition in art.

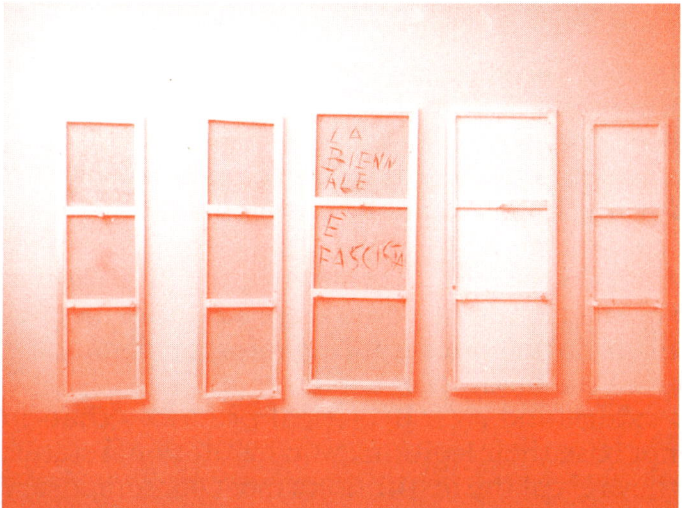

Ugo Mulas, Protest at the XXXIV Venice Biennale, 1968.
Same series. Courtesy ASAC—La Biennale di Venezia.

Every hegemonic order is susceptible to being questioned. Historically, artists have been portrayed as incubators of contestation seeds. While mass movements attacked dominant power structures, the events of 1968 infected the art world, contributing to the crystallization of this tendency.
Art making goes beyond information or dissemination, it is essentially political because it implies a refusal of the status quo—or at least a clear choice—but in any case, it is contestation.
I copied this note from my phone, then pasted it into Google, and the search returned zero results. Such are the pros and cons of fragmented writing methods. Either I pulled it from a printed text I can no longer identify, or I wrote it myself on a day of peak rhetorical inspiration.

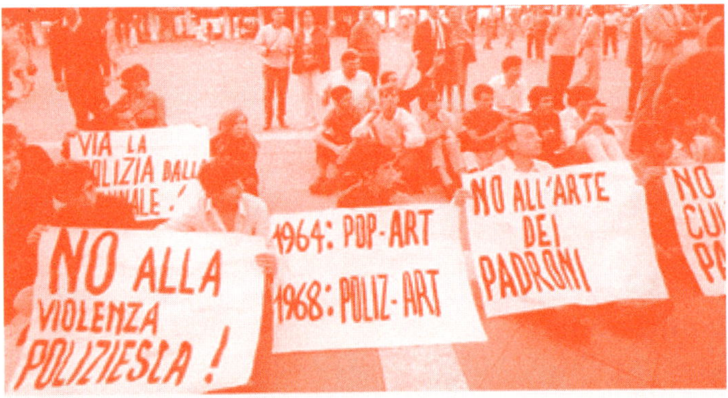

Ugo Mulas, Protest at the XXXIV Venice Biennale, 1968.
Same series. Courtesy ASAC—La Biennale di Venezia.

Despite the rhetoric, today—amid the decline of the public sphere brought on by the crisis of representative democracies—artistic and curatorial practices offer ways to experiment with various forms of public engagement, especially from within institutions.
A diverse range of practices adopt a radical social critique of power-reproduction mechanisms, while not requiring a forced distancing from the institution itself.
Understood as self-critical practices that do not base their legitimacy on institutional status, they reveal the institution's most contemporary potential.
Whoever bought this book should know this.
Thus, a little riddle for you:
How many words belonging to the semantic field of contagion have you found in the text?

Among various contestation efforts, consider a case study from the 1968 Venice Biennale: as Franco “Bifo” Berardi suggests, the myth of the end operates powerfully within ’68, due to its scale and duration, as well as the historical significance we attribute to its aftermath. At the end of July 1968, Rinascita, a magazine owned and supported by the Italian Communist Party, published an investigation as a supplement to Il Contemporaneo that took stock of the most important cultural institutions that had been “contested” at the start of the summer. Among many, there were the Triennale in Milan and the Venice Biennale.

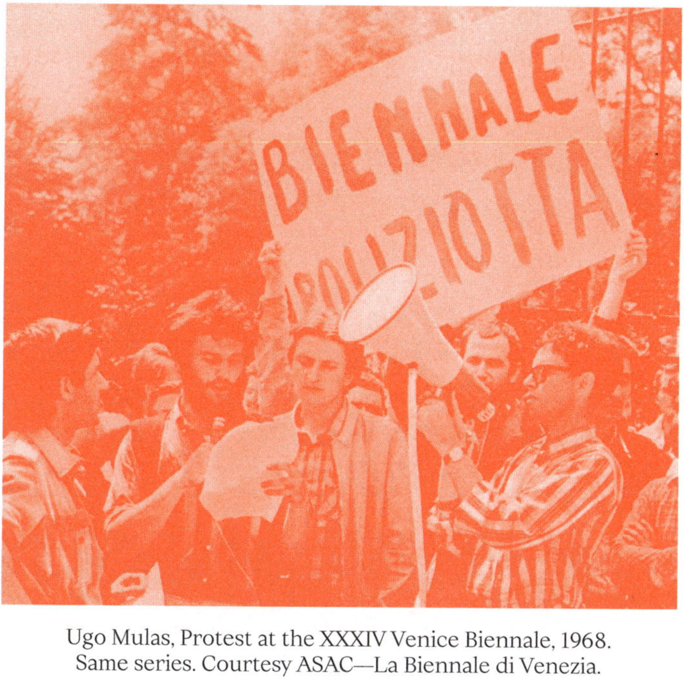

Ugo Mulas, Protest at the XXXIV Venice Biennale, 1968.
Same series. Courtesy ASAC—La Biennale di Venezia.

According to the investigation, the Biennale "is an instrument for mystifying artistic production, for organizing and controlling a culture reserved for the ruling class; the very same class that, in factories, in schools, and in society at large, smuggles its own economic interests and cultural models."
We cannot let this opportunity for struggle slip away at a time when the contestation of capitalist power is erupting across the globe and uniting students and workers.
Thus the call for artists to withdraw their works, and the concrete organization of the Biennale boycott. These actions must arise from the organized mobilization of all conscious and militant social forces, to strike at the heart of capital's repressive apparatus. The vernissage is the moment when capital's culture becomes market; thus, this year, on June 18, 1968, the contestation must take the form of direct struggle.
Comitato di boicottaggio della Biennale
(Biennale Boycott Committee)

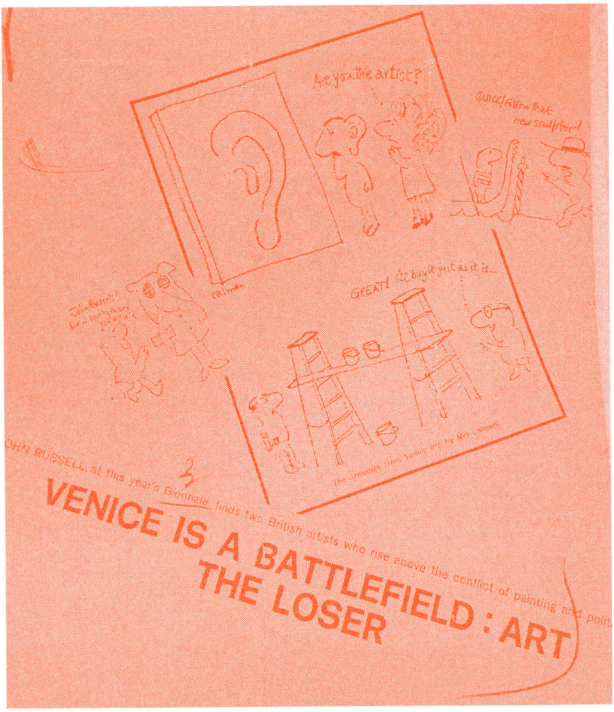

Archival research and photograph by the author.
Source: ASAC—La Biennale di Venezia (Archivio Storico delle Arti Contemporanee), Venice.

Numerous copies of this letter—evidently never delivered to the artists invited to the Biennale—are carefully preserved in the Biennale Foundation's archives, in a yellow folder on which an unknown hand has written, in bold, "VARIOUS CONTESTATIONS."

I stumbled upon it accidentally.
A rough, quick critical analysis: aside from the atmospheric 1968 urgency to join the struggle (which I strongly support), the pragmatic aspects referenced remain vague. Moreover, the terms boycott and protest are used synonymously, a terminological flattening that weakens and blurs the deeper motivations behind the struggle.

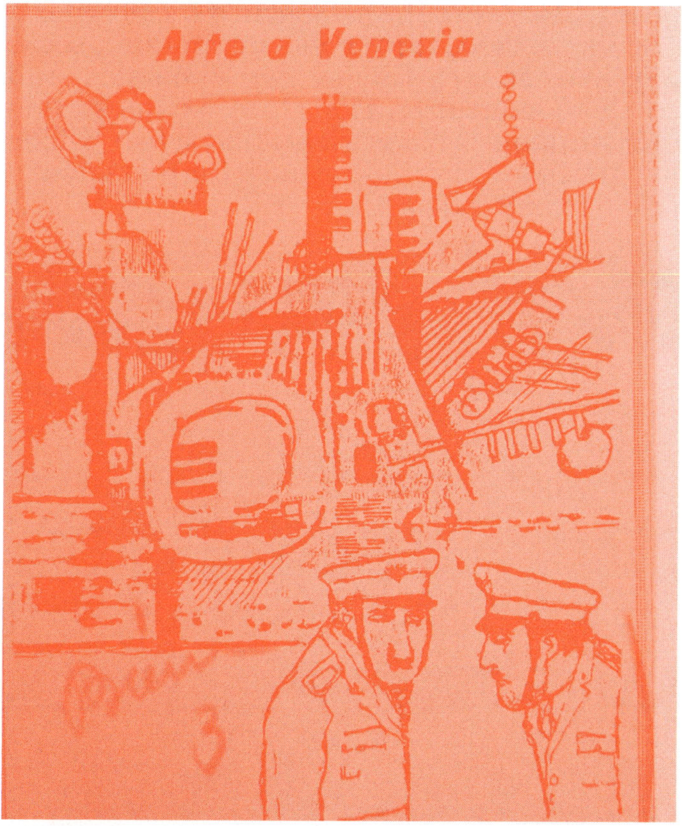

Archival research and photograph by the author.
Source: ASAC—La Biennale di Venezia (Archivio Storico delle Arti Contemporanee), Venice.

On the troubled nature of derivative protests and overlapping struggles, Carla Lonzi wrote a strikingly lucid text in which she described the Venetian contestation as a programmatic extension of the Triennale occupation. She accused the artists of having joined the student protests without reflecting on the structural reasons that would have justified a contestation—namely, the power exerted by the institution at the expense of genuine artistic inquiry.

By definition, an institution tends to control values and establish hierarchies. The Biennale is not a place of conservative reactionaries, but it continues always to be an entity meant to be contradicted. Insofar as it hosts artists, it also hosts revolutionaries.
In other words, it hosts a form of humanity that poses a danger to the established social order—one that society, through its institutions, seeks partly to absorb for its own dynamics, and partly to neutralize. Therefore, a contestation of institutions will invariably find artists willing to participate; but the grounds for that contestation must be clear.

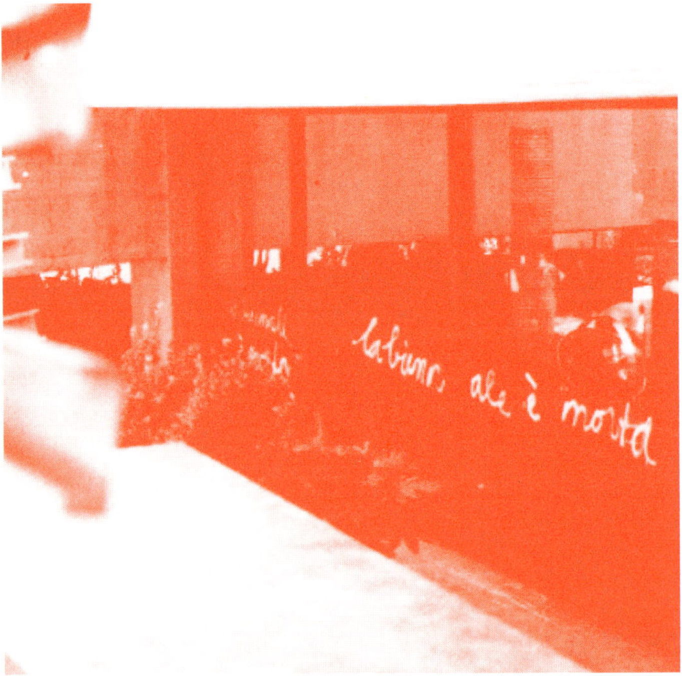

Ugo Mulas, Interior, XXXIV Venice Biennale, 1968. Same series. Courtesy ASAC—La Biennale di Venezia (Archivio Storico delle Arti Contemporanee).

The protests of '68 did not merely resolve themselves into a multiplicity of fragmented and unorganized sectoral clashes that fed mini-powers of Foucauldian memory. The revolt against pre-established authority was born from the desire to exercise a form of power equal and opposite to the existing one.

If I ever end up working for a biennale—not unlikely, considering how they've proliferated across the globe—I'll try to make some extra cash on merch that states, in bold type:

A CULTURAL INSTITUTION ALWAYS HAS TO BE CONTRADICTED.

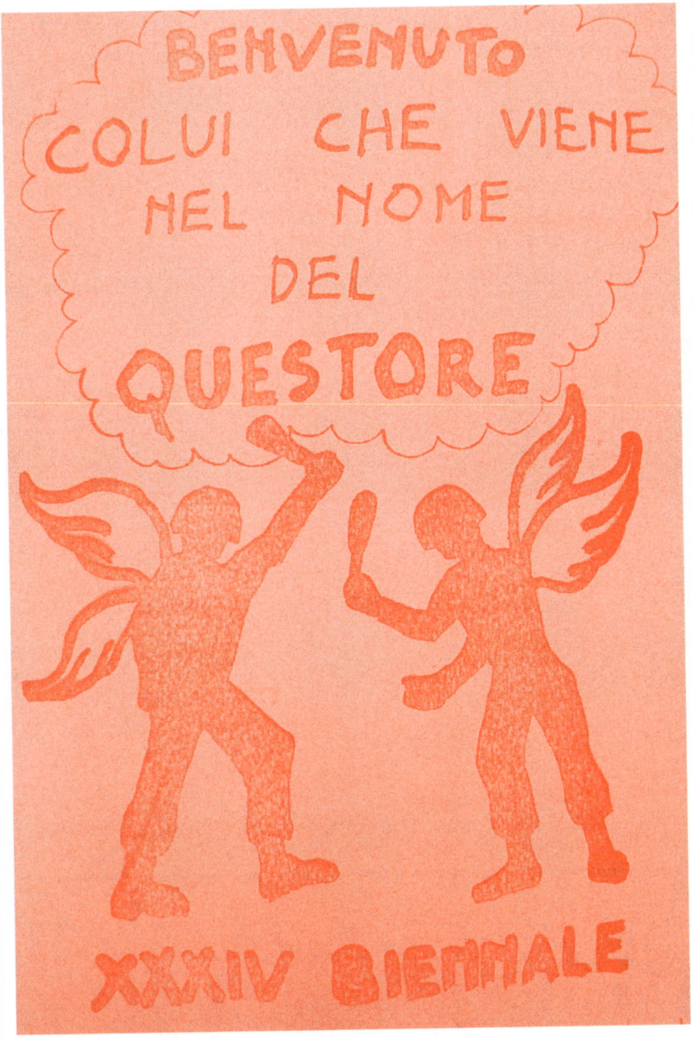

Archival research and photograph by the author.
Source: ASAC—La Biennale di Venezia (Archivio Storico delle Arti Contemporanee), Venice.

Institutions are political apparatuses of representation that organize systems of value-control and enact the performative power of the (usually) nation organism within the mesh of a cellular system. Within institutions, symbolic and political negotiations take place.
In light of the wider politicization and transdisciplinarity of art, Alex Farquharson describes the institution as a kind of compensatory public space—an oasis of openness or a forum of possibility. Following Gerald Raunig's work, a more contemporary articulations of the institution has been explored through multiple frameworks, such as new institutionalism, institutional experimentalism, relational institutionalism, and instituent practices.

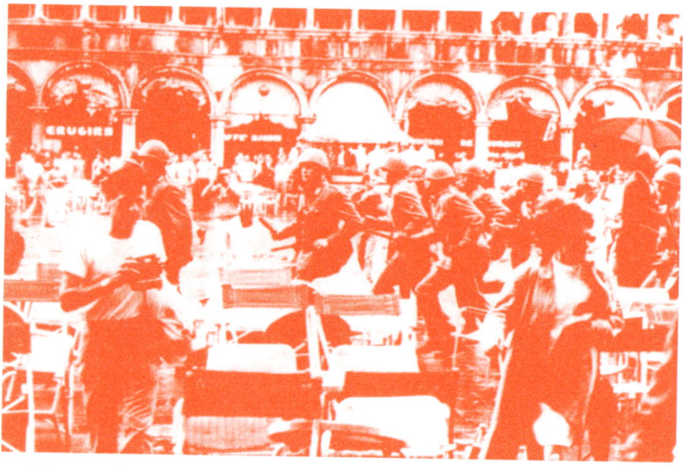

Ugo Mulas, Protest at the XXXIV Venice Biennale, 1968. Same series. Courtesy ASAC—La Biennale di Venezia.

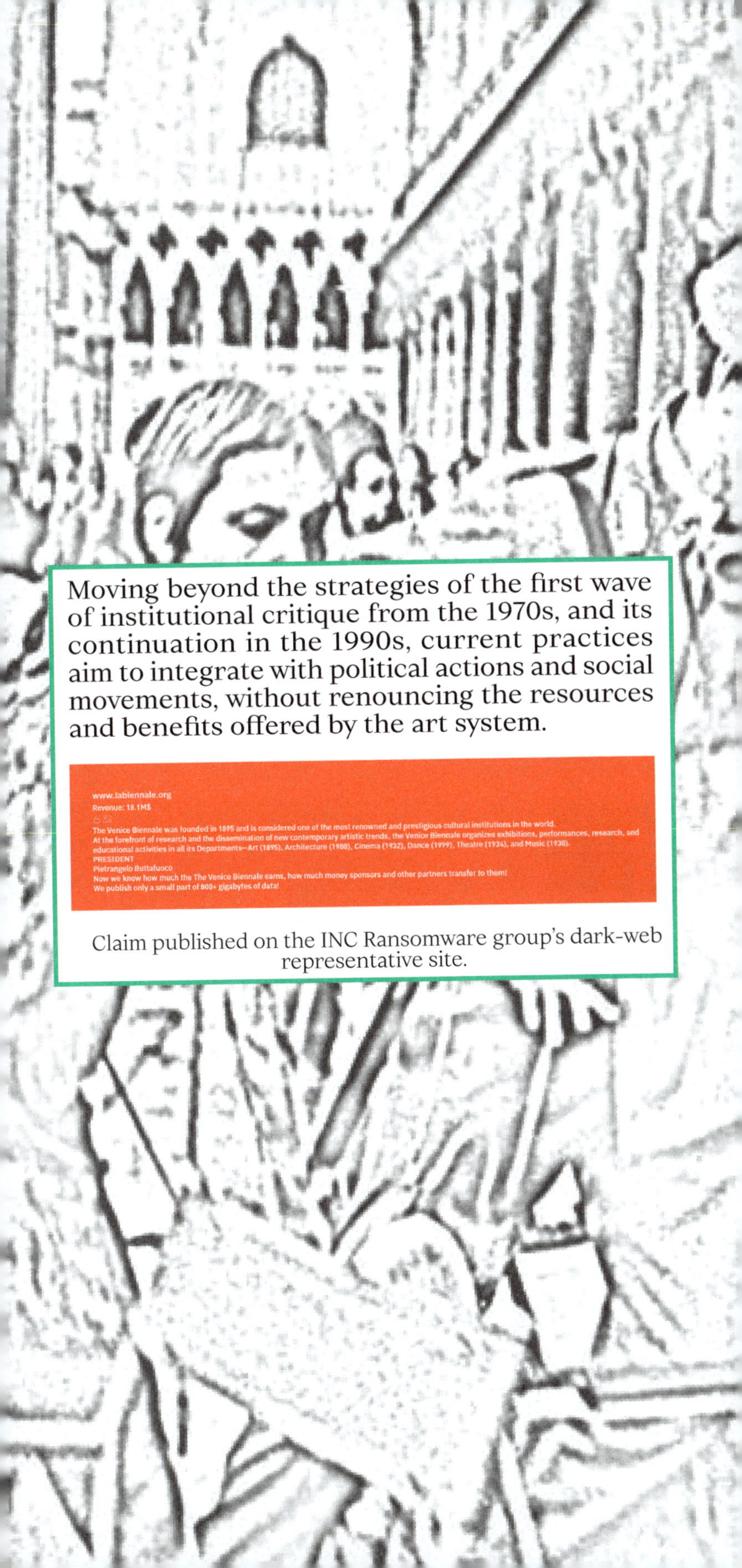

Moving beyond the strategies of the first wave of institutional critique from the 1970s, and its continuation in the 1990s, current practices aim to integrate with political actions and social movements, without renouncing the resources and benefits offered by the art system.

www.labiennale.org
Revenue: 18.1M$
The Venice Biennale was founded in 1895 and is considered one of the most renowned and prestigious cultural institutions in the world.
At the forefront of research and the dissemination of new contemporary artistic trends, the Venice Biennale organizes exhibitions, performances, research, and educational activities in all its Departments—Art (1895), Architecture (1980), Cinema (1932), Dance (1999), Theatre (1934), and Music (1930).
PRESIDENT
Pietrangelo Buttafuoco
Now we know how much the The Venice Biennale earns, how much money sponsors and other partners transfer to them!
We publish only a small part of 800+ gigabytes of data!

Claim published on the INC Ransomware group's dark-web representative site.

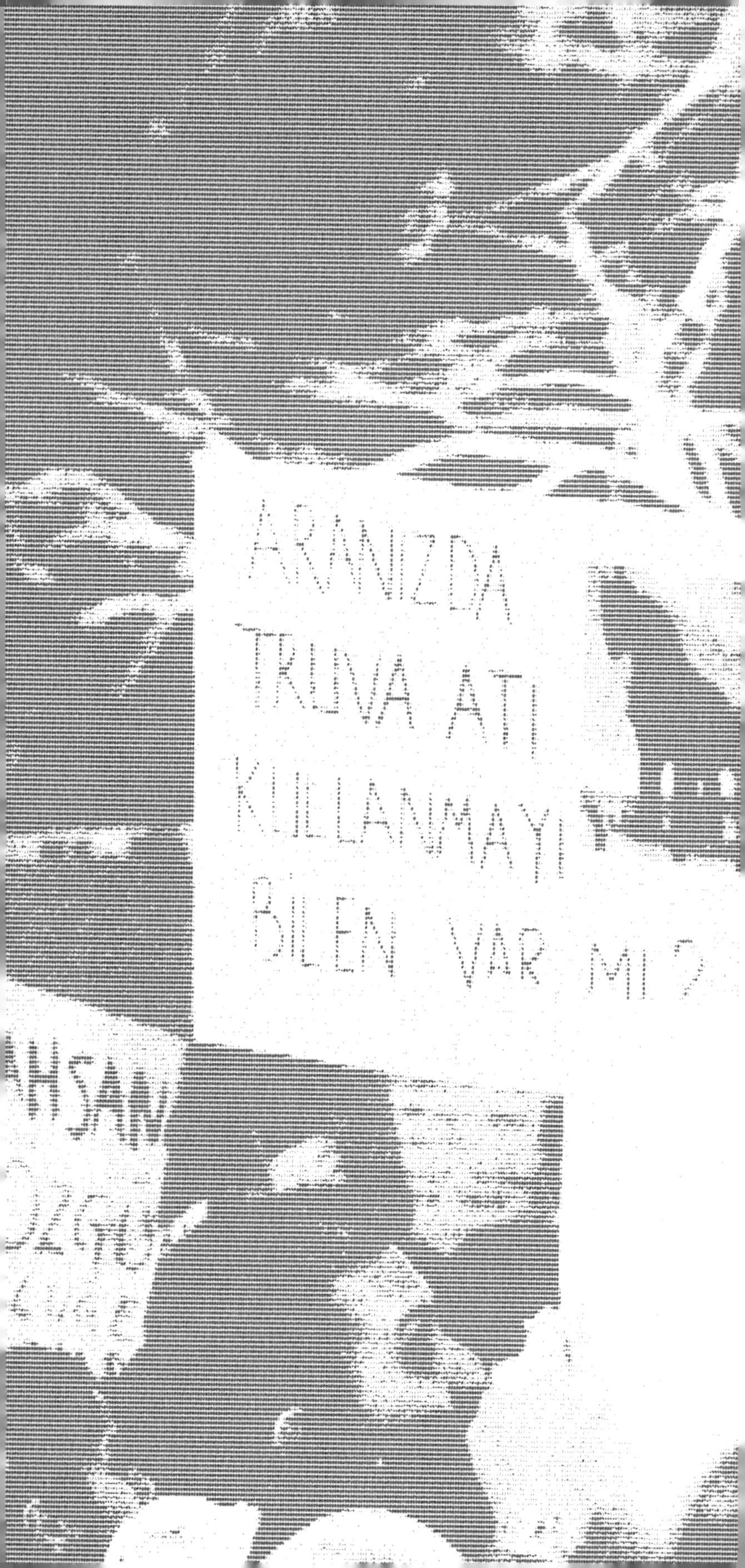
ARANIZDA
TRUVA ATI
KULLANMAYI
BİLEN VAR MI?

As the billboard asked: Does anyone know how to use a Trojan Horse? This book was written in the summer of 2024 and later edited through the 2025 protests, under the pall of routine, often absurd repression in Turkey. To avoid causing trouble for our kind and generous partners, we adopted a cautious linguistic strategy, deliberately diluted wording that removes any practical or symbolic references to sabotage, and aims instead for questions and metaphors that can travel safely.

Exit Monument

Peter Lang

Echoing the iconic figure known as the keeper of heaven's gates and founder of the first truly ecumenical institution, people named Peter often have a penchant for keys. Likewise, Peter Lang embodies this mastery, unlocking countless doors in and out of institutional context. His polymathic approach transforms the monument from a barrier into a doorframe—a passage inviting us to leave behind fixed meanings and enter spaces of possibility. For Troy, he conceives a "monument to an exit," which creates thresholds, challenges permanence, and navigates the ever-changing dialogue between history, memory, and power.

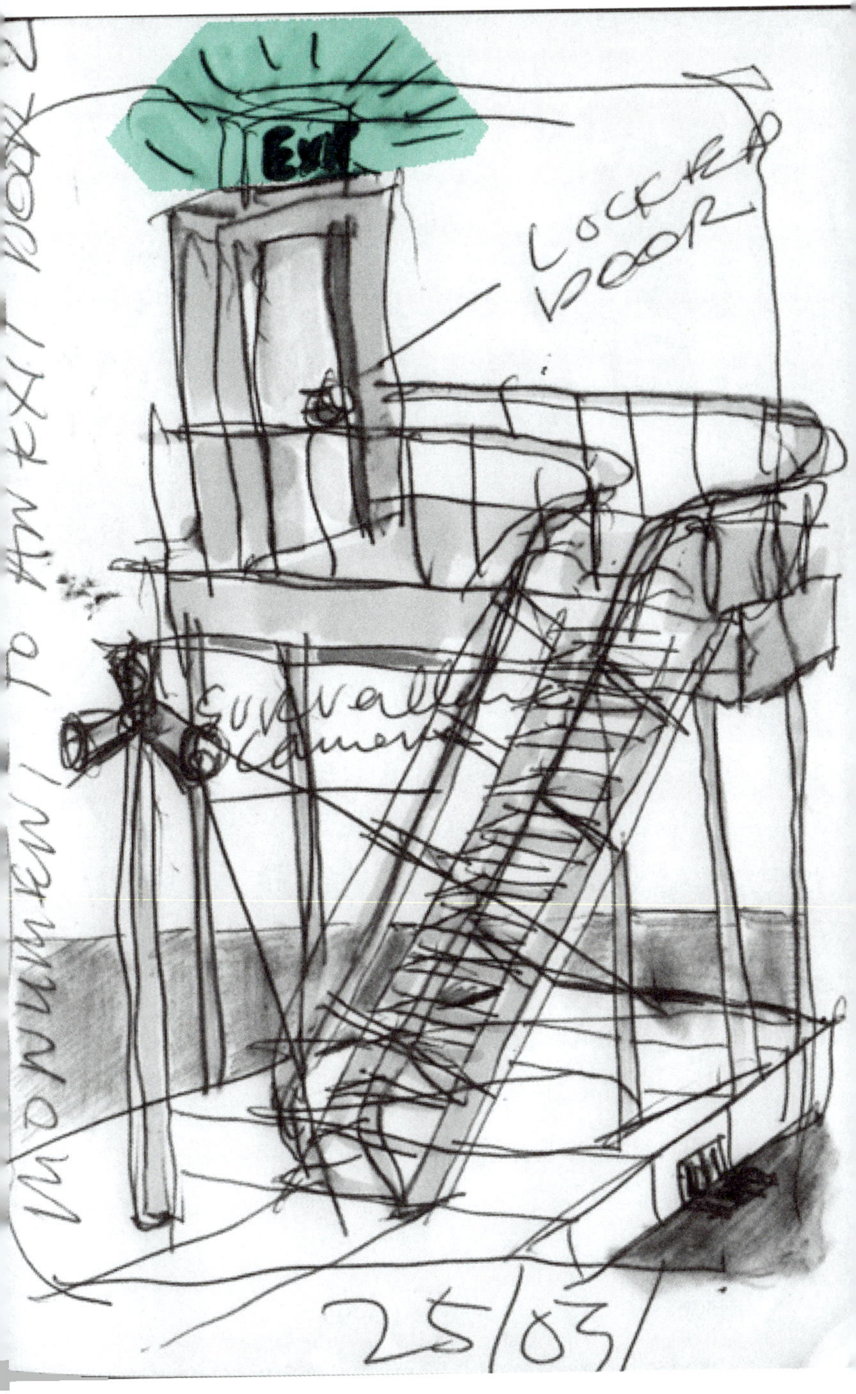
EXIT
LOCKED DOOR
25/03

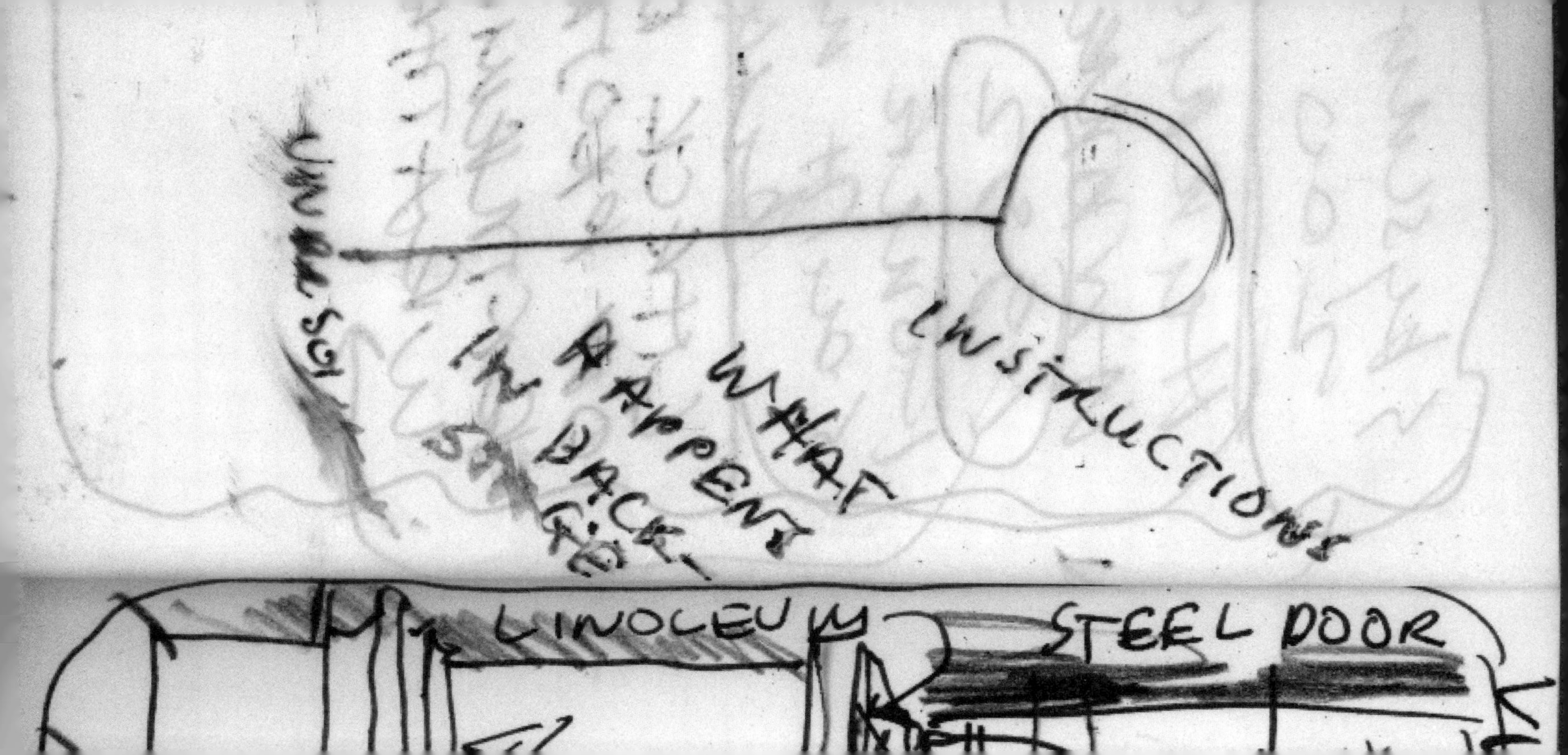
INSTRUCTIONS
WHAT HAPPENS IN BACKSTAGE
LINOLEUM
STEEL DOOR

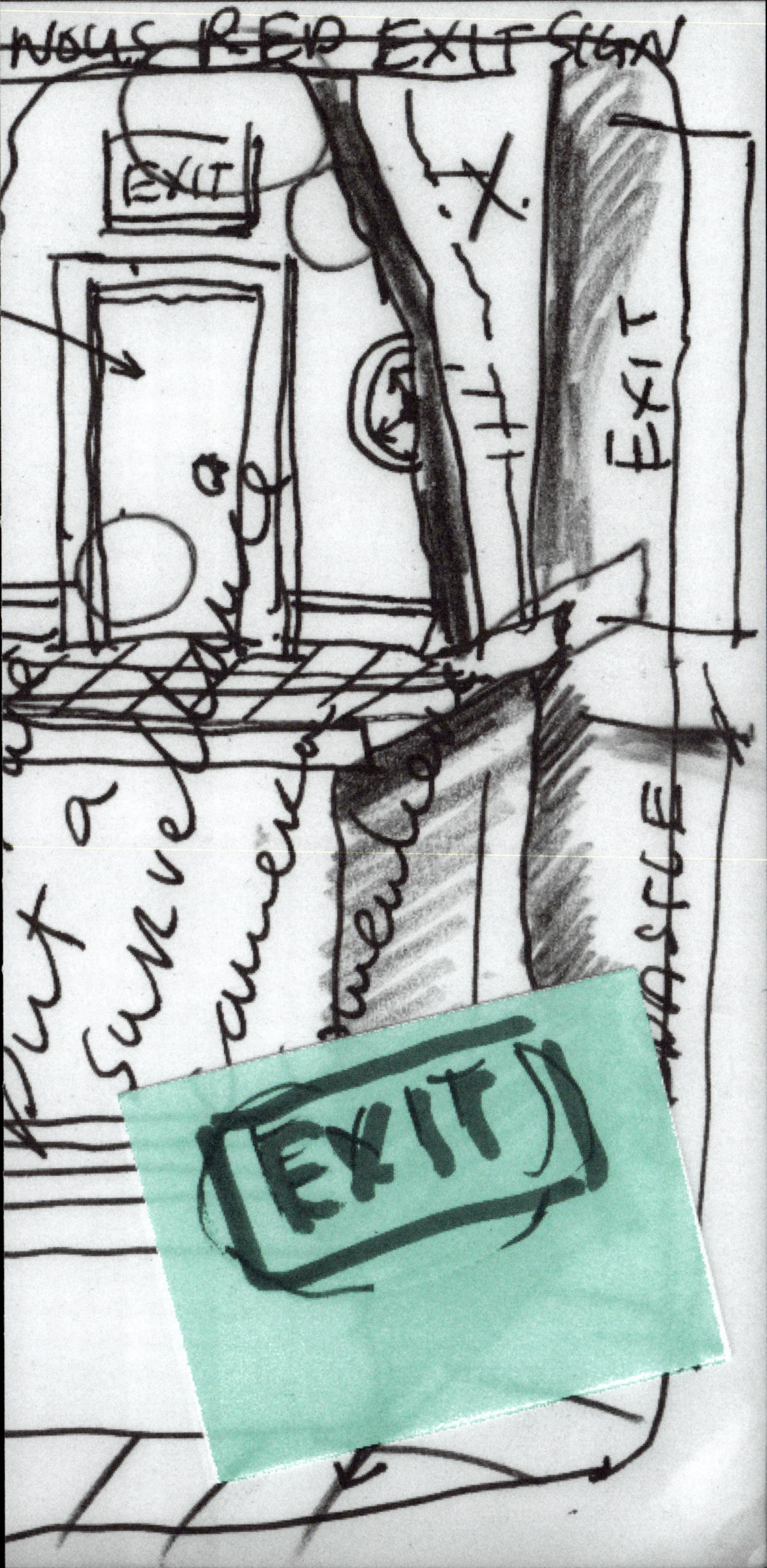
RED EXIT SIGN
EXIT
EXIT
EXIT

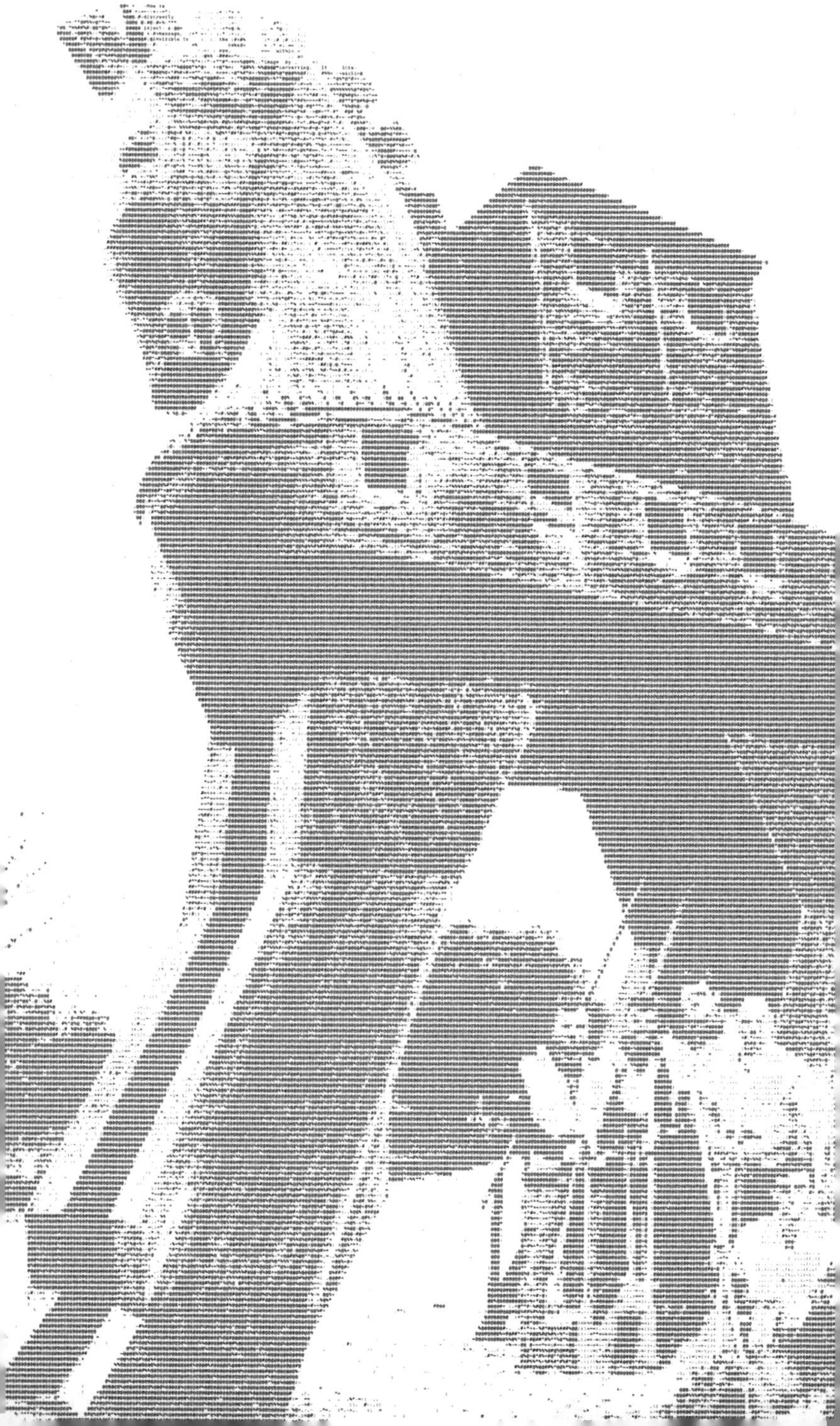
How to
discreetly
inject a
message,
invisible to
the
naked
eye,
within
image by
converting
it
into
ascii

If you came here hoping for a manual on tactical innovations in the profanation of museums, we must apologize: this is not that book. Perhaps our meaning has slipped. Because under the appetite to disrupt institutions sits a quieter, more practical question, posed by Mierle Laderman Ukeles in the Maintenance Art Manifesto: "After the revolution, who's going to pick up the garbage on Monday morning?"

Breaking the Fast: A Gastroscopic Conversation

Interview with Caroline Barneaud + Stefan Kaegi (Rimini Protokoll)

To continue the process of de-Odysseusizing the Trojan Horse, we aim to silence our brains to think with our guts. Renowned for expanding theatre beyond conventional stages, Caroline Barneaud and Stefan Kaegi devise works in which the body, the city, and even the digestive tract become sites of revelation. After twenty-four hours of collective fasting, we enter a moment of conceptual and physical hunger in which digestion is not merely a process but a method: situating thought in the belly and unspooling meaning through heat, discomfort, proximity, and waiting. The conversation unfolds at the intersection of hunger and performance, both literal and symbolic.

Participants: Caroline Barneaud (CB); Stefan Kaegi (SK); Natalia Agati (NA); Matteo Locci (ML); Başak Tuna (BT).

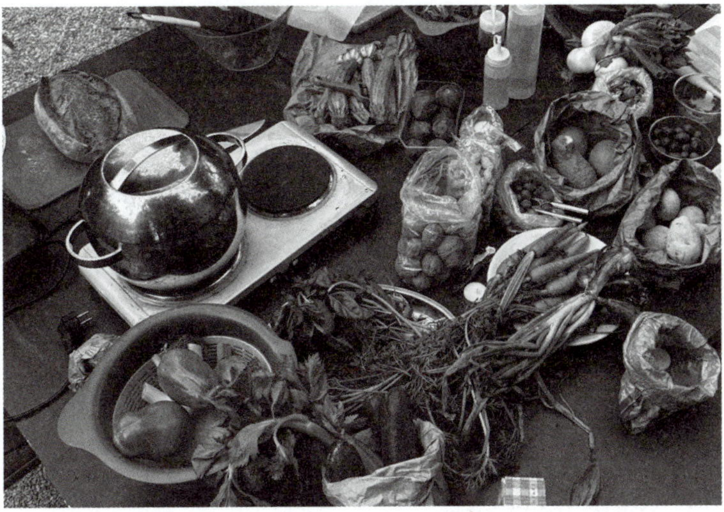

It is a muggy Roman summer day. We are not used to fasting. We are tired. There's a faint, shared halitosis. This isn't about clear answers or neat conclusions. It's a moment of fermentation. Thoughts come slowly, all over the place, shaped by being tired, trusting your gut, and low blood sugar. The mind steps back. The belly takes over. Somewhere between ritual and recovery, sharing this meal preparation becomes the method.

CB: Oh wow you really brought a lot of food! I don't see garlic. Remember I'm allergic to garlic.

The atmosphere is refreshing. The table is set, but nothing is ready to eat. Vegetables still need cooking, fresh beans wait in their pods, and nuts remain sealed in their shells. They all ask for our time, divide our attention, and test our patience. There are bitter vegetables that need trimming, soaking, and blanching. There's no way to rush it. Then there are rolled, baked and stuffed items, carefully prepared by our break-fast master Edoardo.

NA: We know. No garlic whatsoever.

EF: Before we begin, a small matter of metabolic strategy. We'll be eating in about an hour or so. In preparation, we offer you two options: two distinct paths through the next stretch of time. One is to remain as you are: to stay at your current level of hunger and simply wait, pacing yourself toward the coming meal. The other involves a calculated risk: a small intervention in the form of a candy. This will mess with your ketogenic state, briefly elevate your blood sugar, granting you a flash of energy... but at a cost. Within a few minutes, the hunger may return with sharper teeth. Your stomach may even enter a mild state of tension, somewhere between urgency and gastro-philosophical hunger. So: which process do you feel more inclined to choose? Shall we wait together in balance, or stir the storm a little?

SK, CB: we stay put.

Thank god they said no!
A sugar spike would have made the entire interview agitated, unfocused, and miserable.
But still, the question had to be asked.

BT: That´s a pity.

Oddly, Stefan seemed unsettled by his own restraint, as if skipping the candy made him appear too careful. Maybe to compensate, he offered a playful counter-proposal.

SK: We could start chewing some food without ingesting it... then pass it along to the next person. Like a ritual.

PS: That's possible.

SK: Cows do that for their calves, don't they?

NA: I think it's birds. If you propose it, we'll follow. Still, our suggestion is to wait one hour and cook for the experiment before we break the fast. So, I would suggest we all take one eggplant, salt it, and wait. Please slice with one principle: we go slow tonight. While we're salting the eggplants, we would like to ask you to introduce your current work, rooted in the stomach, *Holy Shit.*

Cutting begins, hunger is bearable. People are tired. Questions drift past unheard. Misunderstandings take the lead.

BT: What is the meaning of shit that you haven't thought about before this work and that you are realizing?

CB: Two words: Fecal Transplant. In the beginning and the end. We are really moved by the idea that parasites shape so much of your emotional state. However, we were a bit disappointed to find out that it's not used as often as we thought at first. Besides ours, there's a lot of scientific speculation around fecal transplants. Including the theoretical possibility that you can change the mind of a person, the spirit, the psychology; and thus a fecal transplant can also potentially change your personality.

SK: For instance, what if we change the microbiome of Trump, what happens? Swap the shit of Caroline and me, and I get some of what she lacks and she gets what I lack, and vice versa. Changing the microbiome is theoretically possible.

CB: So, depending on your genetics, context, what you eat, and whether you are stressed or not, a microbiome that is very good for Stefan may be very bad for me. And so, yes, it's utopian, though practically unrealistic.

Sudden interruption and stomach sounds.

CB: Oh my goodness. Did you hear that? We should probably put the microphone on our bellies, it's talking. Do you hear the sound? I heard it from over here. It was really strong... I think it's happy. However, I have no direct understanding of it even after a year working on this project. What are all these signals coming up from the stomach? We know the brain sends information down there. That's why we get diarrhea when we're nervous, but there's at least as much information going up. Scientifically we just don´t know enough.

ML: I have no idea what you are talking about. Are you saying that you are disappointed by the level of understanding of the gut that you have at this moment?

CB: Yeah, it's a bit frustrating. We know a lot of information is sent every second from the gut to the brain, but we can't read it.

ML: Is it an issue of specialization, not being expert enough in the field? Or is it more of a global lack of information?

SK: It's a problem that neuroscientists also have. They kind of give up. I have this good friend who is one of the leading neuroscientists in Germany, Jonathan Haynes. We called him and said: look, we've talked so much about the brain with you; can you tell us something about all this input that comes from the gut? He goes: "Look, it's definitely wrong to say you think with your guts." So he was totally against this expression, including the gut feelings. Being negative, his answers open up a more existential approach to the stomach. He immediately connected to the idea that it's impossible to think starting from the gut. He accepts that it influences—that it creates emotion, which is scientifically proven—and it's based on experience: right now we're very hungry and I feel the gut taking over. However, he also said something interesting: "The gut is too vague. It's not relevant yet in neuroscience, because it's too vague." I felt it was stressful for him to expand "thinking" beyond the brain. It was like: no, no, no. The brain is enough. Anyway, through a gastroenterologist we heard about exploring the intestine with a camera, to see a place you normally cannot access visually, and we were advised to use a PillCam.

ML: Excuse our triviality, is that the Mossad technology you once mentioned?

Mossad triggers a sudden attentive reaction and awakens the group.

SK: It wasn't exactly invented by them; the technology came out of the Israeli Ministry of Defense, very small cameras that an Israeli doctor later demonstrated with a live stream from the small bowel.

ML: We were wondering why the stomach? Why the gut? It seems that it's a very effective metaphor device to talk about so many other things and this was very enriching.

Touching his stomach, Edoardo suddenly noticed that the stomach is never at rest.

EF: The stomach and the intestine are always in motion. Even when the body rests, like today, when we haven't given them things to process, they're at work. Actually, when one is fasting, one puts them to rest a little. It's the only time the stomach really rests.

PS: The moment when we don't eat? No, we can say it's the moment when the gut stays less active.

SK: Did you hear her stomach? It was very loud. So it seems to be doing something. I imagine it's trying to digest itself.

CB: Yeah, it's a never-ending movement. It will never stop working. It's like a river.

EF: A Japanese biologist discovered that when someone is fasting, many processes are activated that otherwise wouldn't be. But even then, the body doesn't activate itself as it normally does. We were joking about the metaphor of... how was it? I don't remember.

Edoardo is usually very focused, despite his experience with fasting, he's probably, like everyone else, just as fatigued.

BT: You said it! I think we're also super tired. Because you don't remember what you said. I would like to eat. I can't take it anymore.

ML: I think Edoardo is touching on something interesting.

EF: It's a kind escape from the logic of consumption. Consumption is always put in the production of one's own body. To stop and fast for a moment, it's an interruption.

SK: You want to propose a vacation for the stomach. I mean, there's the option of striking, at least, I guess. I think it's a strike when it's too much. Sometimes the stomach doesn't accept.

EF: Strikes or holidays. In many cultures and regions, fasting is a very important moment—in Arabic, Christian, and Jewish traditions. Fasting is a moment of detachment; it's like our body's shabbat. Ramadan is exactly this. It's the moment when...

BT: Coming from Turkey, I have to say it's more extreme than ours. It's without water. On average, 12 hours of fasting.

We have been fasting for 25 hours now.

SK: In this respect, what I find interesting, both in capitalism and evolution, is outsourcing. You probably know the theories: once we had fire and began to cook, we started to pre-digest. Cooking already does part of digestion. That's the moment in evolution, as far as I understand, when the brain starts to grow, because we don't need as much energy down here.

CB: An externalization of digestion, done outside the body, so it's like what we do now with technology.

SK: I find it super interesting. We constantly try to outsource everything. Now that we have the bigger brain, we also try not to use it for remembering things, so we keep external archives. With A.I., we outsource research, creativity, and information. So where does the idea come from that, in a capitalist society, we try to be as lazy as possible with our body, or try not to use our capacities?

PS: It's the reptile we are in, right? It's not a Trojan Horse conversation, we are more like crocodiles, trying to avoid extra movements, extra energy. We stand still. Hey, if you feel like eating a little bite, you could. Anyway, maybe I interrupted a conversation. Was there a good discussion? I got distracted. I'm sorry.

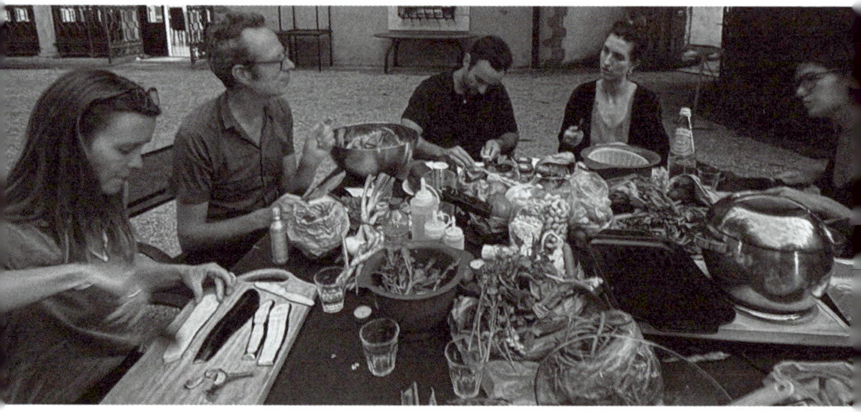

NA: We all have low blood pressure; we're distracted. But yes, we were discussing a good point.

A long pause while the group tries to pick up the thread of the conversation.

PS: Outsourcing!

SK: What would be the next functions we would outsource? Obviously we've already outsourced a lot of our physical activity.

CB: We're also outsourcing what the intestine does to make nutrients. We take vitamins and other things because we remove them from food by processing it too much. Then we add some of them back into the food we eat. It's the perfect capitalist circle: you spend a lot of money transforming food into something that has nothing in it, and then you develop individualized medicines to compensate for the problem you created by transforming the food.

The conversation is once again distracted by the stomach noises, and the thread is lost.

ML: OK, so, Edo, master of the breaking the fast ceremony, shall we interrupt?

EF: I was thinking again about that discussion on capitalism, maybe the real problem will always be when life itself can be reproduced. When it becomes possible to reproduce the human body. That still isn't possible, right?

SK: Yes, it exists in the tap, in the glass. Yes. But there are no clones.

Another distraction—background chatter about what to put in the brioches: cheese, olives, and other similar things.

ML: I'm not an expert in cloning. By mistake, I just ate a fagiolini to try it while cutting.

NA: An involuntary move. Your stomach is taking over.

SK: We're not hungry.

Collective laughter.

ML: Anyway, I have to be honest. I can't cope with my current self and the supposed role of interviewer. Usually I can ask questions and I'm very engaged in the conversation. Today, I'm really not.

Edoardo starts serving the brioches.

SK: let´s eat: Eat, eat.!
Go, go. You go first, Matteo, you need it. There was one more thought of yours about the outsourcing talk that I tried to reconstruct, and I don't fully get it.

CB: Yeah, yeah, fermented food reproduces what the intestine is doing.

BT: In Turkey we pickle everything.

CB: Yeah, it's the same process.

PS: I'm lost. No idea what you are talking about. Let's eat!

SK: In what way will the conversation develop after we start eating?

ML: How long will it take until we start operating normally? Seconds? Minutes? How long would it take for my thoughts to leave the stomach and reach the head?

EF: Immediately. As soon as you introduce sugar. The second you put sugar in, you have ten minutes. Except if you're on a keto diet. You take it, you smell it, and then you eat it. The first bite will open your stomach.

Stefan is excited.

SK:... Mmm... I remember when I did my two weeks without eating. The moment I started to eat, I totally exaggerated, I cooked a huge risotto.

NA: What?

Thoughts still sound foggy.

SK: Yes. Not even drinking, only tea and water. I was about twenty years old. It was a time I drank intensively. I partied a lot. I took all kinds of drugs, and I felt like I wanted to make a radical difference. So I went to the mountains and decided for two months not to see anybody, not to listen to music, not to read novels, and for the first two weeks, not to eat. I was with a dog.

ML: So the fasting was foundational for you?

People are all very distracted.

CB: I'm focusing on the food. Also, it's a bit spongy and I like the texture of it; it's a bit like an intestine. Wow. It was an amazing way to break the fast. Thank you.

A long silence while eating.

EF: Let's throw these vegetables into the soup.

SK: It's interesting that your collective seems focused on negation: not being allowed to see the temple the other day in the performance, or not eating food today. In your performance, what was striking was the act of being forbidden and then obeying the rule you proposed, looking the other way. You created a phantom picture that isn't there, but that your neurons complete.

ML: Notwithstanding that we're flattered and would love to talk about our work, technically today we are interviewing you.

SK: No, it's a round table.

ML: I'm curious how things resonate, not with a Trojan Horse specifically, but with the idea of forcing your way into something.

Matteo gets lost in his own thoughts, people barely listen. Still, he insists:

I see it in your relationship with experts, this drive to enter a specific sect, discipline, or field of knowledge outside your own, which also has a spatial side. Maybe I'd like to propose that we understand what moves you to go into things, and then how you get out of them, and why you move on to something else.

SK: I think the bigger question driving many projects is identity, what we perceive as very clear. Here, in the bowel, in fasting, identity gets lost, and we think: are we what we eat? What are we? Are we the multiple or the single? Are we just another animal?

CB: For instance, you brought a lot of food. Maybe there's a limit to how much we should cook.

The excessive food is part of an exhaustive food preparation protocol. Eating a bite to break the fast; then a one-hour conversation while cooking.

ML: Thinking about agreement, how things move from one place to another. We don't know how you two work together. How do you alternate your practices?

CB: We work together in very different configurations. Sometimes together from the beginning; other times Stefan brings a project, and I come for a bit of production, or something else.

ML: It seems that, between the two of you, you—Caroline—shift roles the most. Is that right?

CB: Yeah, also because I have a full-time job,

A very long existential, pretentious and pseudo-intellectual question from Matteo drains the last attentive energy. We cut it. Başak tries to clarify.

BT: What is your method of Trojan Horse?

ML: But nooo, you weren't listening!

BT: No, I wasn´t, but while not listening I understood I was not interested in your question.

SK: One association I have with the Trojan Horse, I'm hesitant to use it directly, but since you brought it up, it resonates. In all our projects, but particularly in Holy Shit, we've done many interviews and accumulated a lot of knowledge. In a more conventional approach, someone might now sit down and write a novel or a piece, shape all that material into a plot, maybe with an emotional arc to make it appealing. But for us, something else happens, something that resists being reduced to a single output or a linear form. We decide to implant our ideas into something, or somebody. So there's a bit of a Trojan Horse strategy. Instead of bringing it out in a straight line, we like to see it explode or flourish in somebody else. We are not soldiers. The metaphor ends because I wouldn't know where the enemy is, or which fortress we need to invade.

CB: It's a bit of a transplant. The being-together in temporary intimacy—this is close to what happens in the Trojan Horse. We had an idea, a goal, and we invited people to enter a body we made for this to happen. ... And while we were in with them... I'm lost.

Despite eating, it's hard to keep up with our own thoughts. Low energy is common when the body shifts from using stored nutrients to processing incoming food; blood sugar wobbles. Fatigue makes the dialogue heavier.

CB: Hm.

Many seconds later...

CB: Coming back to the idea of the "expert."

For both of us, theater isn't so much about presenting knowledge as it is about creating temporary communities and moments of intimacy. It becomes a mini-laboratory where things can happen differently, outside the usual structures. So maybe it's less about being an expert, and more about holding space for something to unfold in a shared, experimental way.

ML: On our self-appointed experimentality, sorry to interrupt... The brain, my brain, isn't in charge. I feel tipsy, even though we haven't drunk. Anyway, the idea of micro-intimacies is interesting for us; it's also about why one enters the belly of the Horse. In your practice we see a capacity to be disruptive, like an aggressive Trojan Horse, and also genuinely interested in intimacy.

The point is missed again.

CB: Maybe it's time to eat those grilling eggplants?

ML: Let me put it differently, because I may not have been clear. It seems you're drawn both to provocation and to being inside the space, taking time not to disrupt, and connecting worlds that aren't your usual political context.

SK: Those are not for provocation, almost the opposite. It's more about going somewhere I'd normally feel provoked by. That's the reason to enter, to have this intimate kind of context. Hopefully intimate. But first of all, it's to be able to enter without having to hide in a forest. Or, if the Horse is there, then maybe it's the naivety of being an artist, not already a provocateur, not someone who arrives with an ideological attitude, not a journalist who wants secret facts. For instance, in the show Security Conference, we copied an actual security conference that's hosted every year in a big hotel in Munich, the one we rented. We copied it on a smaller scale, but invited experts who would never get invited to the Munich Security Conference. It's more of a meta-conference, I think.

CB: Embodying situations is important in Rimini Protokoll's work, being put in the position of embodying the story, the situation, the role. It's a strategy.

SK: *Société en Chantier*, for example, is a work we made together. You almost swap identities every twelve minutes on a construction site. For about ten minutes you're an urban planner, then you switch, and you're a construction worker. Then an engineer. Then a lawyer. Then someone from Transparency International. Then a property developer making money off construction. Classically, theater plays the "as-if" game. But in these simulation games, we address the spectator as a construction worker, both by the performer and by the situation. You might even dress certain things or carry things. It's physically done.

ML: What was the "as if" in the embassy project for instance?

CB: You're referring to a project called This Is Not an Embassy. It was organized with the National Theatre of Taipei, about the specific situation of Taiwan, which is not recognized as a country but acts as one in many ways, including the economy. There are only twelve countries in the world that officially recognize Taiwan. Our protagonists found creative ways to establish small bilateral situations, or communication acts. One of them is a diplomat; another an NGO diplomat. Another founded a company that's now the biggest exporter of bubble-tea products, making Taiwan known in trade around the world. To your question: the "as if" is, let's pretend we are opening an embassy together here. It wouldn't be possible in reality, but in the theater we're protected by the freedom of the arts. So it becomes possible.

ML: But this freedom of the arts eventually has some form of repercussion. The theatrical device is clear. But how does it deploy? How does it extend beyond the representation?

CB: I feel like an honorary consul of Taiwan now. And it won't stop. I think some other people in the audience felt the same. I have a responsibility to defend Taiwan, in a way, because of my show.

SK: Empathy is interesting to discuss, also in relation to digestion, hormones, neurons. It's a central mechanism of theater: you look at others, tell others; you try to identify with others; you go through a process, you might suffer with them, or maybe not. It's classic drama theory, but it still happens. And that's very different from visual art.

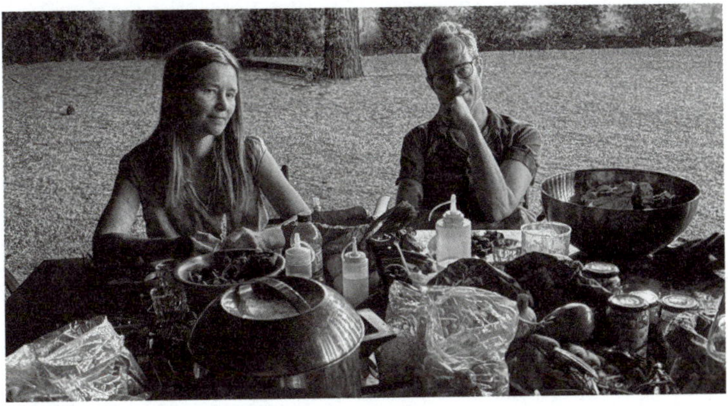

Sniff, sniff. Something smells like it's burning.

BT: I think it's the aubergine.

CB: I realize I'm not hungry anymore.

SK: It's weird how, once hunger is gone, you can't remember how it felt. I already think: oh, I was hungry. Cheers.

CB: For me it was very difficult around 7 p.m. I was at the British Academy; people were talking to me and I wasn't able to reply. I felt better later. Now I'm tired, but I'm okay. I feel good, but a little sleepy. Yes, sleepy.

Many weeks later while editing the interview.

CB & SK: Even if this isn't really productive for a book :-) it's definitely not a problem for us to be out.

We hope we'll do another experiment and fail again with you all. Maybe not being efficient was a kind of unconscious collective escape strategy. :-)

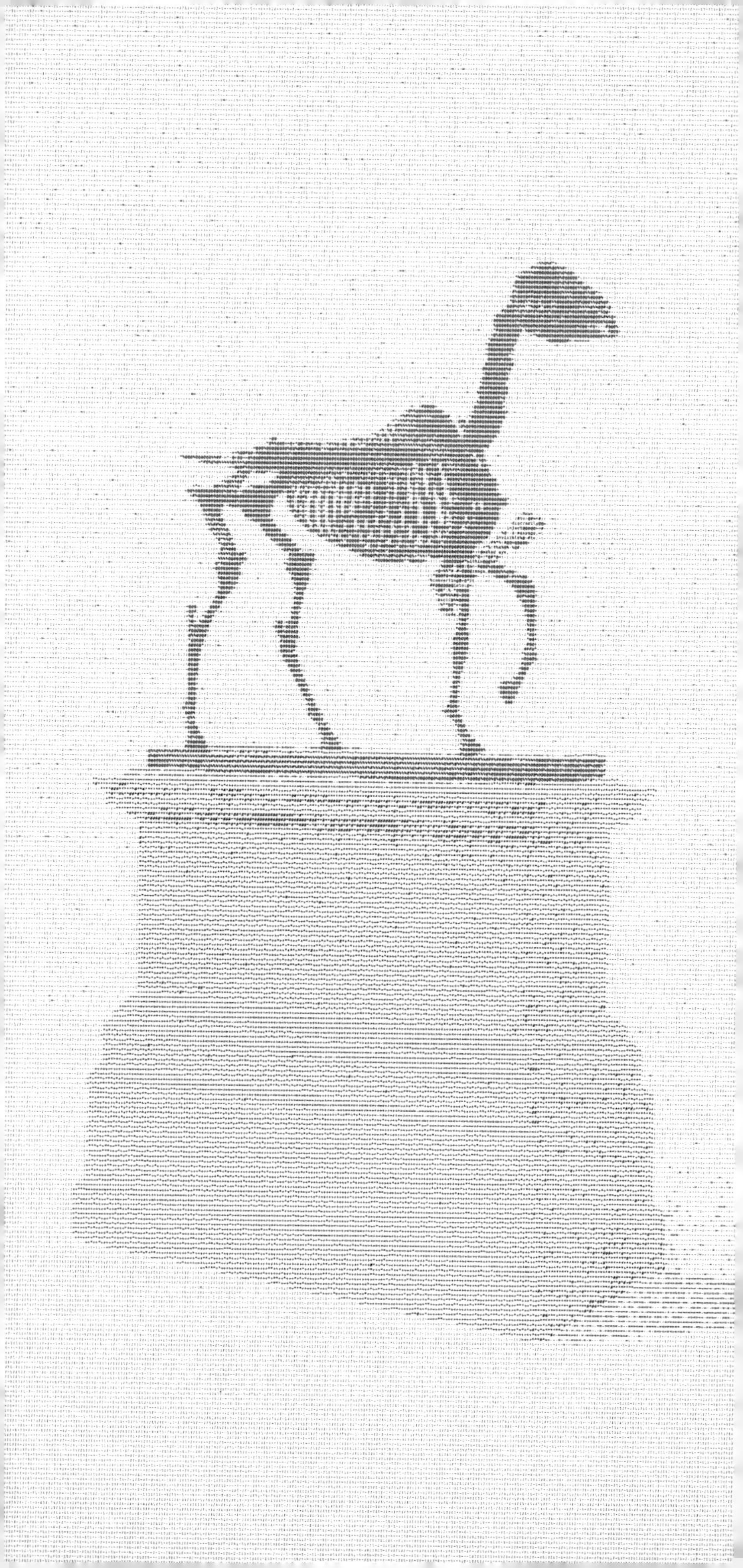

Exit Poll: Is this book worth the effort? Yes or No. Tear the page if not.
Gift Horse, Hans Haacke, 2014.

Bibliography

Agamben, Giorgio. *L'uomo senza contenuto.* Macerata: Quodlibet, 1970.

Ahmed, Sara. *What's the Use? On the Uses of Use.* Durham, NC: Duke University Press, 2020.

AMO / Koolhaas, Rem. *Door. In Elements of Architecture: 14th Venice Biennale.* Venice: Marsilio, 2014.

Badovinac, Zdenka, Bojana Piškur, and Jesús Carrillo, eds. *Glossary of Common Knowledge.* L'Internationale, 2018.

Bishop, Claire. *Radical Museology, or What's "Contemporary" in Museums of Contemporary Art.* London: Koenig Books, 2013.

Bishop, Claire. *Artificial Hells: Participatory Art and the Politics of Spectatorship.* London and New York: Verso Books, 2012.

Bourdieu, Pierre. *The Rules of Art: Genesis and Structure of the Literary Field.* Stanford, CA: Stanford University Press, 1995.

Boltanski, Luc, and Ève Chiapello. *The New Spirit of Capitalism.* London and New York: Verso Books, 1999.

Borja-Villel, Manuel. *Campos magnéticos: escritos de arte y política.* Barcelona: Arcadia, 2020.

Cabeza de Vaca, Fran, Sofia Olascoaga, and Adela Železnik, eds. *From/To — Letters from/to the Constituent Museum.* L'Internationale, 2022.

Caleo, Ilenia. *Performance, materia, affetti: Una cartografia femminista.* Rome: Bulzoni, 2021.

Christianopoulos, Dinos. *They Buried Us.* Translated by Emily Jones. *In Poems of Resilience.* London: Penguin Books, 2020.

Debord, Guy. *La société du spectacle.* Paris: Buchet-Chastel, 1967.

Deleuze, Gilles. *Qu'est-ce que l'acte de création?* Lecture at Fondation Femis, Paris, 1987.

Derrida, Jacques. "Rhetoric of Cannibalism." Seminar, Paris, 1991.

Duncan, F. Cameron. "The Museum: A Temple or the Forum." *The Journal of World History*, special issue "Museums, Society, Knowledge," 1971.

ESCI (Exoteric Society of Critical Illusionism). *Manifesto.* Rome, 2019.

Flusser, Vilém. *Bodenlos: Eine philosophische Autobiographie.* Düsseldorf: Bollmann, 1992.

Flusser, Vilém. *Bodenlos: Uma autobiografia filosófica.* São Paulo: Annablume, 2007.

Foucault, Michel. *Surveiller et punir: Naissance de la prison.* Paris: Gallimard, 1975.

Fraser, Andrea. "From the Critique of Institutions to an Institution of Critique." *Artforum*, New York, 2005.

Pollock, Griselda. *Vision and Difference: Feminism, Femininity and the Histories of Art.* London: Routledge, 1988.

Groys, Boris. *Art Power.* Cambridge, MA: MIT Press, 2013.

Han, Byung-Chul. *Psicopolitica: Il neoliberismo e le nuove tecniche del potere.* Milan: Nottetempo, 2014.

Harney, Stefano, and Fred Moten. *The Undercommons: Fugitive Planning and Black Study.* New York: Autonomedia, 2013.

Hegel, Georg Wilhelm Friedrich. *Phänomenologie des Geistes. Bamberg: Joseph Anton Goebhardt,* 1807.
Homer. *The Iliad.* Translated by Emily Wilson. New York: W. W. Norton & Co., 2023.

Ingold, Tim. *The Perception of the Environment: Essays on Livelihood, Dwelling and Skill.* London and New York: Routledge, 2000.

International Organization for Standardization. ISO 3864: S*afety Colors and Safety Signs — Design Principles for Safety Signs and Safety Markings.* Geneva: ISO, 1984.

Kunst, Bojana. *Artist at Work: Proximity of Art and Capitalism.* Winchester: Zero Books, 2015.

Lamont, Peter. *Magic in Theory: Theoretical and Psychological Elements of Conjuring.* Hertfordshire: University of Hertfordshire Press, 2005.

Manaugh, Geoff. *A Burglar's Guide to the City.* New York: Farrar, Straus and Giroux, 2016.

Margulis, Lynn. *Symbiotic Planet: A New Look at Evolution.* New York: Basic Books, 1998.

Wark, McKenzie. *Capital Is Dead: Is This Something Worse?* London and New York: Verso Books, 2019.

Meisner, Albert. *La soi-disant utopie du Centre Beaubourg.* Paris: Éditions Entente, 1976.

Mouffe, Chantal. *Agonistics: Thinking the World Politically.* London and New York: Verso Books, 2013.

Neufert, Ernst. *Bauentwurfslehre.* Berlin: Bauwelt, 1936.

Perroni, Sergio Claudio. *Nel ventre.* Milan: La Nave di Teseo, 2023.

Rancière, Jacques. *The Emancipated Spectator.* London and New York: Verso Books, 2009.

Rancière, Jacques. *Le partage du sensible: Esthétique et politique.* Paris: La Fabrique Éditions, 2000.

Sacchi, Annalisa. *Inappropriabili: Relazioni, opere e lotte nelle arti performative in Italia (1969–1979).* Padua: Marsilio, 2023.

Sholette, Gregory. *Merciless Aesthetic.* Zagreb: What, How & for Whom, 2016.

Steyerl, Hito. "Politics of Art: Contemporary Art and the Transition to Post-Democracy." *e-flux Journal*, 2010.

Velotti, Stefano. *Dialettica del controllo: Limiti della sorveglianza e pratiche artistiche.* Rome: Castelvecchi, 2017.

Venturi, Robert. *Complexity and Contradiction in Architecture.* New York: The Museum of Modern Art, 1966.

Zevi, Luca, ed. *Il nuovissimo manuale dell'architetto.* Rome: Mancosu, 2003.

Žižek, Slavoj. *The Universal Exception: Selected Writings, Volume Two.* London: Continuum, 1993.

Contributors

Aldo Giannotti is a visual artist who has lived and worked in Vienna since 2000. His practice often involves staging participatory situations and using drawing as a central medium to question and redefine the meaning of spaces and institutions. Over the years, Giannotti has collaborated with and exhibited in numerous institutions, including Albertina (Vienna); MAMbo (Bologna); Kunsthalle Wien; Kunstpavillon (Munich); Lentos Museum (Linz); Kunsthaus Graz; ar/ge kunst (Bolzano); Künstlerhaus Dortmund; Museum der Moderne (Salzburg); Austrian Cultural Forum (London); Donaufestival (Krems); and the Museum of Contemporary Art (Zagreb).

Cesare Pietroiusti born in Rome in 1955, began his career in psychiatry before transitioning into art, where he focuses on the relationship between social psychology and artistic practice. His work explores everyday paradoxes, particularly themes of economics, value, authorship, and social interaction. He is a founding member of the collective Lu Cafausu and co-founded the Fondazione Lac o Le Mon, a center for artistic research and experimental pedagogy in San Cesario di Lecce. Pietroiusti has exhibited internationally and co-founded the artist-run space Jartrakor in Rome, the magazine Rivista di Psicologia dell'Arte, and Nomads & Residents in New York. He was also a coordinator of the "Oreste" projects. He is no longer the president of Palaexpo.

DEMOCRACIA is an artistic collective based in Madrid, Spain. Formed in 2006, the group focuses its artistic production on collectivity, dissent, and conflict. DEMOCRACIA's work is characterized by social interventions that politicize spaces and situations through the apparatus of propaganda. Their concerns are expressed through forms that subvert and reposition the aesthetic materials and textual rhetoric of Western political culture. In doing so, their practice offers a critique of social, political, and economic institutions, systems, and conventions.

Emanuele Caporrella has been drawn to the allure of exits from an early age. This fascination became a driving force as he moved through life, constantly seeking new ways to exit and explore. He departed from school, post offices, supermarkets, institutions, military service—and even from -ATI, which he joined back only to leave again. His exits ranged from the Colombian jungles to European crises, from official art scenes to punk groups, each departure marking a new chapter in his ever-evolving journey. His passion extended to exiting museums, cinemas, and theaters—spaces that, to him, represented more than just temporary escapes.

Francesca Schinzani lives and works across Italy. She identifies as an independent researcher, though her work also situates her as a historian of contemporary theater. Her writing examines the performing arts through methods informed by poststructuralist feminist theory. She is currently experimenting with forms of compromise—for instance, researching dissent during a residency at the Venice Biennale. Schinzani is enrolled in CAMPO (Sandretto Re Rebaudengo Foundation, Turin) and has collaborated with the Santarcangelo Festival in various capacities over the years.

Francesco Restuccia is a postdoctoral fellow in Philosophy and Aesthetics at the Sapienza University of Rome and a founding member of -ATI. His doctoral thesis focused on Vilém Flusser's critique of idolatry in the age of new media. His main interests include the history of aesthetics, media theory, and the philosophy of technology. He regularly translates essays from Portuguese, French, and German into Italian. He has published articles on the thought of Flusser, Benjamin, Baudrillard, Kapp, McLuhan, and Huizinga, as well as the book Il contrattacco delle immagini: Tecnica, media e idolatria a partire da Vilém Flusser (2021).

Ilê Sartuzi is an artist who lives and works between London and São Paulo. He graduated from the University of São Paulo and holds an MFA from Goldsmiths, University of London. With a conceptual approach, his interest in the dramatic arts has given a theatrical quality to his objects. These works are animated by mechanical movements that interpret dramaturgy and choreography, often in a repetitive exercise that leads to no catharsis but instead reveals the functioning of the machines themselves. More recently, Sartuzi has incorporated procedures of misdirection and sleight of hand, with a particular focus on investigating institutional infrastructures.

Mabel Tapia is an independent curator and researcher who has served as artistic deputy director of the Reina Sofía Museum and as coordinator of L'Internationale, a confederation of modern and contemporary art institutions. She has co-directed the DSRA Document and Contemporary Art postgraduate program at ÉESI–École européenne supérieure de l'image in Bourges, France, and coordinated the Red Conceptualismos del Sur platform. Tapia has worked as an editorial coordinator for several publications, including Losing the Human Form and A Really Useful Knowledge. She is part of the editorial collective for Des-bordes, a digital publication intersecting politics, visual culture, and artistic practices. Tapia's research focuses on twenty-first-century artistic practices, exploring archives, heuristic proposals, and political practice. She is the author of Las palabras no anidan: Lettres d'amour (2024).

Meriç Öner is an architect, curator, and researcher who has worked on design and architectural culture since 2005. She was the founding associate director at Salt, where she shaped the institution's critical approach to studies of the built environments. Her inquiries into material cultures initiated local and international conversations and facilitated the public presentation of multiple narratives and timelines through exhibitions, workshops, talks, and screenings. During her tenure as director, she focused on Salt's role as a co-learning institution, advancing both the access to and dissemination of digitized archives. She launched the Office of Useful Art in partnership with Asociación de Arte Útil. She also developed long-term collaborations with local institutions, most notably with Kadir Has University, which led to the digitization of the unfinished Istanbul Encyclopedia (1945–1975) by Reşad Ekrem Koçu and its archival materials. Since 2022, she has been leading Meriç Öner Culture Works, providing strategic consultancy and developing exhibitions, publications, and independent programs on material cultures, technologies, and geographies.

Panagiotis Samsarelos, born in Larisa, Greece, in 1978, is a visual artist and a founding member of -ATI. With over 20 years of experience, his career spans cartoons, contemporary art projects, theatrical performances, short film productions, and applied art initiatives. Samsarelos's work encompasses sketches, paintings, visual and interactive installations, as well as ready-made sculptures. Drawing on historical references and utilizing archival materials such as photographs, videos, and various documents, he creates images that transcend traditional narrative boundaries and incorporate satire.

Peter Lang is an independent artist, author, educator, and curator. He is a former Professor at the Royal Institute of Art in Stockholm, where he taught postgraduate courses from 2013 to 2019. He previously held the position of Associate Professor at Texas A&M School of Architecture. He earned a PhD in urban studies and Italian history from New York University and a Bachelor of Architecture from Syracuse University. In Stockholm, Lang founded R-lab, a public platform for critical research and creative artistic practice, and subsequently launched the initiative "Marvels and Catastrophes," which works to understand and engage in the culture of disaster. Lang is currently an instructor at NABA Rome in the master's program in Visual Arts and Curatorial Studies. He is a co-founder of the video animation production studio YellowGloveLab, which focuses on public art and the environment.

Raivo Puusemp is an American conceptual artist of Estonian origin, best known for his pioneering work at the intersection of art and politics with a peculiar Trojan-esque manipulative spirit. His artistic practice throughout the 1970s was characterized by a deep interest in systems, language, and the invisible structures that govern social and institutional behavior. Central to Puusemp's methodology was the idea of disseminating concepts that would be realized by others. People were his Trojan ground, but so were actual cities. In 1975, Puusemp undertook what would become his most emblematic work by running for and being elected mayor of Rosendale, a small village in New York State, in order to dissolve it. Since then, he has ceased making art—not a former artist, but an artist without pieces.

Rimini Protokoll (Caroline Barneaud + Stefan Kaegi) Caroline Barneaud is a curator, dramaturg and producer in the performing arts, currently leading artistic projects at Théâtre Vidy-Lausanne. Her practice expands the scope of performance by bridging art, public space, and social engagement while supporting experimental and collaborative approaches.Stefan Kaegi is a theatre-maker known for site-specific works that expose and infiltrate everyday spaces through performance as well as documentary performances on stages. As co-founder of Rimini Protokoll, he explores reality-based storytelling, often involving experts rather than actors and technological systems to question structures of power and perception. Kaegi and Barneaud have developed a long-term collaboration that blurs the boundaries between theatre, installation, research, and lived experience. Meaningful to this publication, their work crafts performative strategies that echo the logic of the Trojan Horse, subtly infiltrating systems and contexts, while dissolving traditional divisions between artists, experts, participants, performers and cultural workers.

Rocío Quillahuaman was born in Lima in 1994 and moved to Barcelona in 2005. She studied audiovisual communication at the University of Barcelona and has worked as both a writer and screenwriter. At the age of twenty, she began drawing portraits for fun, but the hobby quickly grew out of hand—she has since created more than three hundred. A self-taught artist, she later ventured into making animated videos that gained wide popularity on social media for their critical and humorous tone. The distinctive visual language of her work, combined with her sharp, sarcastic humor and incisive observations on contemporary culture and society, has established her as a prominent voice among a new generation of artists.

RYBN.ORG, founded in 1999, is an artist collective based in Paris that leads extradisciplinary investigations into complex systems and phenomena within the realms of economics and cybernetics – high-frequency trading, financial algorithms, flash crashes, market infrastructures, opaque tax-avoidance schemes, offshore financial circuits, artificial intelligence, and digital labor, etc.

SPORA, initiated in 2021, is a transdisciplinary and experimental project driven by mycelium, both as a methodology and as a lens for observing the almost invisible. Co-conceived by Charlotte Janis (artist) and Roberto Dell'Orco (artist and landscape architect), SPORA is based in the artist-run space Le Wonder. Their mycelium-centered activities include exhibitions, educational workshops, installations, and performances, forest walks, landscape interventions, meeting cycles, and university research programs.

Stalker, founded in 1995, is a collective that has carried out research and actions in territories with particular attention to marginal realities and areas of transformation. Its intervention method is historically based on exploratory, listening, relational, convivial, and collaborative spatial-planning practices, activated by creative interaction devices with the investigated environment, its inhabitants, and the archives of memory. Since 2009, the collective has continued its research through different paths led by the founders, among them Primavera Romana, Laboratorio di Arti Civiche, Museo Relazionale, No-working, and Stalker Walking School.

Stephen Wright is a theorist, farmer, art writer, and curator who teaches the practice of theory at the European School of Visual Arts and currently co-directs the Künstlerhaus Stuttgart alongside Tamarind Rossetti. His writing primarily focuses on the politics of usership, particularly in the context of collaborative, extradisciplinary practices that feature variable coefficients of art. These practices challenge traditional notions of art, raising the possibility of art without artworks, authorship, or spectatorship.

Todo por la Praxis (TXP) is an artist collective currently composed of Diego Peris and Jo Muñoz, based in Madrid, Spain. Their work centers on research and the production of art, with a primary focus on the social function of art and direct action. Their objective is to activate artistic practice as a means of contributing to transformation, creating spaces and tools for critical reflection. The imaginaries they construct engage with various forms of dissent and political resistance through collaborative practices, aiming to amplify narratives that intervene in public space. A praxis that for a long time responded to needs is now a praxis that is being questioned.

-ATI Team

Matteo Locci is a multimedia artist based in Rome. His work highlights the changing relationships between power, architecture, technical images, and participation, focusing on how attention is triggered, produced, circulated, and how it disappears in neoliberal participatory governance. Most of his artistic experiments are conducted with the interdisciplinary collective -ATI and the artistic collective Funduk.

Natalia Agati is an artist and a PostDoc researcher in Architecture and Urban Studies . She has participated in many projects with several universities, artistic institutions and independent collectives. In her multidisciplinary and critical posture—from architecture to urban studies and artistic research—she explores the mechanisms of spatial control and the loss of control, visibility and invisibility, analyzing the epistemologies of blindness enacted by the neoliberal governance provoking them through art and performance as a research method to re-enchant the world inventing new forms of life. Among her numerous professional and existential identities, in 2014 she co-founded -ATI, with which she conceptualizes and produces installation and performance.

Merve Yücel is an Istanbul-based architect and researcher focusing on the intersection of logistics, ecology, and infrastructure. After working in various architecture offices, she served as exhibition and project manager for the Istanbul Design Biennial (2011–2019). She holds an MA from Goldsmiths, University of London. A frequent collaborator with the interdisciplinary collective -ATI, Yücel's work spans curatorial, artistic, and editorial practices, exploring alternative forms of embodiment, solidarity, and imaginaries related to bodies of water.

Başak Tuna is an interdisciplinary designer and artist based in Rome. With a background in industrial design and an MA in Contextual Design from Design Academy Eindhoven, her work spans spatial design, combining a hands-on, experimental approach with a focus on materiality. She explores the potential of everyday materials through dismantling and reassembling. Her practice delves into themes of infrastructure, transformation and human-environment relationships, questioning the role of design in shaping our surroundings. She is an active member of -ATI.

with

Maria Rocco is an architect and PhD in Urban Studies and founding member of -ATI she is an activator of Laboratorio CIRCO research group and curates the Progetto delle Memorie for the Laboratorio di Città Corviale. Her main research interests concern formal and informal phenomena of production and control of space, issues of spatial justice, processes of production and bottom-up innovation of urban policies. She investigates these themes through action research rooted in the territory and the relationship with its inhabitants, hybridizing the tools of architecture and the arts.

Edoardo Fabbri is an architect and researcher at the Faculty of Architecture in Rome. He holds a PhD from the Department of Philosophical Studies at the Federico II University in Naples. Co-founder of the design and research collective Archibloom with which he won the international competition "Europan 15". He is a board member of the publishing and research project 'Piani di salvezza' and was a member and promoter of the 'laboratorio di Archeologia Filosofica'. For the publishing house Efesto in 2020, he published 'Architettura come arché. Appunti sull'hortus apertus'.

Set Margins' #71
(www.setmargins.press)

First edition, 2025

A book by -ATI
-ATI team is composed of Merve Yücel, Başak Tuna, Matteo Locci and Natalia Agati.

Editor: Merve Yücel with the support of Kerim Bayer
Translations: Matteo Locci
Graphic Design: Başak Tuna
Interviews: Matteo Locci, Natalia Agati, and Başak Tuna with the support of Maria Rocco and Edoardo Fabbri

Typeface: Ortica, designed by Ben Bovani

Steganographic contribution by RYBN.ORG

Supported by:

SAHA

Kunstuniversität Linz
University of Arts Linz

Thanks to Meliha Coşkun for the first invitation and for opening the first door. Thanks to Deniz Erbaş and Seyhan Boztepe, curators of Çanakkale Biennial 2024, for their help and support. Last but not least, thanks to EESI students for collaborating on the first out-of-the-image-tour and the evacuation plan observation at the Centre International de l'Art Pariétal, Lascaux.